ADDISON-WESLEY

DESTINATIONS IN SCIENCE

Authors
David C. Brummett
Karen K. Lind
Charles R. Barman
Michael A. DiSpezio
Karen L. Ostlund

Contributing Authors
Jim Hopkins
Vallie W. Guthrie
Michael B. Leyden
Gerry M. Madrazo, Jr.
Sheryl A. Mercier
Jerome M. Shaw

Activity Consultant
Doug Herridge

Addison-Wesley Publishing Company
Menlo Park, California ▪ Reading, Massachusetts ▪ New York ▪ Don Mills, Ontario ▪ Wokingham, England ▪ Amsterdam
Bonn ▪ Paris ▪ Milan ▪ Madrid ▪ Sydney ▪ Singapore ▪ Tokyo ▪ Seoul ▪ Taipei ▪ Mexico City ▪ San Juan

ISBN 0-201-45050-X 2 3 4 5 6 7 8 9 10-VH-99 98 97 96 95

CONTENTS

Unit A
Ecosystems

Unit B
Biomes

Unit C
Forms of Matter

Unit D

Sound and Light

Unit E
Air and Water

Unit F
Transport Systems

Consultants and Reviewers

Special Consultants

Reading
Bonnie Armbruster, Ph.D.
Center for the Study of Reading
University of Illinois at Urbana-Champaign
Champaign, Illinois

Assessment
Steve Rakow, Ph.D.
Associate Professor of Education
University of Houston–Clear Lake
Houston, Texas

Special Needs
Valerie Wales, M.S.
Coordinator
Special Education Resource Center
Mansfield, Ohio

Multicultural
Gerard Fergerson, Ph.D.
Assistant Professor of Health Policy
New York University
New York, New York

Arlene Maclin, Ph.D.
Research Professor of Physics
Hampton University
Hampton, Virginia

Luis Martinez-Perez, Ph.D.
Associate Professor of Science Education
Florida International University
Miami, Florida

Barbara F. May
Language Enrichment Teacher
Thomy Lafon School
New Orleans, Louisiana

A. Barretto Ogilvie, Ed.D.
Dean of Continuing and Professional Education
Seattle Central Community College
Seattle, Washington

Jennifer K. Patterson
New Orleans Public Schools
New Orleans, Louisiana

Tone Shimizu
Educational Consultant
Berkeley, California

Albert Snow, Ed.D.
Director of Science Education
The Discovery Museum
Bridgeport, Connecticut

Multicultural Photo/Art Reviewers
Cynthia Cooksey
Marlene C. Davis
Cammie Harris
Marie Kitajima
Edna Ahgeak MacLean
Mattie McCloud
Renya Ramirez
June Tanamachi

Environmental
Linda Furuness, Ph.D.
School of Education
Indiana University
Indianapolis, Indiana

Science, Technology, and Society
Jon E. Pedersen, Ph.D.
Assistant Professor of Curriculum and Instruction–Science Education
University of Arkansas
Fayetteville, Arkansas

Urban
Doris Williams
Teacher
Martin Luther King Junior High
Oakland, California

Safety
Jay A. Young, Ph.D.
Chemical Safety and Health Consultant
Silver Springs, Maryland

ESL
Rosa Leon
Coordinator
Bronx School District
Bronx, New York

Cheryl McElvain
E.L.D. Educational Consultant
Morgan Hill, California

Irene Musman
Coordinator
Philadelphia School District
Philadelphia, Pennsylvania

Alice Parra
Teacher
Hughey Elementary School
El Paso, Texas

Content Consultants

Jimmie D. Agnew, Ph.D.
Associate Professor of
Science Education
Elon College
Elon, North Carolina

Kurt Brorson, Ph.D.
Division of Monoclonal Antibodies
Food and Drug Administration
Bethesda, Maryland

Brenda Bussard
Educational Consultant
Fremont, California

Diane Doser, Ph.D.
Department of Geological Sciences
University of Texas at El Paso
El Paso, Texas

Eric Engles, Ph.D.
Education Consultant
Felton, California

Anita Gerlach
Santa Fe High School
Santa Fe, New Mexico

M. Frank Watt Ireton
American Geophysical Union
Washington, DC

Barry Lessow, Ed.D.
Assistant Professor of Teacher
Education
Indiana University
Bloomington, Indiana

Chelcie Liu, Ph.D.
Physics Instructor
City College of San Francisco
San Francisco, California

Elizabeth Looney
Teacher
Woodrow Wilson High School
San Francisco, California

Maja Nowakowski, Ph.D.
Health Science Center
State University of New York
New York, New York

Rosalind Philips
Teacher
New Century High School
Olympia, Washington

Richard H. Shippee
Chairman of Life Science Department
Vincennes University
Vincennes, Indiana

Deborah Tippins, Ph.D.
Assistant Professor of
Science Education
University of Georgia
Athens, Georgia

Reviewers

Robert Burtch
Teacher
Batavia Middle School
Batavia, Illinois

Bradley N. Martin
Teacher
Las Lomitas School District
Menlo Park, California

Nancy Rankin
Science Specialist
Oak Knoll Elementary School
Menlo Park, California

Bruce Schulert
K–12 Science Consultant
Lansing School District
Lansing, Michigan

Marilyn Trow
Educational Consultant
Ames, Iowa

Marjorie Zellner
Teacher
Encinal Elementary School
Atherton, California

Monica Zeringue
Teacher
Rudolph Matas Elementary School
Metairie, Louisiana

Field Test Teachers

Natalie Barman
Park Tudor School
Indianapolis, Indiana

Lisa Coats
Betsy Ross Elementary School
Prospect Heights, Illinois

Sheila Gallagher
William A. White Elementary School
Kansas City, Kansas

Susan Harper
W.T. Jackson Elementary School
Atlanta, Georgia

Gay Littrell
Blair Elementary School
Fairchild AFB, Washington

Patricia Yencho
Fair Oaks Elementary School
Redwood City, California

Dear Travelers,

You are about to begin an incredible journey. *Destinations in Science* will take you to some special places to study science. You may go to real places you can find on a map, such as the Appalachian Mountains. There you will investigate how living things interact with their environment. Or, you might take a trip to an airport to explore sound and light.

Some of the destinations, such as the pizzeria, can be found in your neighborhood. Others, such as a trip on a space shuttle, can be found only in your imagination, at least for today. From the space shuttle you will look back on the earth to learn about different animal and plant communities.

Welcome to an exciting way of thinking about your world. You'll discover that science is *everywhere*—think about it.

Destinations in Science is a trip worth taking!

Bon Voyage!

The Authors

The Authors

APPALACHIAN
TRAIL
GEORGIA
TO MAINE
A Footpath for
Those who seek
Fellowship with
the Wilderness
1934
The
GEORGIA APPALACHIAN TRAIL CLUB

Appalachians

Your group is hiking on a wilderness footpath called the Appalachian Trail. This trail, located in the Appalachian Mountain range, is more than 3,300 kilometers long. It runs from Mount Katahdin in Maine to Springer Mountain in Georgia, passing through 14 states along the way.

The environments change along the trail. In the northern mountains, for example, there are more evergreen trees. The northern animals also differ from those found in the south. Meadows, lakes, and streams have their own characteristic plants and animals.

Living things depend on one another and on the nonliving parts of their environment to survive. While you hike along the trail, you too depend on the forest resources. Even when you are not in the wilderness, you depend on the environment for your daily needs.

- How do living things get energy?
- How do living things depend on one another?
- What nonliving parts of the environment do living things depend on?

Unit A

ECOSYSTEMS

Activities

Features

Chapter 1

Getting Food

A gurgling stream flows through a forest of evergreen and broad-leaved trees. Fragrant wildflowers grow along the edge of the stream. You hear the rush of the water, the whisper of the wind through the trees, and the quiet buzzing of insects. Occasionally there is a loud crackle as acorns fall to the ground or a squirrel scurries across the forest floor.

At your campsite, the smoky smell of last night's campfire lingers. Your stomach gurgles in anticipation of breakfast. This is the second day of your hiking trip. You roll up your sleeping bag and fold your tent. Your backpack is stuffed, and you're ready to hike another segment of the Appalachian Trail.

You can find a great variety of plants and animals in the Appalachian Mountains. There are evergreen trees, and trees that change color in the autumn. Ferns and shrubs carpet the forest floor. Blueberry and huckleberry bushes grow along the side of the trail. Insects, birds, and other animals depend on these plants for survival.

Everything you need to survive for the next few days is strapped to your back. Your backpack is filled with food and clothing. Your canteen is filled with water. And your shelter—your tent—is strapped to the outside of your backpack. Other living things in the Appalachians get what they need to survive from their environment.

SCIENCE JOURNAL

What do you need to survive? In your Science Journal, list some of the things living things need to survive.

Explore Activity

What do living things need?

Process Skills
Making models, Observing

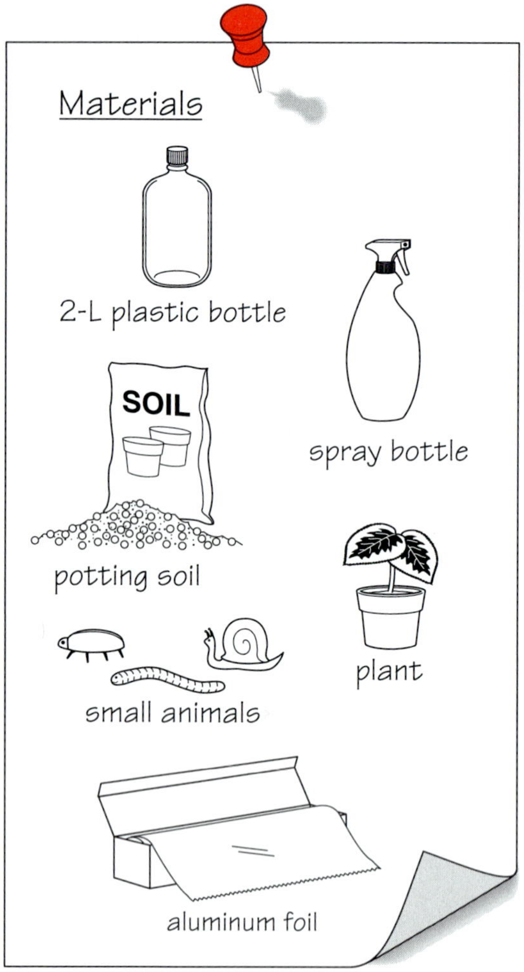

Observe and Collect Data

1. Cut off the top of a 2-liter plastic bottle. Use care when cutting. Also, handle the small animals with care throughout the activity.
2. Put about 10 centimeters of soil in the bottle. Place the roots of the plant into the soil. Place one or more small animals, such as garden snails, earthworms, or beetles, in the bottle. Moisten the soil by spraying it with water.
3. Cover the top of the bottle with aluminum foil. Make sure your animal cannot escape.
4. Use the spray bottle to water the plant when the soil is dry. Record your observations in your Activity Journal.

Share Your Results

Observe the environments prepared by other students in the class. How are the environments similar? How are they different?

Draw Conclusions

1. How had the environment you created changed by the end of the week?
2. What do the living things you observed in your environment need to survive?
3. How is your model like a forest? How is it different?

Apply What You Know

If you wanted to create a special container that would allow you to observe large animals, what would you be sure to include in the container?

Which living things produce and consume food?

Sunlight sprinkles through the leaves of the tall trees that surround your campsite. You find a warm, sunny spot and sit down on a stump to eat your breakfast. The sun's energy does more than make things warm. The sun also helps produce the food that you are eating.

During a process called photosynthesis (fōt′ō sin′thə sis), plants use water, carbon dioxide, and energy from the sun to produce a kind of sugar. Photosynthesis is carried out by all plants, algae, and even some kinds of bacteria. These living things use the food they make to live and grow.

Living things, such as plants, that make their own food are called **producers** (prō do͞os′ərz). The trees above you and the ferns that cover the ground are producers. The sun is the source of the energy for these producers to make their food. Where do you think the carbon dioxide and water they need for photosynthesis come from?

Plants are producers. They make their own food.

You cannot make food by sitting in the sun. You need to eat to get energy to live and grow. Living things that do not carry out photosynthesis get their energy from other living things. Since they consume, or eat, other living things, they are called **consumers** (kən so͞om′ərz). Some consumers eat plants and others eat animals.

You're not the only consumer around the campsite. A small tree frog is climbing on a tree nearby. This tree frog gets its energy by eating insects. As the tree frog hops away, one of your fellow campers points out a caterpillar that is crawling on a leaf. The caterpillar eats leaves to get its energy.

Many of the living things you have seen on your hiking trip are consumers. The birds that woke you this morning eat seeds and insects. The fish in the stream also eat plants and insects. Even the insects are consumers. They eat plants or other insects. What are some consumers in your area? What do they eat?

Be a Scientist

HANDS-ON ACTIVITY

What are nearby producers and consumers?

1. In your schoolyard or in a nearby park, measure a square of grass that is 1 meter on each side. Use a piece of string to outline the square.
2. Examine the square for producers and consumers. Look for evidence of consumers. You might find tracks or the remains of seeds that have been nibbled on.
3. ACTIVITY JOURNAL In your Activity Journal, draw or describe the producers and consumers or evidence of consumers you observed in this square. Which did you find more of? Why?

Caterpillars are consumers. They consume plants.

How do consumers get their food?

When a caterpillar eats a leaf, it does not have to worry about the leaf running away. A snake, on the other hand, has to catch the food it eats. An animal, such as a snake, that captures and kills its food is called a **predator** (pred′ə tər). An animal, such as a mouse, that is caught by a predator is called the **prey.**

Predators catch prey in different ways. Some hunt for food; others wait silently and capture animals that come close by. Some predators go where their prey live or eat, and then dig or fish them out.

Prey have different ways to avoid their predators. Some animals blend into their environment and the predator has a hard time finding them. Other prey look like dangerous animals or animals that taste bad, and predators are not tempted to eat them. Some prey can run or fly quickly to avoid their predators, and some can dart into holes too small for their predators.

The timber rattlesnake is the same color as its surroundings. This predator hides on the forest floor, waiting. When a mouse comes within reach, the snake captures its prey.

The fox sneaks up on its prey. This is called stalking. The fox will surprise its prey and it may not have time to escape.

This woodpecker finds its prey in the bark of trees. These predators go to where the insects live and dig them out of the bark with their long, sharp beaks.

SCIENCE JOURNAL

Have you played hide-and-seek? Playing hide-and-seek is similar to predators finding their prey. Play hide-and-seek with your friends or family. What skills help you hunt? What skills help you hide? Record your answers to these questions in your Science Journal.

BACK HOME

What are some relationships between living things?

After hiking up a hill, you lean against a rock for a rest. The rock is covered with flakes of brownish-green lichen (lī′kən). You take off your backpack and pull out your binoculars to look at the view. As you look through the binoculars, you see a colorful butterfly flitting among some wildflowers.

Living things depend on one another for survival. This kind of partnership between living things is called **symbiosis** (sim′bi ō′sis). There are three different kinds of symbiosis. In some symbiotic relationships, both partners benefit. Some symbiotic relationships are helpful to one partner and harmful to the other. In a third kind of symbiosis, one partner benefits and the other is neither harmed nor helped.

The lichen growing on the rock you leaned against is made up of a fungus and a simple plant called an alga (al′gə). The alga makes food for the lichen by photosynthesis. The fungus attaches the alga to the rock and absorbs the minerals the alga needs to survive. This kind of symbiosis, in which both partners benefit, is called mutualism (myo͞o′cho͞o əl iz′əm).

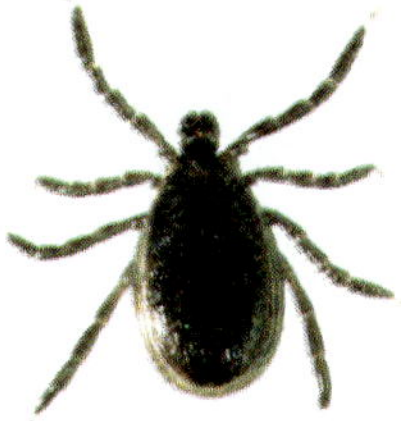
Deer tick

Your trail guide warned you about deer ticks. These ticks harm other living things by feeding on their blood. This kind of symbiosis, in which one partner benefits and the other is harmed, is called parasitism (par′ə sit′iz′əm). The partner that benefits, such as the deer tick, is called a parasite. The partner that is used as a source of food by the parasite is called a host.

The alga and fungus that make up lichen help each other survive. This is an example of mutualism.

Deer ticks can carry another parasite, a tiny organism that causes Lyme disease. Symptoms of Lyme disease can appear 3 to 32 days after a tick bite. Symptoms can include a rash in the shape of a bull's eye, fever, headache, and aching joints and muscles. Lyme disease must be treated promptly to avoid serious complications.

Another kind of symbiotic relationship is called commensalism (kə men′səl iz′əm). In commensalism, one member of the partnership benefits, but does not help or harm the other member of the partnership.

Flowers provide food for the butterfly. The butterfly also carries the pollen from one flower to another, helping the flowers to reproduce. What kind of symbiosis is this?

SIDE TRIP

Rain Forest

High up in the rain forest are plants, called bromeliads (brō mē′lē adz′), that grow on trees. The trees give the bromeliads a place to grow where they receive a lot of sunlight. The bromeliads neither help nor harm the trees. This relationship is an example of commensalism, since one partner benefits and the other partner is neither helped nor harmed.

How are you doing?

1. What is the difference between producers and consumers?
2. Some predators, such as wolves, hunt in packs. How might this help them catch their prey?
3. **Think** Do you think a successful parasite kills its host? Explain your answer.

How do different consumers get energy?

The deer, like most herbivores, has flat teeth that help it grind the plant parts it eats.

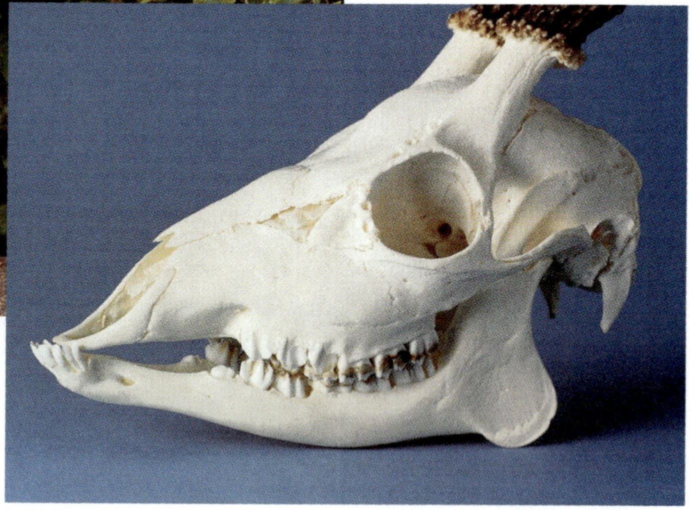

You hear a stick snap in the woods as you pull on your backpack. When you look in the direction of the noise, you spot a white-tailed deer. You see the deer's jaw moving back and forth as it munches on some leaves.

The deer is a consumer. It gets its energy from consuming other living things. The tree is one source of food for the deer. The tree is a producer. It makes its own food. Consumers, such as the deer, that eat producers are called **herbivores** (hər′bə vôrz′).

While you're watching the deer, you spot a chipmunk beneath a tree. The chipmunk eats seeds and nuts that fall from the trees. Since the seeds and nuts are made by producers, the chipmunk is also said to be an herbivore. What are some herbivores that live in your area?

The weasel, like most carnivores, has sharp teeth for killing and eating other animals.

You hear a rustle of leaves. A brown weasel races after the chipmunk, which scampers up a tree. Startled by the noise, the deer also bounds away. The weasel is a consumer. It eats chipmunks, mice, birds, and other small animals. A consumer that eats other consumers is called a **carnivore** (kär′nə vôr′).

A large, hairy wolf spider crawls out onto the trail in front of you. The wolf spider is another carnivore. It eats insects. What are some carnivores that live in your area?

Spiders are carnivores.

What happens to the bodies of dead plants and animals?

Chanterelle mushrooms recycle once-living things.

While you are hiking, you have to climb over a dead tree trunk lying across the trail. The wood is soft and rotted in places. You notice insects and mushrooms on the trunk. What kind of consumers are these?

Mushrooms and molds are called fungi. Fungi are not plants and they cannot make their own food. Most fungi get energy by feeding on the bodies of once-living things. Fungi digest, or break down, dead plants and animals. Living things that get energy by breaking down the bodies of dead things are called **decomposers** (dē′kəm pōz′ərz).

Fungi are not the only decomposers in the Appalachians. Tiny decomposers, called bacteria, live in the forest soil. Bacteria break down dead plants and animals and animal wastes. Worms and some insects are also decomposers. Earthworms are common decomposers that you might find in your neighborhood.

Decomposers are important. As decomposers break down dead matter, minerals and other materials are released into the soil and air. These materials are then reused by living things.

YOU CAN HELP

Reduce your garbage by making a small compost pile in your backyard with scraps of leftover fruits and vegetables. Decomposers will break down the waste.

Be a Scientist

How can you make a fungus garden?

1. Put a damp paper towel in a jar. Place some dead leaves, twigs, or food in the jar. Put the lid on the jar and put it in a cool, dark place.
2. **Predict** what the things in the jar will look like in several days. Record your prediction in your Activity Journal.
3. After several days, observe the material without opening the jar. Record your observations. How are your classmates' jars similar? How are they different?

There are many kinds of fungi, bacteria, worms, and insects decomposing this fallen tree.

What are some other kinds of consumers?

After a long morning of hiking, you're hungry. What are your favorite foods? It's too bad you can't carry a pepperoni pizza in your backback! A pepperoni pizza contains food that comes from both plants and animals. As you've learned, animals that eat producers are called herbivores. Animals that eat consumers are called carnivores. Animals that eat both producers and consumers are called **omnivores** (äm′ni vôrz′).

Most people are considered omnivores. In cold regions, where plant life is scarce, some people are carnivores. People who live in some Inuit communities of northern Canada, Alaska, and Greenland eat mostly fish and meat. People can also be herbivores. People who are herbivores, or vegetarians, get the protein and vitamins they need from vegetables, fruits, grains, and nuts.

There are many other omnivores in the Appalachians. Black bears, skunks, raccoons, and foxes eat both plants and animals. Some omnivores in the forest also eat people's food. If you don't want visitors at your campsite during the night, hang your food from a tree or lock it in a box so that it doesn't get eaten by another omnivore. What are some omnivores in your area? What do they eat?

Sometimes raccoons eat producers.

Other times raccoons eat consumers.

Turkey vultures are scavengers.

Not all the carnivores and omnivores in the Appalachians act as predators. Instead of hunting and killing animals, some carnivores and omnivores feed on the bodies of animals that were dead before they found them. An animal that consumes dead animals, but does not kill the animals itself, is called a **scavenger** (skav′in jər). Consumers that eat animals killed by accidents or by other predators are considered scavengers. Black bears, raccoons, and foxes sometimes act as scavengers.

One of the most familiar scavengers in the Appalachians is the turkey vulture, or buzzard. With its two-meter wingspan and distinctive style of soaring in groups, this bird is easy to spot. The turkey vulture's diet comes from animals that have been killed by automobiles or by other causes.

Rotten meat contains chemicals that are deadly to many creatures. However, these chemicals do not harm turkey vultures because their bodies have adapted to using rotten meat for food.

How are you doing?

1. Describe the role of a decomposer in the Appalachians.
2. Are human beings omnivores, herbivores, or carnivores? Explain your answer.
3. **Think** Herbivores' teeth tend to be flat, and carnivores' teeth tend to be sharp. What do the teeth of omnivores look like?

Science & Literature Connection

All Things Are Linked

This story comes from the Lega people who live in the country of Zaire in Africa. It appears in the book The Crest and the Hide *by Harold Courlander.*

There was a certain chief in a certain village. He had many slaves. Whatever he wanted to be done, he ordered it. If it was a wise thing he wanted, his various counselors said to him: "Yes, it is good." If it was not a wise thing, they said, just the same, "Yes, it is good," because if they disagreed with him he grew angry, saying, "What! Do you say the chief doesn't know what he is doing?" But the lowest of his counselors never said yes or no. If the chief asked him about a certain thing he would think for a while and then reply: "All things are linked."

It happened one time that the chief could not sleep at night because of the croaking of frogs in the marshes. Night after night he could not sleep, and decided at last that the frogs would have to be exterminated. He told his counselors what he intended to do. One by one, as usual, they applauded him, saying, "Yes, it is good." Only the lowest of the counselors did not speak. The chief said: "You, counselor, have you no tongue in your mouth?" The man thought for a while, then he said: "O chief, all things are linked." The chief thought: "This man knows nothing else to say."

The chief sent his slaves out to exterminate the frogs in the marsh. They killed frogs until no more frogs remained. They returned, saying, "Sir, the frogs are done with." That night the chief slept well, and he slept well for many nights thereafter. He was pleased with life.

But in the marshes, the mosquitoes began to rise in swarms because there were no frogs to eat their larvae. They came to the village. They came into the chief's house and bit him. They made his life a misery. The people of the village suffered. So the chief ordered his slaves to go out and kill mosquitoes. The slaves went out, they tried, but the mosquitoes were too numerous. They continued to plague the village. The chief called his counselors. He scolded them, saying, "When I asked you about killing the frogs, you answered, 'It is good.' Why did you not say, 'If the frogs are killed the mosquitoes will multiply?' Only one of you said something for me to think about. He said, 'All things are linked,' but I did not understand his words."

The mosquito hordes made life unlivable. People left their houses and fields and went away. They went to distant places, cleared new fields, and began living again. The old village became deserted except for the chief and his family. Finally, the chief, too, took his family and went away.

Because of what happened there came to be a saying:

"'Yes, it is good' caused a village to become deserted."

Think About Your Reading

1. Which animal, the mosquito or the frog, is the predator? Which is the prey?
2. What did the counselor mean when he said, "All things are linked?"

Predicting How else would the environment be affected by the removal of frogs? For example, what do you think happened to the animals that prey on frogs? Explain your prediction.

Where to Read More

Jean Craighead George, *The Talking Earth* (New York: Harper Collins, 1983) A Seminole girl finds why it is important to know about the plants and animals in the Everglades.

Looking Back

Words and Concepts

Complete each of the following statements.

1. A living thing that makes its own food is called a(n) ____.
2. Living things that break down the bodies of dead organisms are called ____.
3. An insect caught by a frog is prey, while the frog is the ____.
4. Consider a deer, a fox, and an owl. The herbivore in the group is the ____.
5. A partnership between living things is called ____.

Applied Thinking Skills

Answer the following questions. You can use words, drawings, and diagrams in your answers.

6. A rhino helps a tick bird by providing food. A tick bird helps a rhino by taking insects off the rhino's skin. What kind of symbiosis is this? Explain your answer.

Rhino and tick birds

7. The tick bird eats insects. The rhino eats grass. What kind of consumer is a tick bird? What kind of consumer is a rhino? Explain your answers.
8. How are decomposers important? What would happen to dead animals and plants if there were no decomposers?
9. Five types of consumers are herbivores, carnivores, decomposers, omnivores, and scavengers. Do some living things fit into more than one of these categories? Explain your answer.
10. **Your World** Name three consumers that live near your home. They can be pets or wild animals. Tell what type of consumer each one is. Explain your classifications.

Show What You Know

How can you classify living things?

Observe and Collect Data

1. Draw or cut out from old magazines 15 pictures of living things. Tape the photos or drawings onto index cards.
2. ACTIVITY JOURNAL Separate the cards you made into producers, decomposers, and consumers. Then separate the consumers into herbivores, carnivores, and omnivores. You should have at least one of each category. Make a list in your Activity Journal of the animals in each category.
3. Combine your cards with the cards of one or more classmates. Make up a card game. In your Activity Journal, describe your game.

Process Skills
Communicating, Classifying

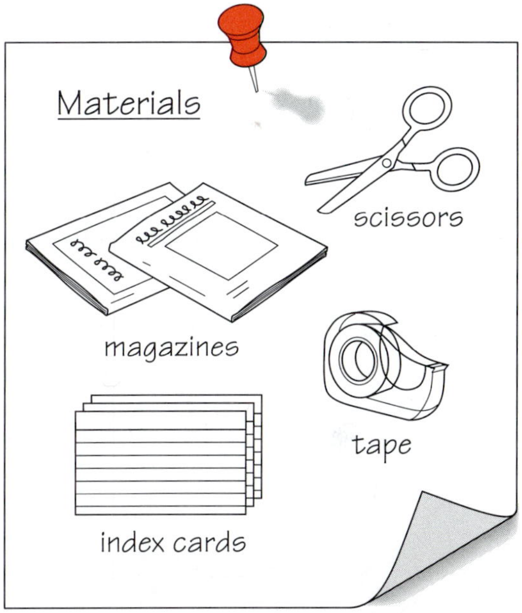

Draw Conclusions

1. Describe the relationships among the living things on your cards.
2. Which consumers on your cards are predators? Which consumers are prey?

Food Webs

As you pass between two trees, you feel something sticky. You stop and take a step backward. You have just walked into a strand of a spider's web. After brushing it off, you notice the rest of the web. It runs between the trees on the trail. You also notice that a beetle is caught in the web. When you look up, you see a small bird with a spider in its beak.

Which animals were predators? Which were prey? When the spider caught the insect, the spider was the predator and the insect was the prey. When the small bird caught the spider, the small bird was the predator and the spider was the prey.

The small bird, in turn, may become the prey of a larger predator, such as the peregrine falcon.

Many animals act as both predators and prey. Predators and prey transfer food energy. The bird got energy when it ate the spider. The spider got energy when it ate the insect. The insect got energy when it ate a plant. And the plant got energy from the sun.

SCIENCE JOURNAL Can you think of other animals that can be both predators and prey? In your Science Journal, write about these animals and where they get energy.

This tufted titmouse eats spiders.

Explore Activity

How is energy passed among living things?

Process Skills
Making models, Inferring

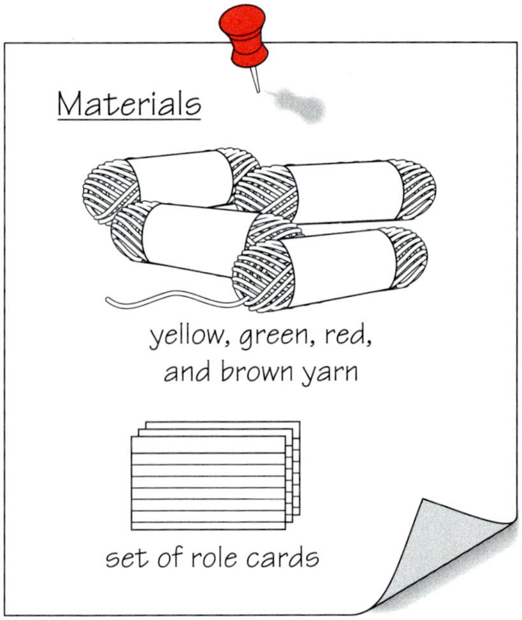

Observe and Collect Data

1. Form a large circle with your classmates. Your teacher will give one role card to each person. The role cards include plants, herbivores, carnivores, omnivores, and decomposers.
2. If you have a plant card, tie a piece of yellow yarn around your wrist. The yellow yarn represents the energy connection between plants and the sun.
3. Students playing roles use the yarn to connect to their food sources. A student playing an herbivore uses a piece of green yarn to connect to a plant. Carnivores use red yarn, both scavengers and decomposers use brown yarn, and omnivores use green and red yarn twisted together.
4. As your teacher gives you more pieces of yarn, make additional connections to food sources.
5. ACTIVITY JOURNAL Your teacher will select one of the "plants" to become extinct. This person tugs on all yarn that is attached to him or her. Students who feel a tug then tug on the yarn of others who use them for food. Record your observations in your Activity Journal.

Share Your Results

Discuss with your classmates how energy is passed among the living things in your energy circle.

Draw Conclusions

1. How do living things depend on each other?
2. How do carnivores depend on energy from the sun?
3. Which group—producers, herbivores, carnivores, omnivores, scavengers, or decomposers—is connected to the most living things?

Apply What You Know

How does the loss of a producer affect other living things?

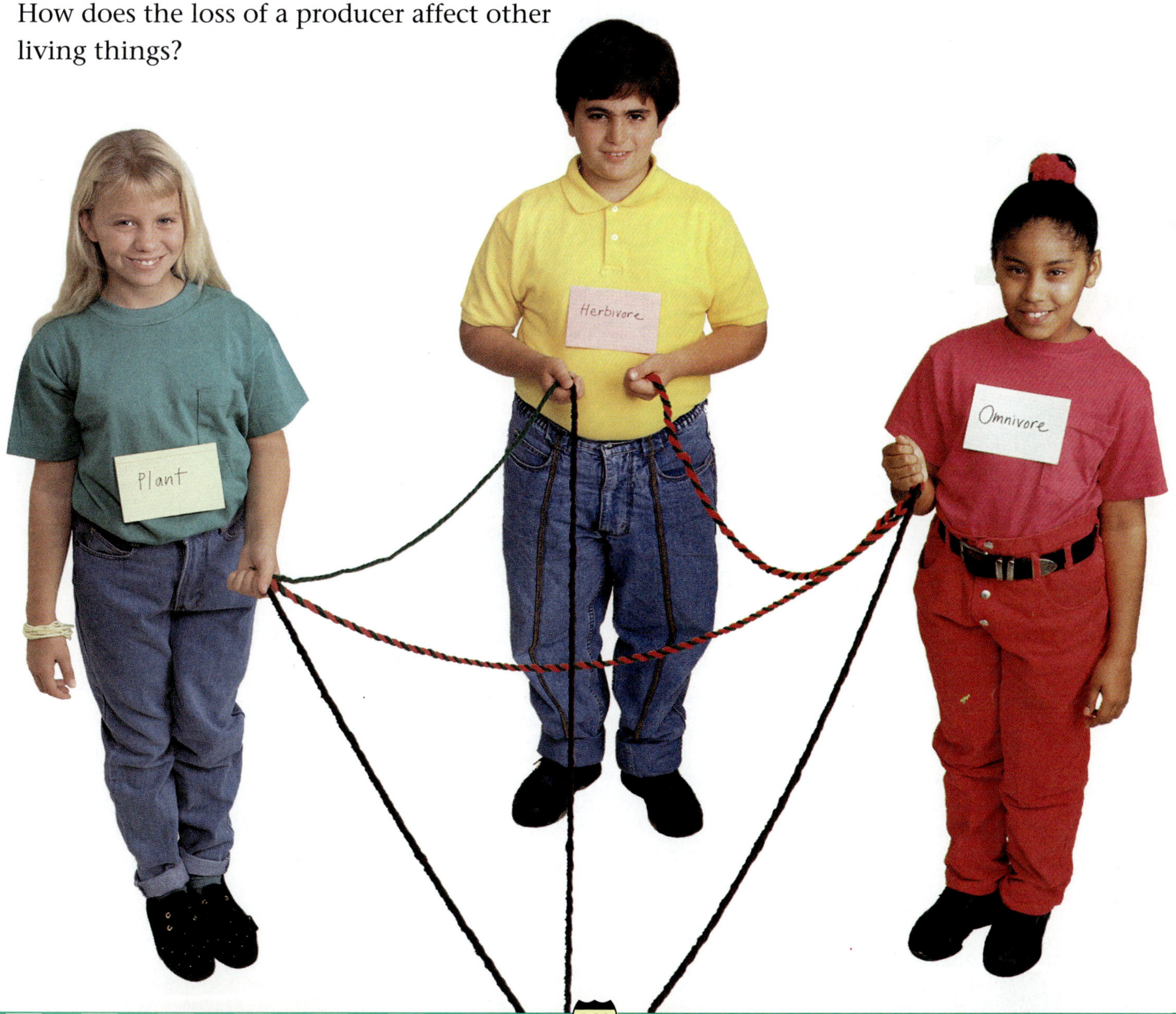

What is a food chain?

At the edge of the trail, you see a mouse feeding on acorns that have fallen from an oak tree. Suddenly, a hawk drops from the sky. Clutching the mouse in its talons, the predator flies away.

The search for food is a search for energy. The path by which energy is passed from one living thing to another is called a **food chain.** All food chains begin with the sun. Producers use the sun's energy to make their food. Producers use some of the energy from this food to live and grow. They also store some energy in their cells and tissues.

Energy and nutrients are passed from the acorn to the mouse to the hawk in this food chain.

When an herbivore feeds on a producer, some of the energy stored in the producer is transferred to the herbivore. Herbivores use most of this energy and store the rest. Carnivores, such as the hawk, get this stored energy when they eat an herbivore or another carnivore.

The food chain gives consumers nutrients as well as energy. For example, the vitamins, minerals, and proteins consumers need to build cells are contained in the food they eat.

Be a Scientist

HANDS-ON ACTIVITY

What happens to energy in a food chain?

1. Meet with three or four people and form a food chain.
2. ACTIVITY JOURNAL The producer gets 30 peanuts. Each peanut represents a unit of energy. Each living thing in the food chain sets aside, or "uses," one-half of the energy it receives, leaving one-half to pass along the food chain. In your Activity Journal, record the number of peanuts passed along.
3. Repeat the procedure until the "energy" reaches the last link in the food chain. What happens to the amount of available energy as the energy moves along a food chain?

This energy pyramid shows the amount of energy available at each level of the food chain. As you can see, the amount of energy decreases as you move up the food chain.

What is a food web?

Mice aren't the only animals in the Appalachians that eat acorns. Chipmunks, squirrels, and insects also eat acorns. And hawks aren't the only animals that eat mice. Weasels, foxes, and snakes also eat mice.

Most living things are part of more than one food chain. The many food chains in an area are combined, or linked, to form a **food web.**

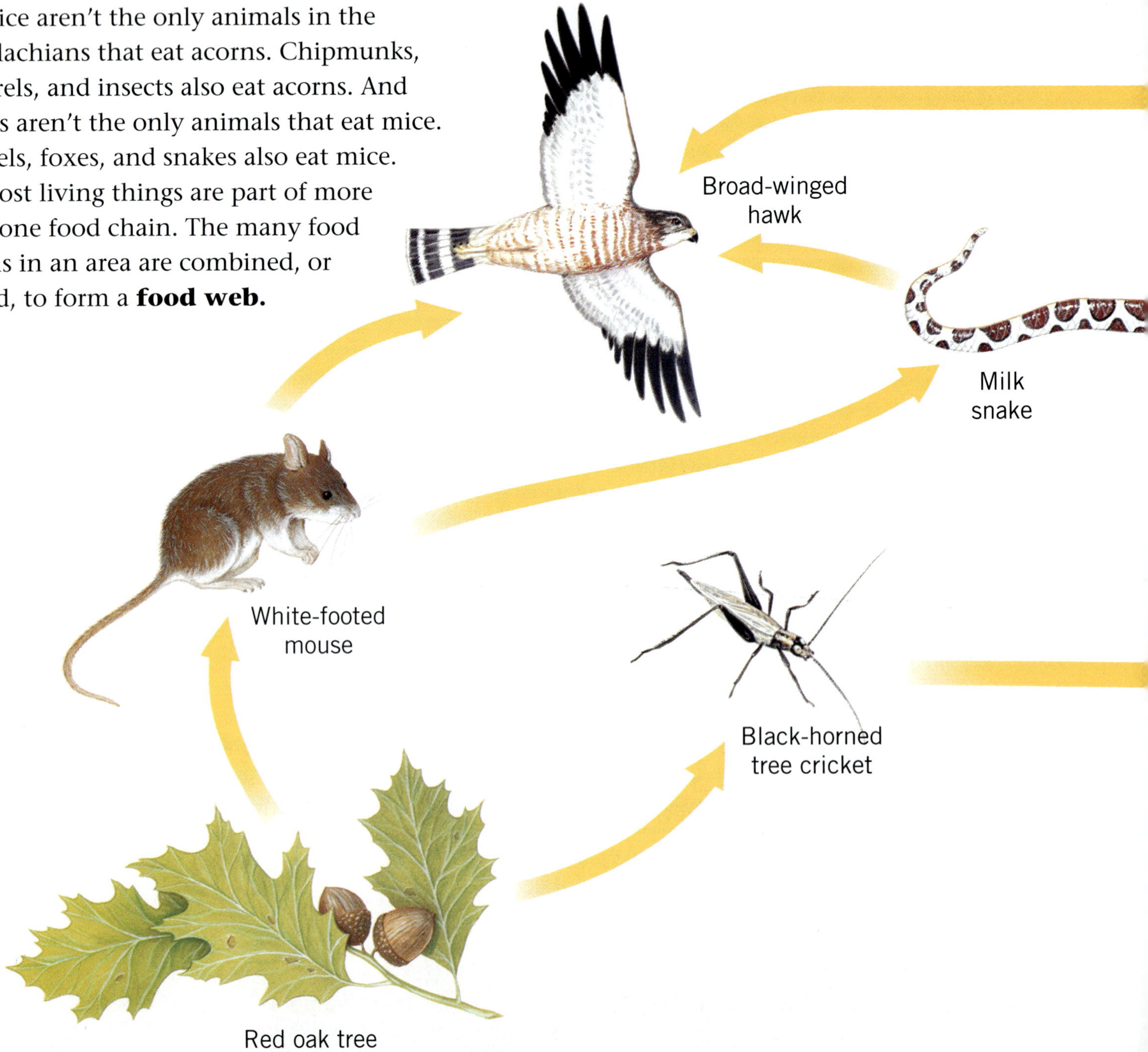

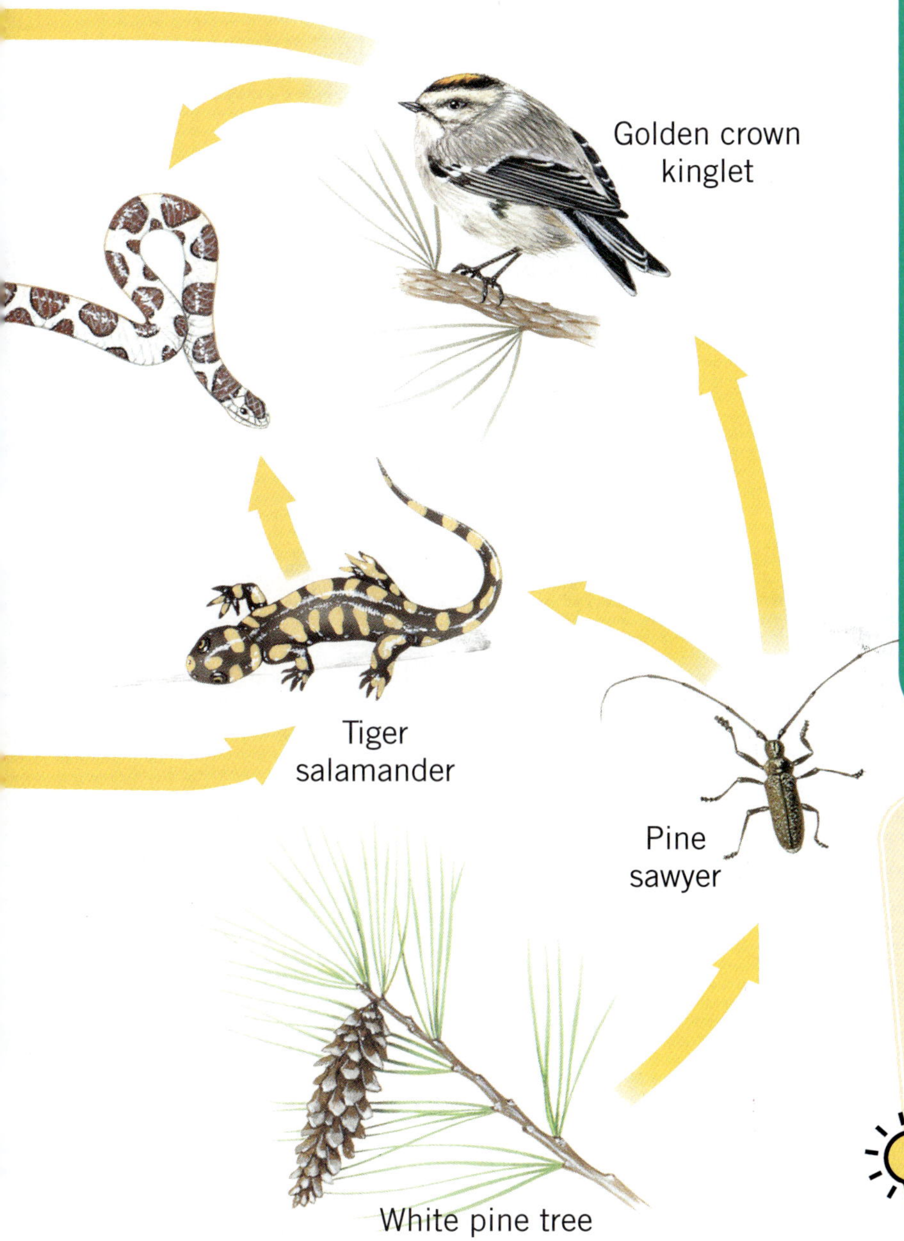

DILEMMA

Deer Overpopulation

In the past, wolves preyed on deer. Then people killed the wolves. Today, deer have overpopulated many areas. Deer must compete for a limited food supply. Many starve to death each year. In most areas, deer hunting is permitted for several weeks. Some people have suggested that natural predators, such as wolves, should be reintroduced in some areas to control the deer population.

Think About It Should wolves be reintroduced? Should the hunting season be extended? Are there other solutions to the problem? Write a letter to a local official and explain your ideas.

How are you doing?

1. Describe how the energy in a producer is transferred to other living things in a food chain.
2. What is the difference between a food chain and a food web?
3. **Think** How would overpopulation of a consumer, like deer, affect a food web?

How can food webs change?

What would happen if all the red oaks were to disappear from the Appalachians? When producers in an environment are destroyed, many living things in that food web are affected. If red oaks disappeared, mice might begin feeding more heavily on different kinds of seeds and plants. But with less food, fewer mice might survive. What might happen to hawks and snakes if there were fewer mice living in the area?

When one part of a food web is affected, many other living things are also affected.

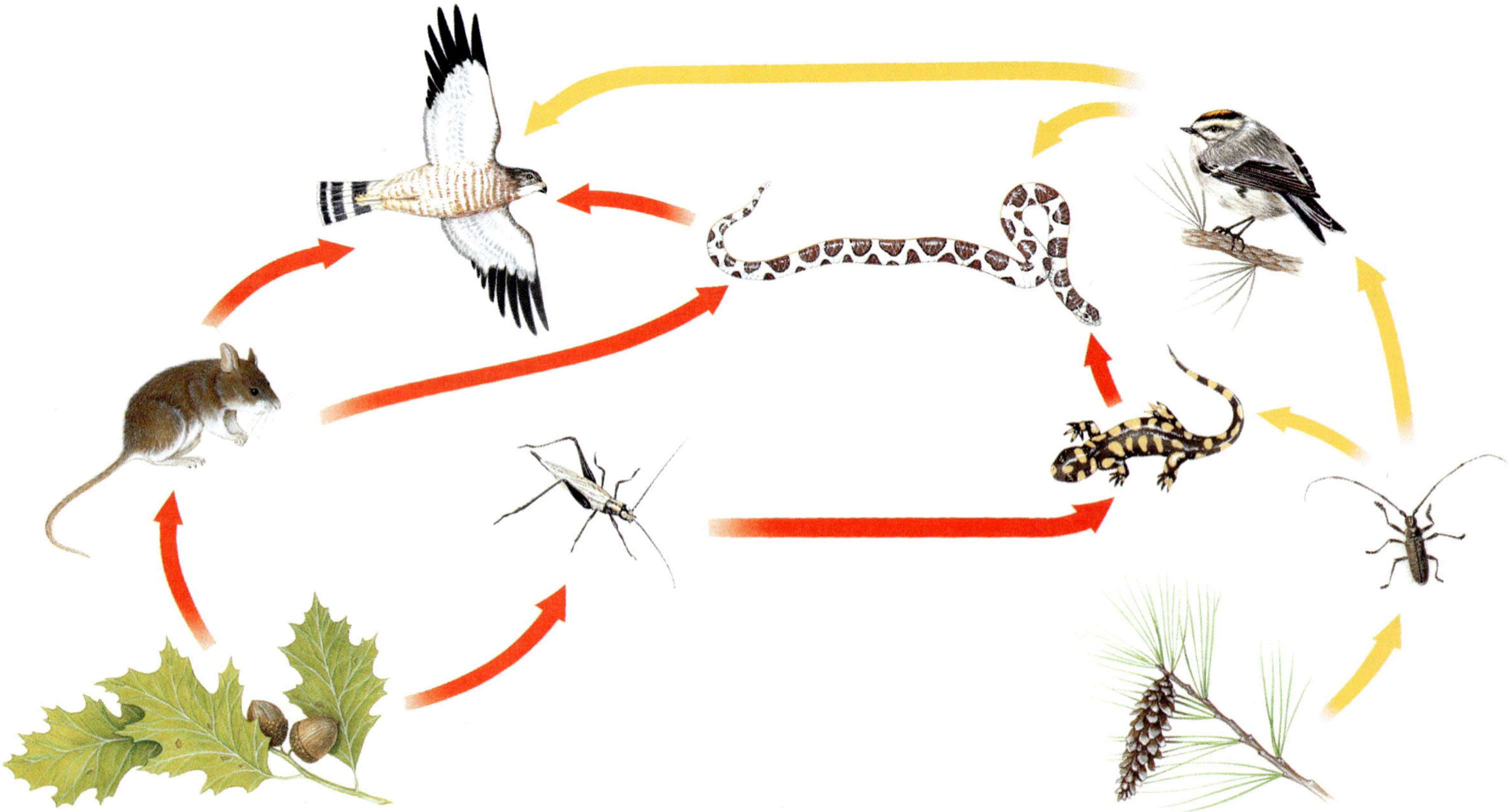

Natural factors can disturb food webs. Lightning, for example, can start forest fires that destroy an area's food webs. If a late frost kills plants, animals also suffer. Food webs can be greatly affected by changes in the environment. Sometimes these changes are caused by the activities of people.

Pesticides, or poisons used to kill insects or other animals, can harm members of a food web. Consumers may take in poison when they eat plants or animals that have been poisoned. Pesticides can also dissolve in rain, streams, and lakes. These poisons may be taken in by producers as they grow. When consumers feed on producers contaminated by poison, the poison is passed through the food web.

Be a Scientist

HANDS-ON ACTIVITY

How do poisons pass through food webs?

Your teacher will assign you a role as a grasshopper, a shrew, or a hawk. A paper bag represents your stomach. Paper squares represent plants to be eaten by the grasshoppers. Shrews, in turn, eat grasshoppers, and then hawks eat shrews. When a consumer eats another animal, the predator takes his or her prey's paper bag. Follow your teacher's directions.

At the end of the activity, meet with other students. Any creatures who have not been eaten should count the number of white squares and colored squares that they have. Your teacher will tell you what the different colored squares mean.

SCIENCE JOURNAL

Observe some of the plants and animals that live in your neighborhood or near your school. In your Science Journal, draw the food webs that connect these plants and animals.

BACK HOME

How do people affect food webs?

One way people affect food webs is by using pesticides. A pesticide called DDT entered food webs when it was used to kill insects. Hawks and other birds that are predators also became contaminated. Some birds, such as peregrine falcons, were wiped out in some areas by DDT. The poison caused their eggshells to weaken and break before hatching time, killing the baby birds.

A researcher in New York captured a few peregrine falcons. He fed them food that had no DDT in it. These birds were able to lay eggs with strong shells. Scientists took care of the young falcons until they were old enough to find their own food. Then they released the birds on steep mountains or city skyscrapers. Today DDT has been banned and peregrine falcons nest in Montreal, Baltimore, and New York, as well as other cities and countrysides.

DDT has been banned and the peregrine falcon population is increasing.

PEOPLE

SCIENCE TECHNOLOGY & SOCIETY

Rachel Carson

Rachel Carson worked as a biologist for the U.S. Fish and Wildlife Service and later became a writer. Her 1962 book, *Silent Spring,* described how pesticides had spread through food chains and warned of the danger pesticides posed to the environment. As a result of Rachel Carson's work and the work of others, laws have been passed to control or ban pesticides.

Kudzu growing in the Appalachians

Another way people have affected food webs is by bringing new species of plants or animals to an area. In the Appalachians, for example, a vine called Kudzu was brought from Japan in the late 1800s. Today Kudzu grows over trees and bushes in many places in the Appalachians.

New species affect food webs in several ways. Kudzu provides more food for some kinds of herbivores. The trees and other producers that kudzu vines cover, however, often die. Because the native plants die, herbivores that depend on native plants may also starve. The introduction of a new kind of living thing into a food web affects every member of the food web. Some members of the food web benefit, but many other members of the food web are harmed.

In some places, people have introduced new species of consumers to an area. How do you think this affects the producers in a food web? How do you think the introduction of new consumers affects other consumers in a food web?

How are you doing?

1. Describe one way food webs change.
2. Choose an animal from the food web shown on pages A32–A34. How would the removal of this animal affect both producers and carnivores?
3. **Think** Compare the effects of removing a producer with the effects of removing a consumer from a food web.

Food Chain Song

Have you heard the song, "I know an old lady who swallowed a fly"? It is a nonsense verse about an imaginary food chain. Parts of the song are accurate. For example, spiders eat flies. Other parts of the song are not accurate. For instance, a horse is an herbivore, so it would not swallow a goat.

Below is an excerpt from the song. Draw a food chain according to the words below. Then, rewrite the words so that they represent a real food chain. Can you think of other songs that tell you something about animals or the environment? Make a list of these songs.

I know an old lady who swallowed a horse.
She died of course.
She swallowed the horse to catch the goat,
She swallowed the goat to catch the dog,
She swallowed the dog to catch the cat,
She swallowed the cat to catch the bird,
She swallowed the bird to catch the spider,
That wriggled and jiggled
and squiggled inside her.
She swallowed the spider to catch the fly,
I don't know why she swallowed that fly,
perhaps she'll die.

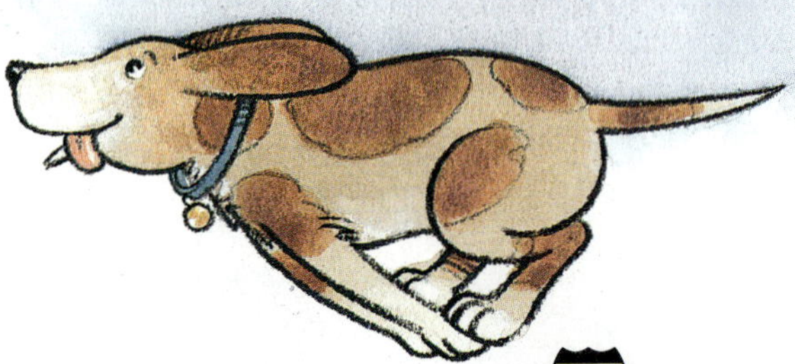

Data Collection and Analysis

How can you predict changes in populations?

Observe and Collect Data

1. In your Activity Journal, draw a food chain connecting the living things listed in the chart below.
2. Make graphs of the population data. Draw a different graph for each plant or animal.

	Year 1	Year 2	Year 3	Year 4
Plants (kg)	120,000	60,000	30,000	15,000
Mice	12,000	6,000	3,000	1,500
Owls	8	4	2	

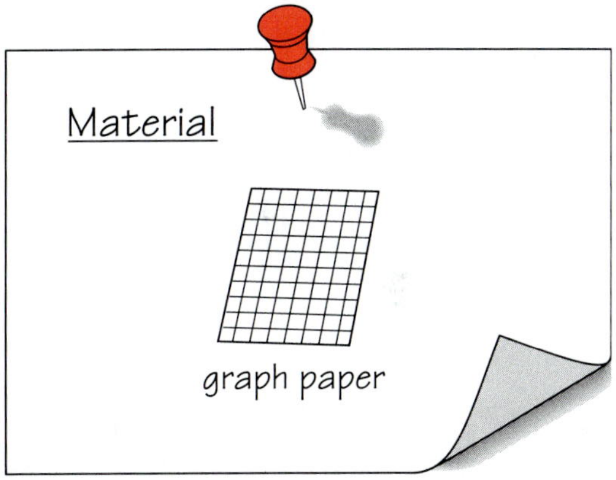

3. **Predict** how many owls there would be in year 4 by extending the lines of your graph. Record your prediction in your Activity Journal.

Draw Conclusions

1. How are the number of plants, mice, and owls in each year related?
2. **Predict** what would happen if the amount of plants increased in year 4.

Looking Back

Words and Concepts

Read each statement. If a statement is true, write *true* as your answer. If a statement is false, change the underlined word or phrase to a word or phrase that will make the statement true.

1. All of the energy in a food web can be traced back to the sun.
2. In a food web, some of the energy obtained by an herbivore is passed on to the carnivore that eats the herbivore.
3. Many linked food chains together make up a food producer.
4. Nutrients, such as DDT, can be passed on to consumers in a food web.
5. Most predators feed on more than one kind of prey.
6. Kudzu is a plant that is native to the Appalachians.

Applied Thinking Skills

Answer the following questions. You can use words, drawings, and diagrams in your answers.

7. How does the amount of energy change in a food chain? Explain your answer.
8. Describe how the introduction of cattle might affect a food web. How would producers, such as grass, be affected? How would consumers, such as deer, be affected?
9. If many producers are removed from a food web, would an herbivore, carnivore, omnivore, or decomposer be affected first? Explain your answer.
10. **Your World** How would an increase in the number of insects affect food webs in your area?

Show What You Know

MINDS-ON ASSESSMENT

Where are you in the food chain?

Process Skills
Inferring, Interpreting data

Observe and Collect Data

1. ACTIVITY JOURNAL List all the foods that you had for lunch in your Activity Journal. If possible, list some of the ingredients that made up each part of your lunch.
2. Choose one food and trace it back to a living thing. If the living thing is a consumer, trace the path back to a producer. Draw or describe how the food reached you.
3. Trade your drawing or description with other students. Compare and contrast your results.

Draw Conclusions

1. Based on the steps it takes to get the food to you, how does eating food from producers compare with eating food from consumers?
2. If you decided to eat more fruits and vegetables and less meat, cheese, and eggs, would you be increasing your consumption of producers or of consumers?

Chapter 3

The Environment

You're tired when you reach the end of the day's hike. Your campsite is in a small meadow near a lake. Even though you have finished your hike, there is still work to do before you settle down for the evening. You must set up a tent and cook dinner.

You are a visitor in the forest. Many creatures have permanent homes in the Appalachian Mountains. One of these animals, a raccoon, comes out of the woods and heads for the lake. The raccoon moves cautiously, searching for food. Someone in camp rattles a mess kit and the raccoon scrambles up a nearby tree and disappears into a hole.

A small tent is your temporary home in the forest. Like you, the raccoon has a place to stay in the forest. The hole in the tree is a den shared by the raccoon and members of its family. The den provides shelter and some security for the raccoons.

You brought your food and water with you in your backpack. The raccoons must find their food and water in the forest. If you don't take care, some of the food the raccoons find might come out of your backpack!

SCIENCE JOURNAL

In your Science Journal, describe how you think the environment meets the needs of other living things in the forest.

Explore Activity

How does the environment affect living things?

Process Skills
Interpreting data, Making a graph

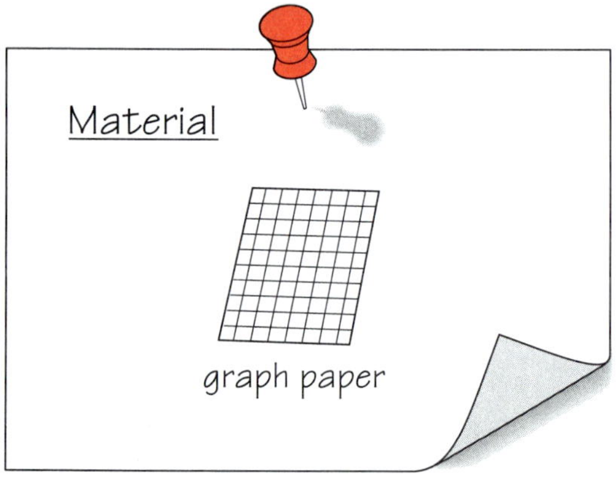

Observe and Collect Data

1. Form four groups. Group 1 is deer. The other three groups are parts of the environment: Group 2 is food, group 3 is water, and group 4 is shelter. Deer stand on one side of a gym or large area, and parts of the environment stand on the other side. One student acts as a scorekeeper.
2. At the beginning of each round, each deer decides whether it's looking for food, water, or shelter. Deer place their hands over their stomachs, mouths, or heads to indicate which element of the habitat they are seeking. Students who represent food, water, and shelter use the same signs the deer use to show what they are.
3. Each deer looks for an environment player that has the sign that the deer is seeking. The first deer to reach the part of the environment it is seeking "captures" that component.
4. Captured environment players become deer in the next round. Any deer that do not find what they are seeking die. They become food, water, or shelter in the next round.
5. ACTIVITY JOURNAL Play fifteen rounds of this game. After each round, the scorekeeper counts the number of deer. At the end of the activity, copy the scorekeeper's data in your Activity Journal. Make a graph of the data.

Share Your Results

What strategies did you and your classmates use as deer to get what you needed from the environment?

Draw Conclusions

1. What do animals need to survive?
2. How does a population change over time?

Apply What You Know

Predict how changes in the population of deer would affect populations of other herbivores, carnivores, omnivores, and producers.

What makes up a habitat?

The lake and forest provide food, water, and shelter for the beaver.

You set up camp along the shore of a lake. A small stream runs into the lake. Beavers have dammed up the stream with sticks, mud, and plants. Dams help protect the lodges made of mud and sticks that the beavers live in. These lodges shelter beavers from bad weather and protect them from predators.

The lake and surrounding forest make up the habitat for the beavers. A **habitat** (hab′i tat′) is a place where a population of plants or animals live and interact with the environment. A habitat provides the food, shelter, and water that a living thing needs.

SCIENCE JOURNAL

In your Science Journal, describe your habitat. How does your habitat provide the things you need to live? What other living things share your habitat?

BACK HOME

The wood duck shares the beaver's habitat.

The cattail has a small habitat.

Animals and plants share their habitat with other living things. One of the animals that shares the beavers' habitat is the wood duck. The lake and forest provide food, water, and shelter for both the ducks and the beavers. Although they share the same habitat, living things play different roles in their habitat. Beavers live in lodges while the ducks live in nests. The beaver and the duck also eat different things. The beaver eats plants from the forest while the duck eats insects that live near the lake.

The habitat for a cattail plant is the side of the lake. The plant gets the food and water it needs in that spot. The cattail has its own role in that habitat. What other plants and animals do you think share the habitat near your campsite?

Career Corner

Forestry Technician

My name is Kirk Ward and I'm a forestry technician. Part of my job is keeping hiking trails clear and making sure campers follow the rules in the campgrounds. I also stock streams and lakes with fish raised in hatcheries and decide which trees should be cut down.

To become a forestry technician, you need a high school education. Many forestry technicians also go to college to study biology and forest management.

How do living things share the environment?

As you look around the lake where you have set up your camp, you wonder what other animals are living nearby. Just as you share your environment with many types of people, the plants and animals of the forest share their environment with living things both like and unlike themselves.

Many different kinds of trees grow in the forest. There are also many trees of the same type, such as silver birch. All living things of the same kind that live in an environment make up a **population.** All silver birch trees in the forest make up the silver birch population.

Silver birch trees aren't the only living things in this forest. Different types of trees, grasses, insects, and other animals also live here. Together, all of the different populations in the forest form a **community.** Members of a community interact in many ways. How do squirrels interact with trees? How do birds interact with the insect populations in the forest?

Members of the population of birds compete for seeds at this bird feeder.

Be a Scientist

How do individuals compete?

1. Spread about 50 seeds on a paper towel. Roll the towel and fold the ends. Moisten the towel and wait a few days until the seeds sprout.

2. Place potting soil in two shallow pans. Place half the sprouts in each pan, spacing them as evenly as possible. Cover the seeds with dirt. Spray the seedlings with water each day. When the seedlings are about 2 cm tall, remove some from one pan so that the seedlings in that pan have twice as much space as those in the other pan.

3. Observe and record the growth of the seedlings for several days. Record your observations in your Activity Journal. How did the growth of the seedlings in the two pans compare? In what ways are the seedlings competing?

All the silver birch trees in the forest make up the silver birch population. The silver birch population is part of the forest community. The forest community includes all the other plants and animals.

What are ecosystems?

Some of the animals that live in and around the lake depend on the lake for food and water. Fish find their food in the water. They may hide and nest among the rocks and weeds of the lake. They use their gills to get oxygen from the water. Fish depend on living things, such as weeds, to survive. They also depend on nonliving things, such as water, rocks, and oxygen.

All living things depend on nonliving parts of the environment to survive. Most living things need water, and they get it from many different places. Most plants take water from the soil. Large animals drink from lakes, ponds, and streams and get water from the food they eat. Insects and other small animals may get water from droplets clinging to rocks or plants.

The living things and the nonliving things in an environment together make up an **ecosystem** (ēk′ō sis′təm). Ecosystems include all living and nonliving things, such as water, air, and soil, in an environment.

Ecosystems have no set size. A lake can be an ecosystem. For insects and worms, a patch of soil and rocks can be an ecosystem. For a family of owls, an ecosystem can be a large part of the forest, including a nearby lake.

This bass finds the food and oxygen it needs in the water of the lake.

This ground beetle lives in a small ecosystem.

This lake ecosystem provides the food, air, water, and soil that living things need.

The owl's ecosystem is large. It depends on living and nonliving things in the lake and surrounding forest.

How are you doing?

1. What does a habitat provide?
2. What is the difference between a population and a community?
3. **Think** Imagine that you find an old tire, a plastic foam cup, and an empty bottle in the forest. Are these things part of the forest ecosystem? Why or why not?

How are materials recycled in an ecosystem?

One of the important nonliving things that plants and animals depend on is nitrogen. Living things use nitrogen to grow and repair their cells. Nitrogen is in the air all around you, but living things cannot use the nitrogen in the air. Nitrogen gas must be changed into another form before plants and animals can use it. The process of recycling nitrogen in the environment is called the nitrogen cycle.

Nitrogen is a gas that makes up most of the air you breathe.

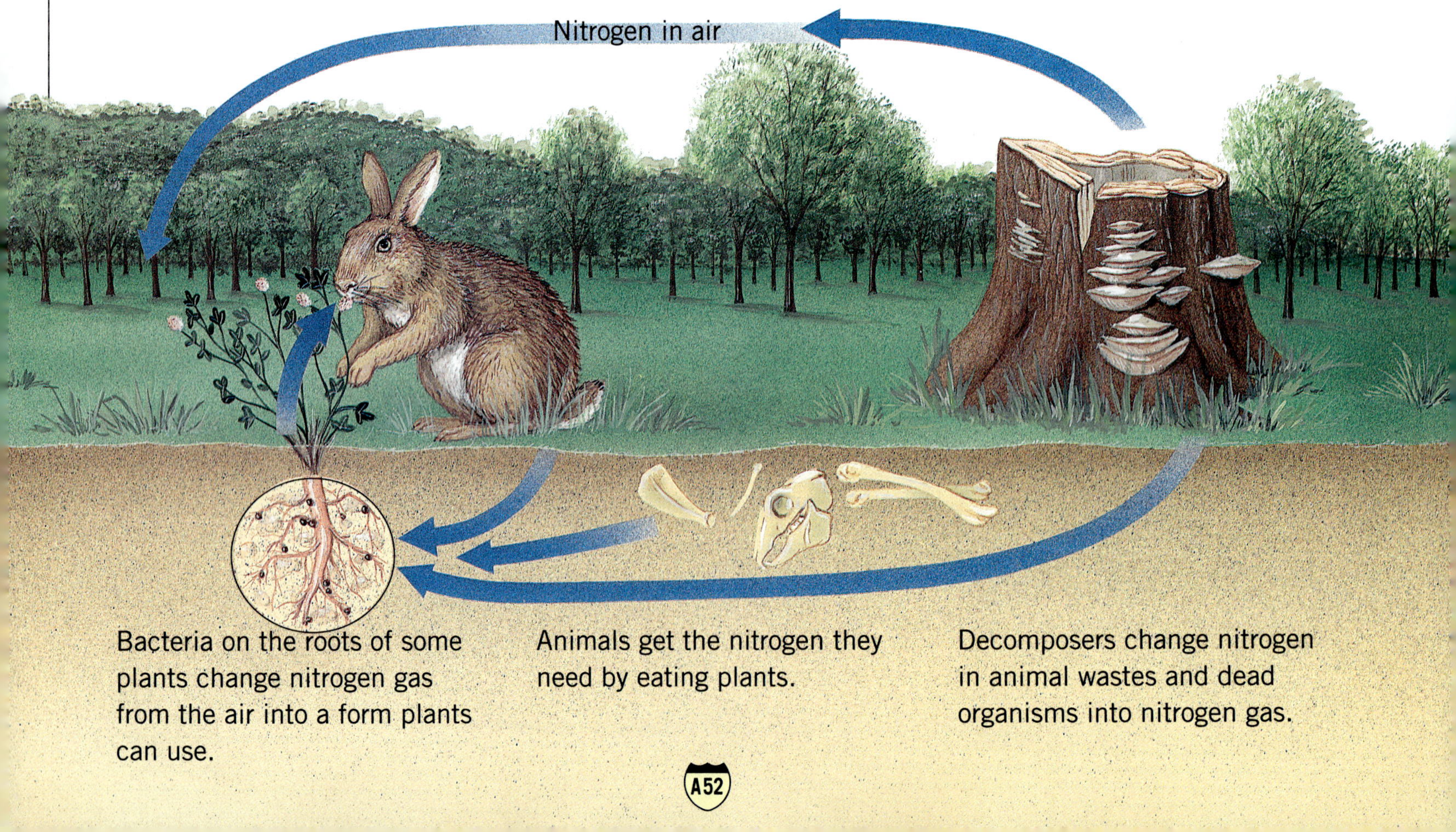

Bacteria on the roots of some plants change nitrogen gas from the air into a form plants can use.

Animals get the nitrogen they need by eating plants.

Decomposers change nitrogen in animal wastes and dead organisms into nitrogen gas.

Amazing!

Most oxygen in the air is made by small organisms in the ocean.

Living things also depend on oxygen and carbon dioxide. Plants use carbon dioxide to make energy. Animals use oxygen to release energy from the food they eat. Producers provide consumers with oxygen; consumers provide producers with carbon dioxide. These two gases are constantly recycled by the earth's living things. This process of recycling is called the oxygen-carbon dioxide cycle.

Carbon dioxide also can be produced through burning.

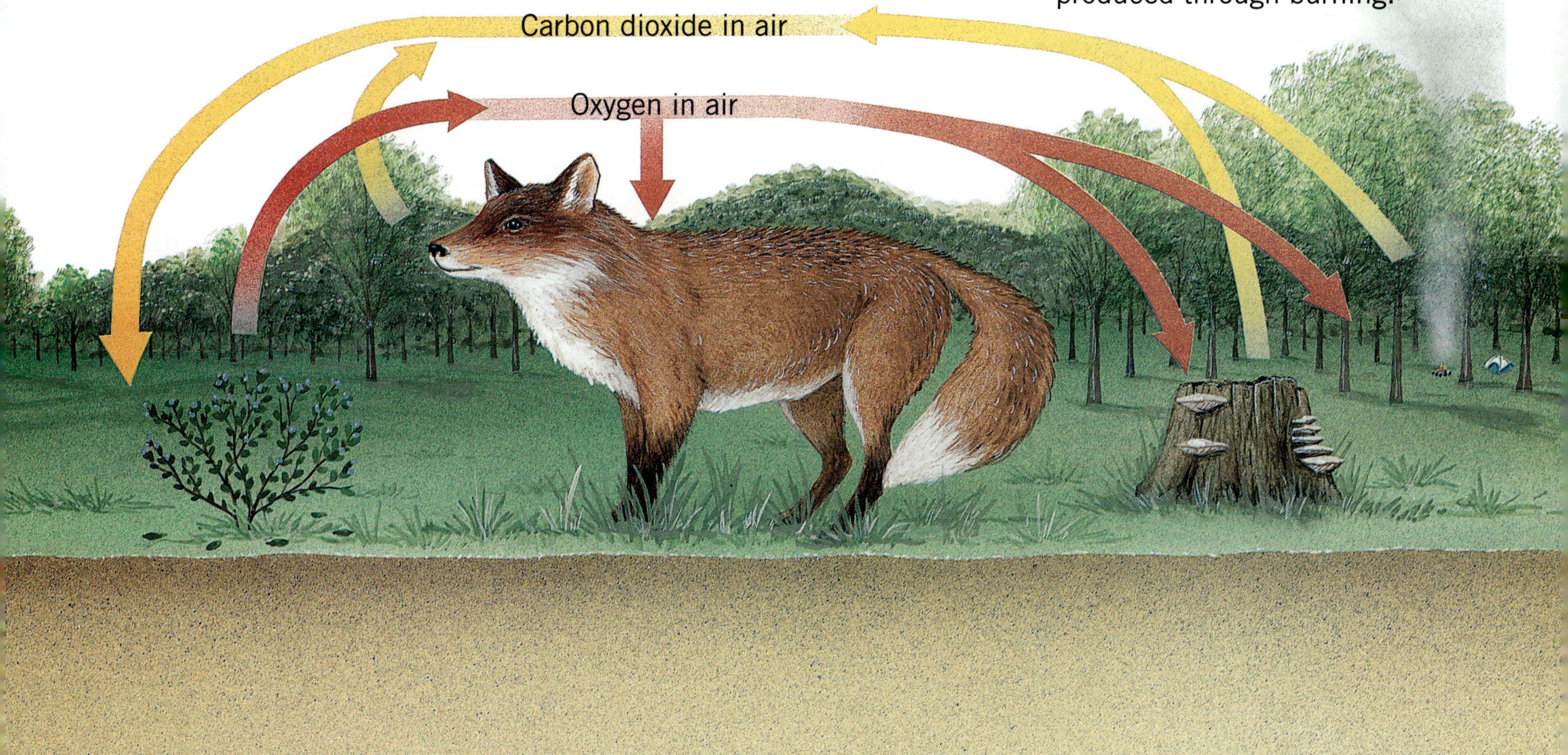

Producers take in carbon dioxide from the air and release oxygen into the air during photosynthesis.

Consumers breathe in oxygen and breathe out carbon dioxide. They use oxygen to get energy from food.

Decomposers take in oxygen and release carbon dioxide as they break down the bodies of dead organisms.

How can ecosystems change?

Sitting by the campfire, you and the other campers trade stories about hiking on the Appalachian Trail. Most of the trail was green and shady. One section, however, was filled with blackened trees. The sun was bright on that part of the trail because no leaves provided shade. A forest fire had destroyed many of the plants and animals that once lived there. Forest fires occur in many forests. Some are caused by lightning. Others are caused by the carelessness of people.

When you looked at the burned-out section of the trail, you noticed tender green shoots of grass and small wildflowers growing. These kinds of plants need a large amount of sunlight, so they thrive in the treeless area. Rabbits and other small herbivores will come to eat these plants. Larger mammals and reptiles that prey on these creatures will soon follow.

Pine seedlings also need lots of sun, and they grow quickly in the fire damaged area. Maple, oak, and birch trees will sprout from roots that survived the fire, and other trees will sprout from seeds that squirrels buried before the fire. As these taller plants grow, they will shade the grass and wildflowers that first arrived and those plants will die. Over the decades, the plants and animals of the forest will return. Fires are a natural part of the forest ecosystem. They change the ecosystem. A series of changes in an ecosystem is called **succession** (sək sesh′ən). The changes that occur in a forest after a fire are examples of succession.

Along your hike, you passed houses and roads. Succession has occurred in these areas too. When people clear an area for building, they alter the ecosystem. Some plants and animals can adapt to the changes in the ecosystem. Sometimes new plants and animals move into an area once it has been developed. Which plants and animals do you think lived in your area before it was built?

There were also areas along the trail where you saw old roads and houses that are now overgrown with plants. Nature may reclaim lands that were once developed.

Be a Scientist

How can you make a model of succession?

1. Place about 4 centimeters of soil in a large wide-mouthed jar. Add water until there is a 3-centimeter layer of water above the soil.
2. Plant an aquatic plant in the jar. Every day, add two seeds to the jar. Do not replace the water as it evaporates, but keep adding seeds.
3. 

Observe the contents of the jar for two weeks. Draw a picture or write notes in your Activity Journal about your observations.

People cause succession when they build things. Building changes an ecosystem.

Succession continues even after people have developed land.

What are examples of slow succession?

Some forms of succession, such as the changes after a forest fire, happen quickly. Other kinds are much slower. If your great-great-grandchildren were to visit your camping spot by the lake, they might find an ecosystem that is very different from the one you see there today.

Like animals and plants, ponds and lakes have a natural life span. Small, shallow bodies of water last for less time than large, deep lakes. The water that flows into a pond or lake carries soil and plant matter. This material settles on the bottom and adds nutrients to the water. These nutrients allow plants and animals to live in the pond. As these plants and animals die, they too fall to the bottom of the pond.

As the pond is gradually filled by soil and dead plant and animal matter, it becomes a marsh. Animals and plants that lived in the pond are replaced by new forms of life.

The marsh gradually becomes drier and grasses and small shrubs start to grow in the area. Over many years trees will begin to grow there too. Eventually the meadow may become a forest. A lake can be changed into a forest in as little as 500 years, though it could take as long as 10,000 years.

Today the lake near your campsite is deep. It is an ecosystem filled with fish and water plants.

Over time the lake may fill with soil and fallen leaves. Eventually it may turn into a marsh.

The marsh may eventually dry up. Land plants and animals will inhabit this ecosystem.

Thousands of years ago, mountains of ice called glaciers covered much of North America.

When the Ice Age ended, short grasses and shrubs grew on the barren landscape.

As the glaciers moved farther north, the climate became warm enough for trees to grow.

Your campsite also looked different to your ancestors than it does to you today. Thousands of years ago, a large part of the Northern Appalachian region was covered with sheets of ice called glaciers (glā′shərz). This period of time is called the Ice Age.

As the Ice Age gradually came to an end, a long period of succession began. During the Ice Age few plants could survive. After the Ice Age ended, small grasses and shrubs grew where the glaciers once were. Eventually pines grew up, creating an evergreen forest. After more time passed, slower growing trees, such as maples and oaks, grew in the pine forest. This created the mixed forest you can camp in today.

How are you doing?

1. Draw a sketch of the oxygen-carbon dioxide cycle.
2. What is the difference between the kind of succession that occurs after a forest fire and slow succession?
3. **Think** Describe the stages of succession that would occur on a vacant lot after a building has been torn down.

Looking Back

Words and Concepts

Choose the term that correctly completes each of the following statements.

1. All of the living things in an ecosystem make up the ____.
   a. habitat
   b. community
   c. population
   d. cycles
2. The series of changes that an ecosystem may undergo is called ____.
   a. the nitrogen cycle
   b. habitat destruction
   c. succession
   d. energy flow
3. During the oxygen-carbon dioxide cycle, oxygen is returned to the air by ____.
   a. producers
   b. consumers
   c. decomposers
   d. parasites
4. Clearing a forest to build a shopping mall will most likely result in ____.
   a. habitat loss
   b. symbiosis
   c. the nitrogen cycle
   d. the oxygen cycle.
5. The place where living things interact with their environment is their ____.
   a. community
   b. population
   c. habitat
   d. food web
6. A scientist studying meadow mice in an area is studying a ____.
   a. population
   b. community
   c. succession
   d. habitat loss

The eruption of Mount Saint Helens changed the surrounding ecosystems.

Applied Thinking Skills

Answer the following questions. You can use words, drawings, and diagrams in your answers.

7. Describe the populations and community in a garden.
8. Describe a small ecosystem that might be part of a larger ecosystem.
9. Draw pictures that show the steps of succession that occurred after the volcano Mount Saint Helens erupted.
10. **Your World** Describe your ecosystem. What are some examples of succession in your ecosystem?

Show What You Know

How do people change habitats?

Observe and Collect Data

1. Count off by threes. Members of group 1 will be herbivores, group 2 will be carnivores, and group 3 will be builders.
2. Herbivores and carnivores construct their habitats. Use green construction paper to represent food, blue construction paper to represent water, and brown construction paper to represent shelter. Each type of animal takes its place in its habitat.
3. Builders then use chairs or desks to build a housing development and/or shopping mall. As soon as two or more elements of any animal's habitat are covered, that animal must leave the area. If a herbivore is removed, any carnivore that eats that herbivore must leave too.
4. ACTIVITY JOURNAL In your Activity Journal, draw a plan showing what the development looked like. Also record how habitats were affected by the building.

Draw Conclusions

1. How many animals were left in the area when the construction was complete?
2. Could houses and a shopping area have been built disturbing fewer habitats? Draw a plan in your Activity Journal showing how this could be done.

Process Skills

Making models, Inferring

Materials

green, blue, and brown construction paper

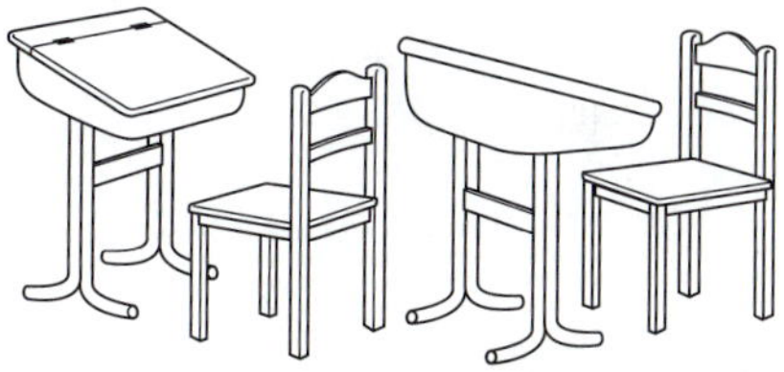

chairs and desks

Ecosystems

Work by yourself, with a partner, or in a group. Select one activity to show what you know about the relationships between living things and their environments.

Sports Promoter Many schools and sports teams have animals as mascots. Pick a mascot for your class. Describe its place in the food web, identify what type of consumer it is, and describe an ecosystem where it might be found. Give reasons why it would be a good mascot.

Artist Identify the producers and consumers that live in a park. Draw or describe their habitat. Design a poster to encourage park visitors to be aware of the habitats there.

Poet/Songwriter Create a song or poem that describes the environment, including the living things, found in the forest.

Zoo Curator Pick a zoo animal. Research its habitat. Create a "natural" zoo exhibit for this animal. Make a sketch or model of your plan.

Museum Exhibit Planner Imagine that you must plan a forest exhibit. List all of the things you will need for your exhibit. For the living things, plan on using lifelike models. Describe how you will arrange the living things and nonliving things in your exhibit.

Puppeteer Make puppets that represent the living and nonliving things in an ecosystem. Present a play with the puppets, showing how the parts of an ecosystem interact with one another.

Glossary

carnivore (kär′nə vôr′) An animal that eats other animals. (page A17)

community (kə myo͞o′nə tē) The different populations of living things that live together in an environment. (page A48)

consumer (kən so͞om′ər) A living thing that eats other living things to get energy. (page A11)

decomposer (dē′kəm pōz′ər) A living thing that gets energy by breaking down dead organisms. (page A18)

ecosystem (ēk′ō sis′təm) The living things and nonliving things, such as air, water, and soil, in an environment. (page A50)

food chain (fo͞od chān) The path by which energy is passed from one living thing to another. (page A30)

food web (fo͞od web) The combined food chains in a habitat or ecosystem. (page A32)

habitat (hab′i tat′) A place where a living thing interacts with its environment. (page A46)

herbivore (hər′bə vôr′) A living thing that eats producers. (page A16)

omnivore (äm′ni vôr′) A living thing that eats both plants and animals. (page A20)

population (päp′yo͞o lā′shən) The living things of the same kind that live in an environment. (page A48)

predator (pred′ə tər) An animal that captures and kills its food. (page A12)

prey (prā) An animal that is caught and eaten by a predator. (page A12)

producer (prō do͞os′ər) A living thing that makes its own food. (page A10)

scavenger (skav′in jər) An animal that consumes dead animals but does not usually kill them itself. (page A21)

succession (sək sesh′ən) A series of changes in an ecosystem and the communities found in an ecosystem. (page A54)

symbiosis (sim′bi ō′sis) A partnership between living things. (page A14)

Unit A Index

Boldface numerals denote glossary terms. Italic numerals denote illustrations.

Credits

Photographs

1(inset) Frank Logue; 1 Larry Ulrich/DRK Photo; 2(inset) Frank J. Miller/Photo Researchers; 2–3 H. Mark Weidman; 3(inset) Frank Logue/Stock South; 4BR Larry Ulrich; 4BL Rod Planck/Tom Stack & Associates; 4T Mary Clay/Tom Stack & Associates; 5 Ken Karp*; 6–7 Michael P. Gadomski/Earth Scenes; 7BL Breck Kent/Animals, Animals; 7BR Frank Siteman/Stock, Boston; 7TC John Cancalosi/DRK Photo; 7TL Karen Lawrence/Stock South; 7TR Marty Cordano/DRK Photo; 8 Elliott Smith*; 9 Elliott Smith*; 10 Tom & Pat Leeson/DRK Photo; 11 Kerry T. Givens/Tom Stack & Associates; 12–13 Zig Leszczynski/Animals, Animals; 12 R. H. Armstrong/Animals, Animals; 13L Stephen J. Krasemann/DRK; 13R Wayne Lankinen/DRK; 14L Tim Davis*; 14R Rocky Mountain Laboratories, Niaid, NIH./Photo Researchers; 15L John Gerlach/DRK Photo; 15R Thomas R. Fletcher/Stock, Boston; 16B Ken Karp*; 16T Stephen J. Krasemann/DRK Photo; 17B Jeff Lepore/Photo Researchers; 17C Oxford Scientific Films/Animals, Animals; 17T Ken Karp*; 18BL Ken Karp*; 18BR D. Cavagnaro/DRK Photo; 18T E. R. Degginger/Earth Scenes; 19 H. Mark Weidman; 20B Jeanne White/Photo Researchers; 20T Erwin and Peggy Bauer/Bruce Coleman Inc.; 21B Gary R. Zahm/DRK Photo; 21T Eric A. Soder/OKAPIA/Photo Researchers; 24B Joe McDonald/Bruce Coleman Inc.; 24T Joseph T. Collins/Photo Researchers; 25 Elliott Smith*; 26–27 Tom Bean/DRK Photo; 26 Art Wolfe/AllStock; 27 Leonard Lee Rue III/Tom Stack & Associates; 29 Ken Karp*; 36L Ron Willocks/Animals, Animals; 36R Alfred Eisenstaedt/LIFE Magazine, © Time Warner; 37 Kevin Vandivier/Viesti Associates, Inc.; 38 Ken Karp*; 39BC Breck P. Kent/Animals, Animals; 39BL E. R. Degginger/Photo Researchers; 39BR Joe McDonald/Animals, Animals; 39(Backgrd) GHP Studio*; 39T James R. Fisher/DRK Photo; 40 Jock Montgomery/Bruce Coleman Inc.; 41 Ken Karp*; 42 Leonard Lee Rue III/Photo Researchers; 42–43 Tom Bean/DRK Photo; 45 Elliott Smith*; 46B S. Nielsen/Bruce Coleman Inc.; 46T John Johnson/DRK Photo; 47L Greg Vaughn/Tom Stack & Associates; 47R Michael Greenlar/The Image Works; 48 Grant Heilman/Grant Heilman Photography; 48–49 Frank Logue; 50–51 Larry Ulrich; 50B Gilbert S. Grant/Photo Researchers; 50T Steinhart Aquarium/Tom McHugh/Photo Researchers; 51 Patti Murray/Animals, Animals; 54B Stan Osolinski/The Stock Market; 54T Breck P. Kent/Earth Scenes; 55L Culver Pictures, Inc.; 55R Michael P. Gadomski/Photo Researchers; 58 Owen Franken/Stock, Boston; 59 GHP Studio*

Special thanks to Malcolm X Elementary School, Berkeley, California; Franklin Year-Round School, Oakland, California; Carl B. Munck Elementary School, Oakland, California; Hintil Ku Ka Child Care Center, Oakland, California.

*Photographed expressly for Addison-Wesley Publishing Company, Inc.

Illustrations

Nea Bisek 8, 25, 28, 39, 59
Carlyn Iverson 30, 31, 32–33, 34, 52, 53B, 56, 57
Maryland CartoGraphics 6
Michael Maydak 22
Jane McCreary 9, 29, 44, 53T
Randy Vergoustraete 60–61
Pat Welch 38

Text

22–23 Harold Courlander, "All Things are Linked," *The Crest and the Hide and Other African Stories of Heroes, Chiefs, Bards, Hunters, Sorcerers and Common People* (New York: Coward, McCann & Geoghegan, 1982). Text copyright © 1982 by Harold Courlander. Reprinted with permission of the author.

Launch minus 10 seconds

. . . 9 . . . 8 . . . 7. . . The three launch engines light. The shuttle shakes and strains at the bolts holding it to the launching pad. The computers check the engines. It isn't up to us anymore—the computers will decide whether we launch.

. . . 3 . . . 2 . . . 1 . . . The rockets light! The shuttle leaps off the launch pad in a cloud of steam and a trail of fire. Inside, the ride is rough and loud. Our heads are rattling around inside our helmets. We can barely hear the voices from Mission Control in our headsets above the thunder of the rockets and engines. For an instant I wonder if everything is working right. But there's no more time to wonder, and no time to be scared.

—*To Space & Back*
by Sally Ride with Susan Okie

Space Shuttle

The space shuttle and its crew are leaving the earth. But, oddly, by leaving the earth they will learn more about it.

The shuttle moves into an orbit 320 kilometers above the earth. From that height, great rivers look like threads winding down to blue oceans. Entire mountain ranges look like crumpled sheets on a bed. Some parts of the earth look green, white, or tan. A large part of the earth looks blue.

- What are conditions like in different parts of the earth?
- What plants and animals live in different parts of the land?
- What plants and animals live in the water?

BIOMES

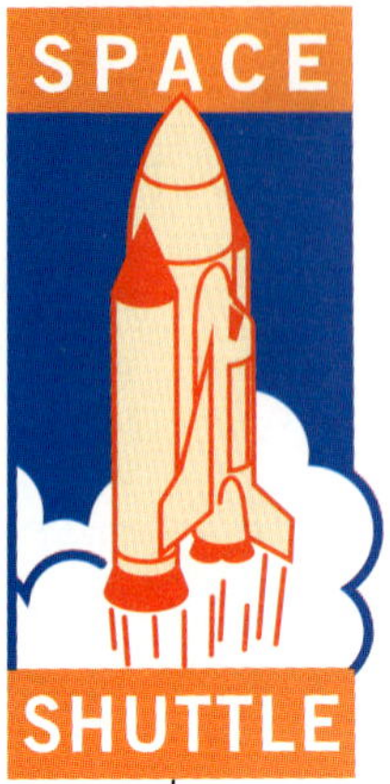

Mae Jamison, Astronaut

Activities

Features

Chapter 1

Biome Features

When you look at something up close, you can see many details. Look at the squirrel on the tree branch, for example. As you move farther away, you can see fewer details, but you also see a larger area.

From the space shuttle, astronauts can see large areas of land and water. Some compare it to a patchwork quilt. It is covered with many different colors and textures. If the astronauts could look at these places close up, they would see that each "patch" has different conditions and living things.

SCIENCE JOURNAL Write in your Science Journal about the details you can see in the pictures on this page.

What conditions affect plant growth?

MINDS-ON ACTIVITY

Process Skills
Inferring, Predicting

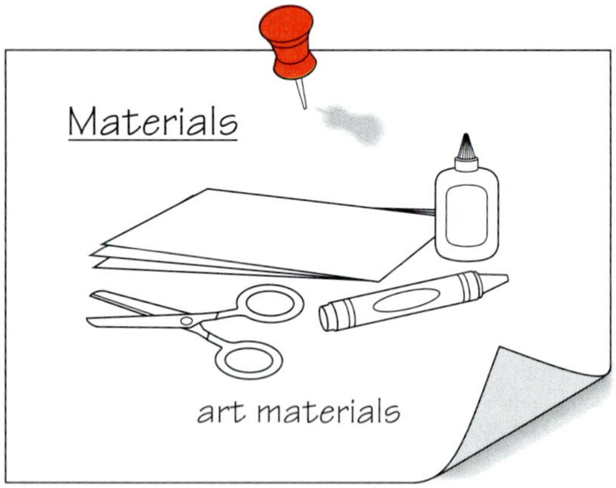

Observe and Collect Data

1. ACTIVITY JOURNAL Draw a picture of a plant that grows near your home. Describe the plant in your Activity Journal.
2. Now imagine that the temperature is 20˚C colder than it usually is in your area. Draw and describe a new picture of a plant you think might grow under these conditions. You can invent a new plant.
3. Draw and describe another plant that would grow in an area that receives half as much rain as your area does.
4. Imagine the soil in your area is different. Describe the different soil. Draw and describe a plant that would grow in this new kind of soil.

Share Your Results

Compare your pictures with those of your classmates. How are the plants you drew similar or different?

Draw Conclusions

Explain how each plant you drew survives the conditions of its environment.

Apply What You Know

Select one of your drawings and add animals that could live under those conditions.

Earth homes: What makes them different?

As the space shuttle orbits the earth, its astronauts spot different kinds of land below. Each kind of land is a home for living things. And each place is different. A large area of the earth that has its own set of conditions and living things is called a **biome** (bī′ōm′).

The earth is divided into six major land biomes. These biomes are the tundra, taiga (tī′gə), temperate (tem′pər it) forest, grassland, desert, and tropical rain forest. Each biome is made up of many ecosystems with similar characteristics.

Each kind of biome shares similar physical conditions. These conditions include temperature, rainfall, amount of sunlight, and type of soil. The shuttle may fly over tropical rain forests in South America, Africa, and Asia. Even though these tropical rain forests are far apart, their physical conditions are similar.

The physical conditions determine which kinds of plants and animals live in a biome. The most abundant plants in a biome are called **climax plants.** Each kind of climax plant needs particular temperatures, soil, amounts of sunlight, and amounts of water to survive. Animals that live in each biome depend on the climax plants for food.

Desert in the southwestern United States

This is what the southwestern part of the United States looks like. What do you think it's like there? What animals live there? What are the climax plants? How much rain falls? What are the temperatures?

SCIENCE JOURNAL

Ask your friends, family members, and teachers if they have lived in different places. Ask them to describe the plants, animals, and weather in those places. Write their responses in your Science Journal.

BACK HOME

Grassland in the central United States

Temperate forest in the eastern United States

As the space shuttle moves east, the land below changes. How might the weather be similar or different from the Southwest? Are the climax plants and animals that live there similar or different? How?

As the space shuttle reaches the east coast of the United States, the land below has changed again. What is growing there? Does it get more or less rain than the other two kinds of land the shuttle has flown over?

What is climate?

If the space shuttle had flown over North America a thousand years ago, the astronauts would have seen many areas that looked similar to the way they do now. The kinds of living things in each part of the land would also have been similar.

These similarities are due to climate. **Climate** (klī′mət) describes the average weather conditions of a biome over a long period of time. Climate determines what kinds of things can survive in a place. Two important conditions that determine climate are temperature and precipitation. **Precipitation** is water that falls from the sky as rain, snow, sleet, or hail.

Winters and summers in Chicago differ from winters and summers in San Diego. Winter is usually colder in Chicago. More snow and rain fall in Chicago too. The climate of Chicago is colder and wetter than that of San Diego.

Of course, it rains in San Diego too. And sometimes it gets cold. Weather can change in San Diego from day to day. But in general, the climate of San Diego is drier and warmer than the climate of Chicago.

San Diego in summer

San Diego in winter

Chicago in summer

Chicago in winter

Be a Scientist

MINDS-ON ACTIVITY

How does your climate compare with climates in other areas?

1. ACTIVITY JOURNAL Describe your climate in your Activity Journal. Include information on temperature and precipitation.
2. Observing the weather will help you learn more about the climate. Look at the weather page in a newspaper and find the listings for temperature and precipitation. Record the temperature and precipitation for several days for both your area and another area.
3. Using the data your class gathered, make a chart for a few cities. Compare the measurements.

How are you doing?

1. What is a biome?
2. What is climate? How does climate affect living things in a biome?
3. **Think** Would one unusually cold winter change the climate of a biome? Explain your answer.

How does the amount of precipitation vary?

Clouds above the Hawaiian Islands as seen from space

A thick blanket of clouds hides the earth's surface as the space shuttle soars over the Hawaiian Islands. Much of the land below the clouds you see is covered by a rain forest. The rain forest gets more precipitation than any other biome.

As the space shuttle circles the earth, its astronauts can see areas where there is less rainfall or where the precipitation is in the form of snow. They also find places where rain falls only at certain times of the year.

Enough rain falls on this forest every year to fill a bucket four times taller than you are!

The amount of precipitation a biome receives is affected by several factors. One factor is how far the biome is from a large body of water. A second factor is the direction in which winds usually blow.

Precipitation affects which plants and animals live in a particular biome. Plants in dry climates, like cacti, store water in their stems. Desert animals, like camels, can also survive with little water. In wet climates, plants like orchids have roots in the air. They get the moisture they need without sending roots into the ground. The animals that live in wet climates also depend on the high level of precipitation for survival.

Be a Scientist

HANDS-ON ACTIVITY

How can you measure rainfall?

1. Get a clear plastic cylinder with a small diameter. Using a ruler and marker, mark a centimeter scale on the side of the cylinder, starting at the bottom.
2. Place a funnel in the top of the cylinder to catch the rain. Use masking tape to attach the funnel to the cylinder.
3. ACTIVITY JOURNAL Place your rain gauge in an outdoor location that is open to the sky. Each day check your rain gauge and record your results in your Activity Journal.

Too hot? Too cold? Just right?

High up in the space shuttle, the astronauts wear special suits to protect themselves from the space environment. Inside the suits and inside the shuttle cabin, the temperature is comfortable and is controlled by instruments. But down on the earth, the temperature varies.

In some places, like ice-covered Antarctica, near the South Pole, the temperature may dive to less than −73°C. At the other extreme, temperatures in places such as the African city of Khartoum have reached a sizzling 48°C.

The temperature of a biome depends on the amount of sunlight it receives. In general, those areas near the equator receive the most sunlight and the temperatures are higher. Farther away from the equator, the amount of sunlight decreases and temperatures are lower. Find Africa and Antarctica on the globe. Which location is closer to the equator? Which is farther away?

The farther from the equator you are, the colder the climate gets.

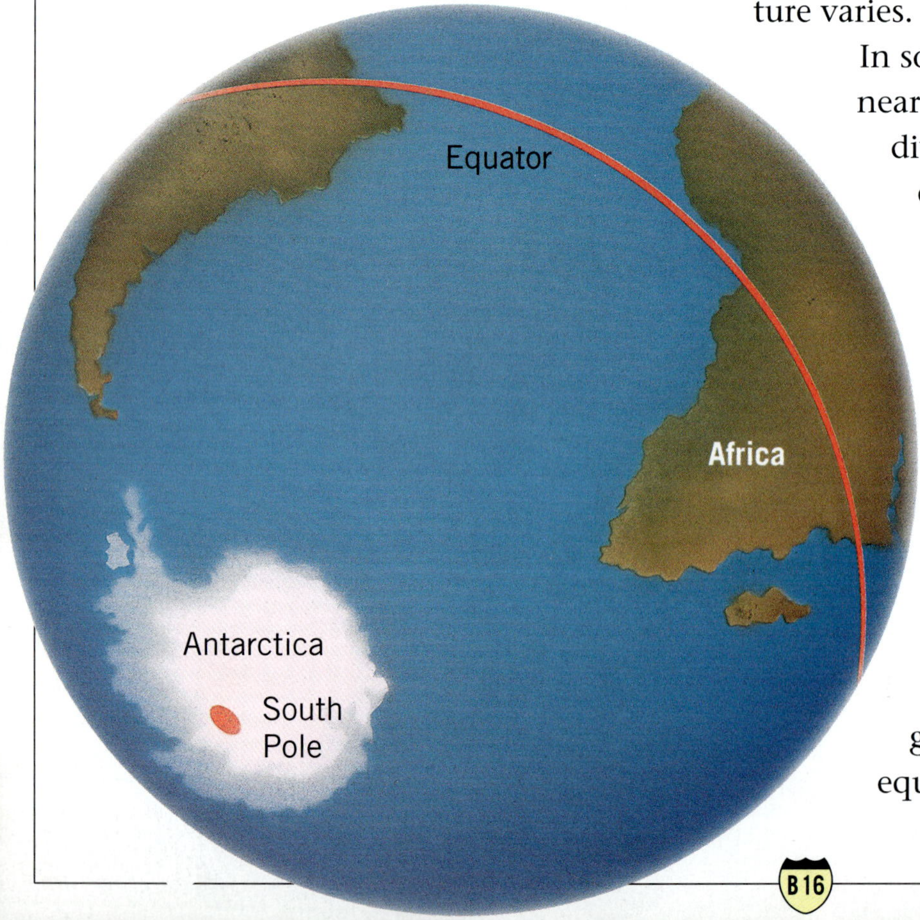

Look at the picture of the mountain on this page. The mountain is called Mount Kilimanjaro. It is in the country of Tanzania in Africa, and it is only about 340 kilometers from the equator.

It is hot at the base of the mountain. But there is snow on the mountain peak. In general, the temperature decreases as you move up a mountain.

Since height, or altitude, affects the temperature of a place, different kinds of plants and animals live at different altitudes. If you were to climb Mount Kilimanjaro, you would see different plants and animals at different altitudes. The climate would also change during your climb.

At the base of the mountain, the climate is hot and dry and farmers grow coffee and bananas. Farther up the mountain, it is colder. Here there is enough precipitation for a temperate forest to survive. Even farther up the mountain, the temperature is lower. Grasses grow at this altitude. The top of Mount Kilimanjaro is so cold that it is covered in snow and ice all year long.

Mount Kilimanjaro is the highest mountain in Africa.

How do light and soil affect plants?

The shuttle flies over some areas of the earth that are drenched in sunlight, and others where less sunlight falls on the ground. Plants need sunlight to make their food. But not all kinds of plants require the same amount of sunlight to survive. For example, some ferns grow in areas with low sunlight while some cacti are adapted to grow under intense sunlight.

Soil also affects the growth of plants. Soil is the loose material on the earth's surface in which plants can take root and grow. Plants take up nutrients from the soil and soil anchors their roots. Most soil is a mixture of a number of things, such as dead leaves, rocks, and sand. Can you think of places where there are different kinds of soil? What kinds of plants grow in these places?

YOU CAN HELP

You can enrich the soil near your home by starting a compost pile. Composting will reduce the amount of trash that you produce.

How are you doing?

1. What are four physical conditions that affect the growth of plants?
2. What kinds of temperatures are you likely to find near the equator? Far from it?
3. **Think** Why do you think there are fewer plants in a desert than in a tropical rain forest? What kind of experiment could you perform to check your answer?

Science & Literature Connection

Chúcaro
Wild Pony of the Pampa

by Francis Kalnay

This is an excerpt from a novel about a boy who finds a very special pony. The boy lives on the Pampa of South America, along with many gauchos, or cowboys.

Looking at it from an airplane flying high, the Pampa seems vast, bare, and bleak. But the gaucho does not fly so high. With his saddle only three feet from the ground, he sees an entirely different picture. From the airplane the prairie appears dead. But from the saddle you can almost hear the Pampa breathing. Plants, animals, and men, in bright colors and distinct forms, come to the foreground. They may seem asleep, but watch and you'll see—they grow and move and smell and sing. Watching still closer, you will find that each blade of Pampa grass has a story to tell, and every second something begins and something ends. Here a prairie flower is born, there an elderly mouse is dead.

The people of the Pampa love these flat prairies. There are no rocks or forests to be cleared, and the soil, that great banker, is very, very rich. The ponies, too, love the Pampa, for they can eat and run to their hearts' content. Even the windmills love the Pampa because the wind blows unbroken, free. The windmills draw the precious water. Water and sun make things grow big and happy.

Sometimes the pampero blows, the strong, cold wind of the prairies. At times it brings the heavy hail that beats down the wheat and corn and even kills the chickens and lambs. And it breaks men's hearts.

Then the sun comes out. Everything takes heart again. The tears are gone and the wounds are healed. Once more you work and sweat and smile.

Think About Your Reading

1. What physical conditions are described in this excerpt?
2. Summarize the two points of view described in the passage.

Collecting data List all the data about the Pampa that you find in the excerpt. Then use books and maps to add to what you know. Draw a picture of a scene on the Pampa. Label the plants, animals, and landforms.

Where to Read More

Phyllis Reynolds Naylor, *To Walk the Sky Path* (Dell, 1973)
Billie Tommie, a Seminole Indian, loves living in the Everglades. Will he always be able to stay there?

Looking Back

MINDS-ON ASSESSMENT

Words and Concepts

If the statement is true, write *true*. If the statement is false, replace the underlined word or phrase with a word or phrase that will make it true.

1. The details of an area become clearer as you move farther away from the area.
2. One factor that affects the environment of a place is temperature.
3. Elevation describes the average weather, including temperature and precipitation, a place usually gets over a period of time.
4. In general, the climate in a desert is warmer and wetter than in a forest.
5. A biome is a large area of the earth that has its own set of physical conditions and characteristic living things.
6. In general, the closer a place is to the equator, the lower its temperature will be.

Applied Thinking Skills

Answer the following questions. You can use words, drawings, and diagrams in your answers.

7. Two people plant flowers at the same time. After one month, one person's flowers are blooming, while the other's have died. Explain what conditions might have caused these differences.
8. How might conditions at the top of a mountain differ from conditions at the base of a mountain?
9. You decide to travel by car from Maine to Florida in January. What changes in climate would you see along the way?
10. **Your World** Describe your biome. Include information about the temperature, moisture, sun, and soil.

Show What You Know

Where are you?

Observe and Collect Data

Process Skills
Interpreting data, Making a graph

1. The data given here show conditions in two biomes. Make line graphs to display the data for each biome.
2. ACTIVITY JOURNAL Study the graphs. Describe in your Activity Journal how the physical conditions in the two biomes differ.

Average Temperature

Place	Jan.	April	July	Oct.
1	1°C	11°C	25°C	15°C
2	10°C	19°C	32°C	22°C

Average Precipitation

Place	Jan.	April	July	Oct.
1	8.4cm	8.6cm	9.4cm	7.9cm
2	1.8cm	0.8cm	2.0cm	1.3cm

Amount of Sunlight

Place	Jan. 1	April 1	July 1	Oct. 1
1	9h 25m	12h 45m	15h 00m	11h 47m
2	10h 30m	12h 30m	14h 20m	11h 50m

Draw Conclusions

1. Describe how each environment changes during the year. What is the climate of each area like?
2. **Predict** in which of these two areas you would expect to find the animal pictured on this page. Explain your answer.

Chapter 2

Land Biomes

Look at the photo from the shuttle. Not all the areas on the earth look the same. Some are covered in clouds, some are white with snow, some are green, and others are brown.

On earth there are different areas called biomes. Biomes have different climates, get different light, and have different kinds of soil. These differences mean that each biome has its own kinds of plants and characteristic animals. The colors on the map below show where the different biomes are.

SCIENCE JOURNAL In your Science Journal, predict what kinds of plants and animals you think live in each biome.

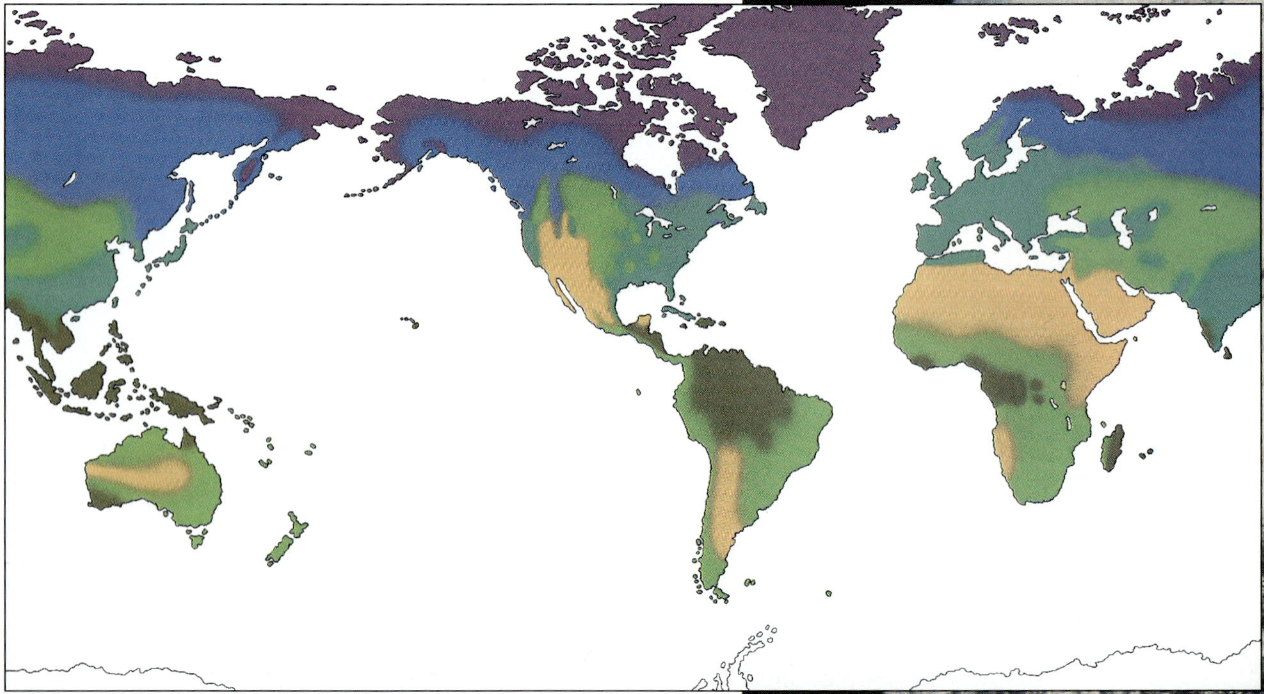

Explore Activity

Can you invent a biome?

MINDS-ON ACTIVITY

Process Skills
Making models, Inferring

Materials

art materials

If you could build your own biome, what would it be like? Could you put any kinds of plants or animals in it? Can different kinds of plants and animals survive under the same conditions?

Observe and Collect Data

1. ACTIVITY JOURNAL In your Activity Journal, make a list of the physical factors of your imaginary biome. Also decide how far north or south of the equator your biome will be located. Will it be near mountains, the ocean, or somewhere in between?
2. Draw a picture of the land in your imaginary biome without plants or animals.
3. **Predict** what plants would grow well on the land. Add plants to your drawing.
4. **Predict** what animals would live among the plants. Draw them. Show what the animals would eat and where they would get their water.

Share Your Results

Compare the biome you invented with the ones your classmates created. How was your biome similar? How was it different?

Draw Conclusions

1. What factors affect the kinds of plants that live in a biome?
2. What factors affect the kinds of animals that can survive in a biome?

Apply What You Know

Predict what would happen if the climate of your invented biome changed. Describe the change and its effects in your Science Journal.

What lives in the coldest biomes?

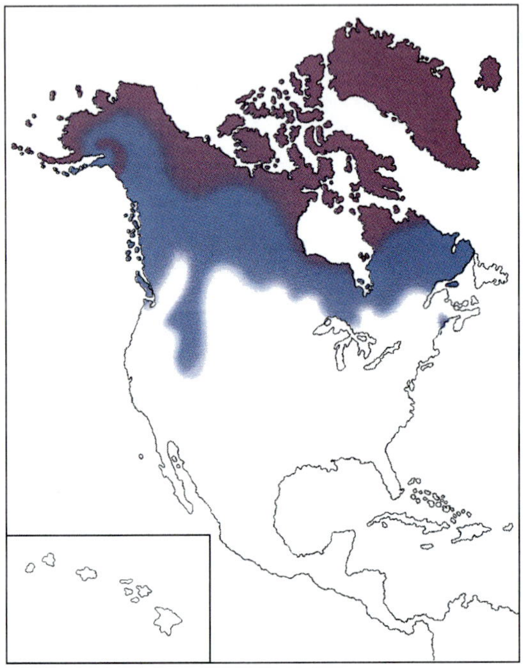

As the space shuttle passes over the northernmost parts of the earth, astronauts see a vast expanse of the earth that appears to be a single color—white. This is the **tundra,** the coldest of the biomes.

In winter, the tundra is covered with snow and the ground is frozen. Spring and summer combined are only about three months long in the tundra. In the summer, the top three or four centimeters of frozen soil melts, allowing short grasses, moss, and shrubs to grow. The tallest plant in the tundra is about as long as your finger. The bottom layer of soil stays frozen all year long.

Although the plants in the tundra are small, the animals can grow quite large. Huge herds of caribou and reindeer graze on the plants that grow here. On the coast, polar bears hunt seals. Arctic foxes, such as the one shown here, hunt animals such as hares and small rodents called lemmings. Many animals in the tundra hibernate or migrate to avoid the harsh winters.

One thing you see in the tundra is snow. Does snow fall where you live? Make a list of ways you think people's everyday lives are affected in places where it snows.

BACK HOME

As the shuttle's orbit shifts to the south, the astronauts notice that the appearance of the earth changes. Things look greener. The land is covered with evergreen trees, such as white pine, black spruce, and balsam fir. This new biome covered with evergreen trees is called the **taiga.** Sunlight strikes the taiga more directly than it strikes the tundra, so the taiga is warmer than the tundra. The taiga also receives more precipitation than the tundra.

The ground in the taiga is moist, not frozen. On the floor of the evergreen forest, shrubs and lacy ferns grow. The forest is home to herds of moose. Porcupines scurry through the shrubs, and birds sing in the trees. In some parts of the taiga, wolves can be found.

BIOME DATA

Biome	Average Temperature	Average Precipitation
Tundra	–28 to 5°C	10 to 40 cm
Taiga	–10 to 14°C	20 to 60 cm

Where do the colors change?

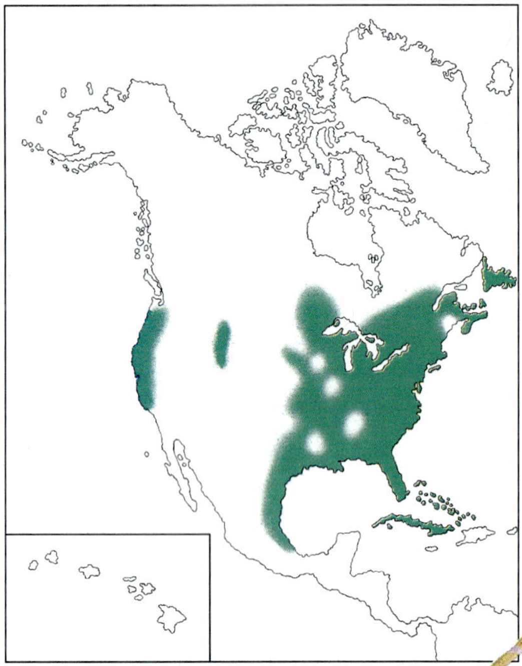

Temperate forest

Astronauts in the space shuttle see parts of the earth in different seasons. For example, during a single mission, the astronauts may see spring in North America and autumn in South America.

In the taiga the forest looks similar in all seasons. That's because the trees in these places are evergreens. Evergreens stay green all year long. Closer to the equator forests change with the seasons. In spring they look green, and in autumn they look orange, red, and yellow. In winter, after trees lose their leaves, these forests look brown. Trees that lose their leaves in autumn are called deciduous (dē sij′o͞o əs) trees.

A forest where trees change with the seasons is called a **temperate forest.** *Temperate* means "not too hot or too cold." Deciduous trees in the temperate forests include maple, oak, hickory, beech, and birch.

Temperate forests are filled with a wide variety of wildlife. White-tailed deer bound through the forests and squirrels dash up trees. Snakes and salamanders slip under rocks. Blazing red cardinals, owls, and other birds wing through the trees.

BIOME DATA

Biome	Average Temperature	Average Precipitation
Temperate forest	0 to 28°C	60 to 100 cm

CULTURAL CONNECTION

SCIENCE TECHNOLOGY & SOCIETY

Using Trees

Long before people from Europe came to America, some American Indians in the temperate forests used the wood of trees to build their homes. They also used wood to make tools, toys, and works of art.

What do we use wood for now? Look around your home and make a list of all the things made completely or partly of wood. Remember, paper is made from wood.

How are you doing?

1. Describe the animals that live in the tundra, taiga, and temperate forest.
2. Describe the kinds of plants found in the tundra, taiga, and temperate forest.
3. **Think** Would you expect wooden buildings to be least common in the tundra, taiga, or temperate forest? Why?

What lives in the dry biomes?

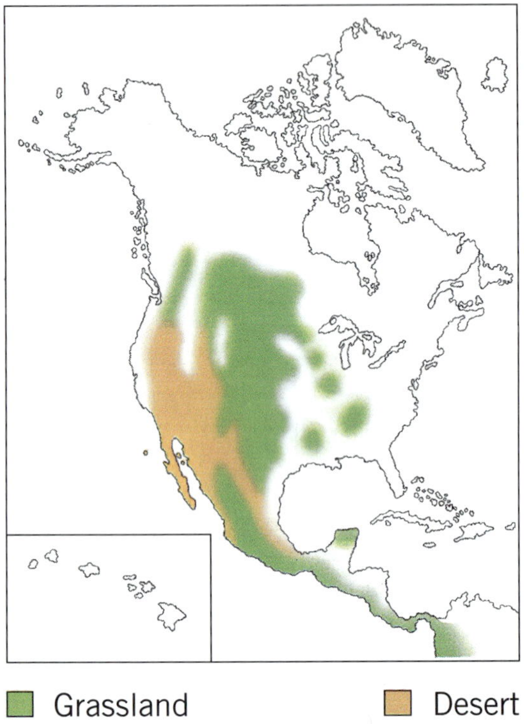

From the space shuttle, the astronauts can recognize the Rocky Mountains and the Mississippi River. They can also see the vast region that stretches between the mountains and the river.

The **grassland** is a region that does not receive enough precipitation to support the growth of trees. As you can tell by the name, grasses are the climax plants in the grassland biome. Both tall and short grasses grow in this biome. Grains, like wheat and oats, cover many grassland areas. The few trees that grow in grasslands are usually near creeks or streams.

The grassland is home to many different kinds of animals. Grasshoppers and locusts cling to plants. Hawks, falcons, and meadowlarks soar in the sky. The grassland is also home to bison, prairie dogs, and coyotes.

DILEMMA

Grasslands, Crops, or Native Plants

When Europeans first came to North America, grasslands covered 200 million acres in the midwestern United States. Then farmers began to plant crops, such as corn and wheat, in place of the native plants. Today, most of the grasslands have been turned into farms.

Think About It Some think this land should be used to produce crops. Others think that grasslands should grow wild to protect plants and animals that have become endangered since their environments have changed. Explain how you would satisfy both groups.

In some places on the earth, rain may not fall for months. These dry biomes are called **deserts.** Some plants that live in deserts, like the cacti, can store water in their stems for very long periods of time. Other plants have very deep roots. Their roots grow far into the ground to reach water.

Desert wildlife includes lizards, such as Gila monsters. There are also kangaroo rats and pocket mice, which are hunted by burrowing owls. The desert is also home to spiders and scorpions.

BIOME DATA

Biome	Average Temperature	Average Precipitation
Grassland	– 2 to 26°C	10 to 60 cm
Desert	– 1 to 48°C	0 to 20 cm

What are rain forests?

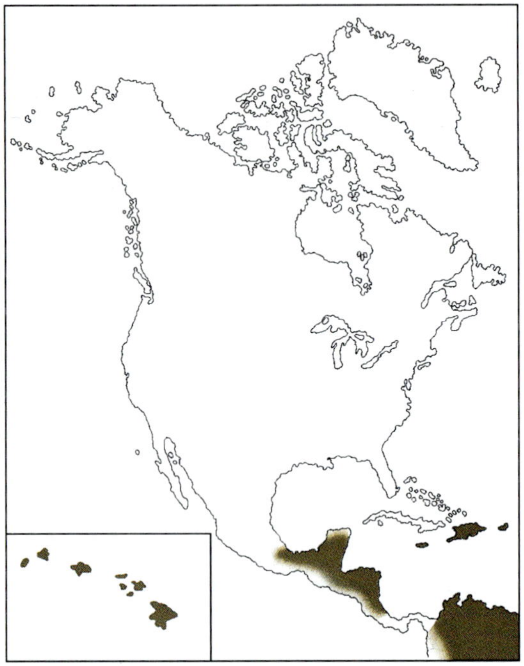

■ Tropical rain forest

The biome that gets the most precipitation on the earth is the **tropical rain forest.** Large amounts of rain and sun help trees grow as high as twelve-story buildings. Their leaves spread out like umbrellas. They form a canopy. Below the rain forest canopy, only a small amount of sunlight reaches the ground.

In the rain forest, vines twist around the trees and grow upward to get their share of sunlight. The roots of orchids cling to the high branches of trees. Like the orchids, many of the forest's animals live their whole lives high in the trees. Monkeys, parrots, butterflies, slow-moving sloths, and snakes move through the trees.

Tropical rain forests contain more varieties of plants and animals than any other place on the earth! Many of the plants contain chemicals that are used by doctors to treat diseases. Large areas of the earth's rain forests have been destroyed for their wood and to make room for farms, buildings, and industries. If this continues, useful chemicals as well as unique plants and animals may be destroyed. Find out what is being done to save the rain forests.

BIOME DATA

Biome	Average Temperature	Average Precipitation
Tropical rain forest	24°C to 28°C	200 to 500 cm

SIDE TRIP

A Cold Rain Forest

Not all rain forests are found in the tropics. Some are found in cooler climates. They are called temperate rain forests. One of these is called the Hoh Rain Forest, which is in the state of Washington.

How are you doing?

1. Which biome gets more rain, the grassland or the desert?
2. Where do most of the animals live in a tropical rain forest?
3. **Think** Since tropical rain forests receive lots of precipitation, why don't more plants grow on the floor of the forest?

How do biomes differ?

The chart below shows typical animals and plants

Biome	Tundra	Taiga	Temperate Forest
Temperature	–28 to 5°C	–10 to 14°C	0 to 28°C
Precipitation	10 to 40 cm	20 to 60 cm	60 to 100 cm
Typical Animals	Polar bear 	Wolf 	Deer 
Climax Plants	Short grass, tiny shrubs 	Evergreens 	Deciduous trees 

that live in each of the earth's biomes.

Grassland	Desert	Tropical Rain Forest
−2 to 26°C	−1 to 48°C	24 to 28°C
10 to 60 cm	0 to 20 cm	200 to 500 cm
Bison 	Vulture 	Jaguar 
Tall and short grasses 	Cacti 	Large trees 

Is a city a biome?

▲ A view of New York City from space

"We can also spot cities, airport runways, bridges, and other signs of civilization," said Mission Specialist Sally Ride, the first American woman in space. A city is not a natural biome. But in many ways it does have its own physical conditions. And it does have plants and animals, including people.

The concrete buildings of a city are like great canyons made by people. Heat, dust, and air pollution get trapped in these canyons. The buildings block breezes and keep them from sweeping the pollution and heat out of the streets. Polluted air can kill some city trees. Polluted air is also harmful to the health of people and animals.

Parks help keep cities cool. The trees and soil don't store the sun's heat. Winds can move freely through a park.

Many animals live in cities. Birds of all kinds visit cities, but pigeons are the most common feathered city dwellers. Rats and mice make their homes in the basements of buildings. And roaches hide in building walls.

If you visit a city park, you might see squirrels and chipmunks. In some city parks, you might even sight a raccoon or a rabbit. Why do you think people are the only large animals?

◀ Cities, like New York City, have their own climate, climax plants, and characteristic animals.

Be a Scientist

HANDS-ON ACTIVITY

How can you keep a city cool?

1. Get three containers. Each one should be a different color. Place a thermometer in each container.
2. Cover the top of each container with paper the same color as the container, making a hole for the thermometer.
3. ACTIVITY JOURNAL Leave the containers in the sun for 30 minutes. Then read each thermometer. Record your results in your Activity Journal. If you were a city planner, what color would you make your buildings?

How are you doing?

1. Describe the driest biome.
2. How do tall buildings affect the city environment?
3. **Think** If you wished to move to a biome with the smallest change in temperature over the seasons, which biome would you choose?

Describing Snow

Which kinds of snow are pictured here?

The Inuit are Eskimos who live on the tundra of Alaska. Snow has always been important to the lives of Inuits. That's why the Inuit have many words for this icy white stuff we call snow.

SCIENCE JOURNAL Read the list at the right and then answer the following questions in your Science Journal. Which of these kinds of snow have you seen? Can you think of other kinds of snow? Give each kind of snow a name. Compare your names with those of your classmates.

Here is a list of some of the meanings for different Inuit words for snow:

snow in air
drifting snow
snow lying on ground
soft, watery snow
newly fallen snow
snow drifted onto homes
hard snow
soft snow
snow for building homes

Data Collection and Analysis

MATH CONNECTION

How does salt affect plant growth?

In some parts of the world, water is very salty. In other parts of the world, it is less salty. If you were a farmer using water from these places to water your crops, how well would your crops grow?

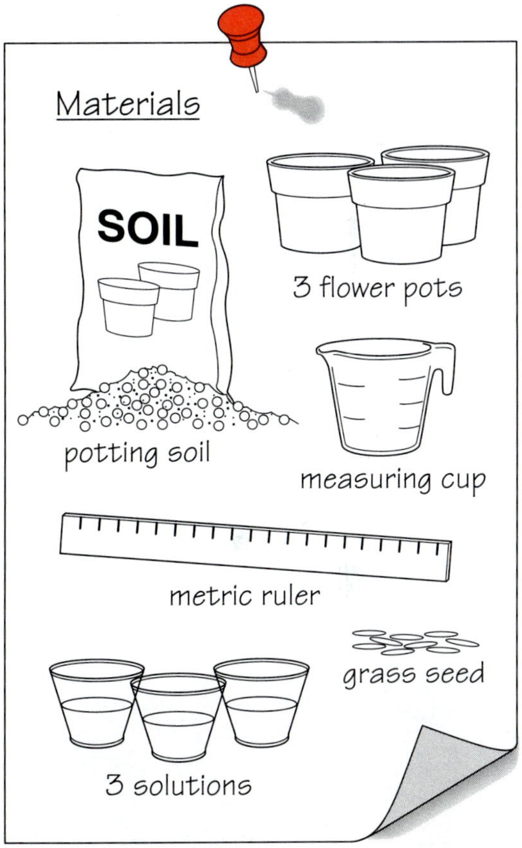

Observe and Collect Data

1. Label three flowerpots 1, 2, and 3. Fill each pot with the same amount of soil.
2. Sprinkle the same number of grass seeds on the soil of each pot. Put all the pots near a window.
3. Once a day, add 25 mL of a water solution. For pot 1, use fresh water with 0% salt. For pot 2, use a solution like ocean water with 3.5% salt. For pot 3, use a solution like the Great Salt Lake in Utah with 22% salt.
4. ACTIVITY JOURNAL After one week, count the number of seeds that sprouted and measure the height of the grass in each container. Record your results in your Activity Journal. Make graphs to record your results.

Draw Conclusions

1. Describe the differences in growth between the pots.
2. How does salt affect the growth of this type of grass?
3. **Predict** what growth you would get if you watered this grass with water from Mono Lake in California, which is a 10% saltwater solution.

Looking Back

Words and Concepts

Choose the letter of the item in Column B that best answers the question in Column A.

Column A	Column B
1. What is the coldest biome?	**a.** Tundra
2. Which biome receives the most precipitation?	**b.** Temperate forest
3. In which biome do trees change color?	**c.** Grassland
4. In which biome are you most likely to find a cactus?	**d.** Desert
5. Tall grasses and bison are found in which biome?	**e.** Rain forest
6. Which region is most affected by buildings?	**f.** City environment

Where do poison arrow frogs live?

Applied Thinking Skills

Answer the following questions. You can use words, drawings, and diagrams in your answers.

7. Where on the earth are you most likely to find a tundra biome? Explain your answer.

8. A poison arrow frog, such as the one shown here, can only survive in a biome moist enough to keep its skin wet. In which biome would you expect to find this animal? Why?

9. A mesquite tree can live in dry areas because its roots dig deep into the ground to find water. In which biome would you expect to find this plant? Explain your answer.

10. **Your World** Describe the plants and animals that live in your biome. Explain how they have adapted to the physical conditions of your biome.

Show What You Know

How can you model a land biome?

Observe and Collect Data

1. Use the materials to build a model of one of the biomes you learned about in this chapter. Indicate the temperature, moisture, and kind of soil.
2. ACTIVITY JOURNAL Draw your model in your Activity Journal and describe the physical conditions of the biome.

Process Skills
Inferring, Making models

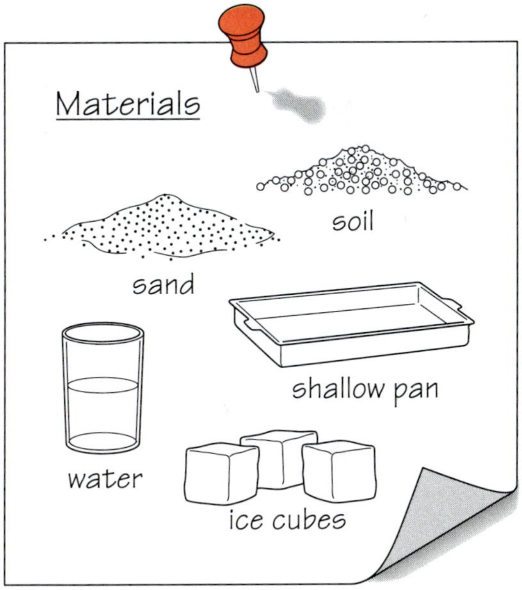

Draw Conclusions

1. What kinds of plants and animals would live in the biome you modeled?
2. How do the physical conditions affect what plants and animals can survive in this biome?

Chapter 3

Water Biomes

"Suddenly from behind the rim of the moon … there emerges a sparkling blue and white jewel. …" That's how astronaut Edgar Mitchell described the earth as he flew over the surface of the moon.

The "white" was the earth's clouds. The "blue" was its oceans. Almost three-quarters of the earth is covered by oceans, seas, lakes, and rivers.

The watery part of our planet has different environments, called **aquatic** (ə kwat′ik) **biomes.** *Aquatic* means "watery." There are two kinds of aquatic biomes. One of these, the marine biome, includes all the earth's oceans. The other, the freshwater biome, includes almost all the earth's lakes, rivers, swamps, streams, and ponds.

The difference between the two aquatic biomes is the amount of salt in the water. Other factors that affect which plants and animals live in an aquatic biome are the temperature, the amount of oxygen, the amount of light, and the water pressure of the biome.

SCIENCE JOURNAL Describe in your Science Journal a local water biome. What plants and animals live there?

Explore Activity

How salty is the ocean?

Process Skills
Observing, Estimating, Predicting

Observe and Collect Data

1. Your teacher will give you four mystery solutions. To taste the samples, dip a clean cotton swab into one of the samples and touch the wet cotton to your tongue. Throw the swab away after you use it. Take a sip of water to clear your tongue between tastes. Do not drink any of the solutions. Repeat the taste test with the other three mystery solutions.
2. In your Activity Journal, list the numbers of the cups in order from the one you think tastes least salty to the one you think tastes most salty.
3. Label the small cups with the marker. Use the spoon to put one spoonful of sample 1 into cup 1. Put one spoonful of sample 2 into cup 2. Repeat with the other solutions.
4. Over a few days, let the water in the cups evaporate. Look at the amount of salt left at the bottom of each cup. Based on what you see, write the numbers of the cups in order from the one with the least salt to the most salt.

Share Your Results

1. How many other groups of students got the same results for Step 2?
2. How many got the same results for Step 4?

Draw Conclusions

1. Compare your estimates in Step 2 to your observations in Step 4. With which procedure are you more likely to get the correct order? Explain your answer.
2. **Predict** which solution is as salty as the ocean.

Apply What You Know

How do you think living things are affected by the amount of salt in water biomes?

What lives in moving fresh water?

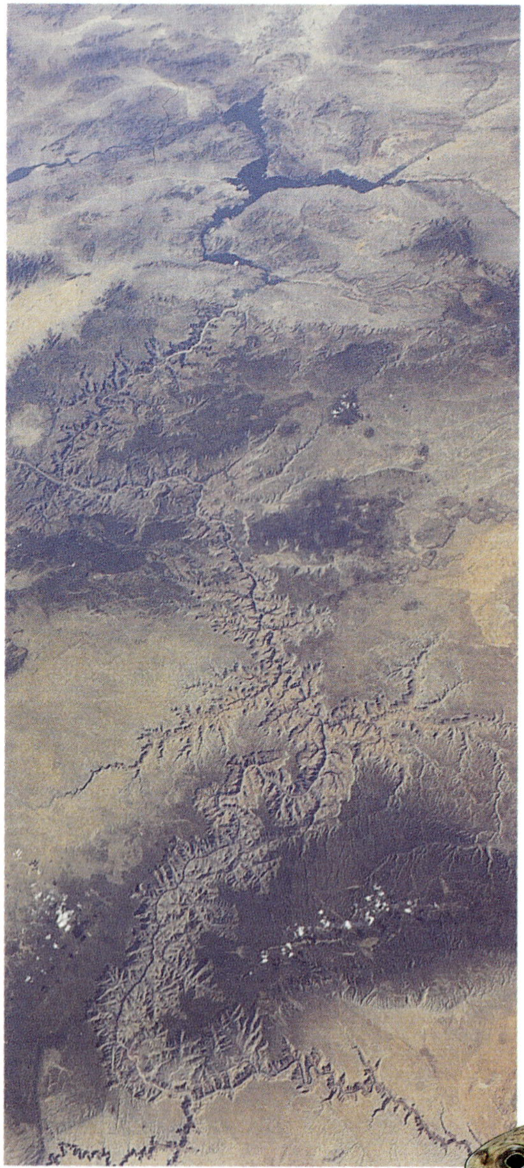

A view of the Colorado River from space

From the space shuttle, the Colorado River looks like a shiny thread winding through the Grand Canyon. But on the earth below, the thread turns out to be a river of rushing water.

If you looked for living things in a river or stream, you'd discover that the speed of the water has an effect on what lives there. Some kinds of plants and animals thrive in areas where water moves quickly. Other living things are adapted to slow-moving sections of water.

A fast-moving river has a lot of air mixed in with the water. That means that plants and animals have a good supply of oxygen. This is especially important for river trout, since these fish need a lot of oxygen to live. On the other hand, the fast-moving water makes it difficult for plants to grow along the bottom of the river.

Where the river is moving slowly, algae and mosses can color parts of the riverbed green. Moving in and around the algae and mosses you might see worms, crayfish, and minnows. Large plants, such as water hyacinths, float on the surface of rivers and streams that flow very slowly or don't move at all. Slow rivers also have larger animals, such as turtles and frogs.

Career Corner

Marine Biologist

Have you ever wondered how many fish there are in the sea? I'm Kenneth Oda, and I have a pretty good guess how many Pacific herring there are in the San Francisco Bay. I'm a Marine Biologist and I work for the Department of Fish and Game. I estimate how many Pacific herring there are so fishing businesses know how many they can catch without upsetting the water ecosystems. To become a Marine Biologist, I went to college for four years and studied biology.

The fast-moving water in this part of the Colorado River provides thrills for these rafters.

What lives in still water?

A view of a lake from the space shuttle

The astronauts in the space shuttle can see a large lake. But from space they can't see all the living things in the lake.

Many different kinds of plants live in still, fresh water. In some lakes, tall grasses, like cattails, grow along the sides of lakes and ponds. Lilies float on the water. Algae also lives near the water's surface. Other plants grow under water only in the shallow areas where sunlight can reach the bottom.

The animals that live in shallow lakes are different from the animals and plants that live in deep lakes. Since sunlight can reach more of the bottom in a shallow lake than in a deep lake, there are more plants in shallow lakes. Fish, such as catfish and carp, tend to live in shallow lakes and ponds.

SCIENCE JOURNAL

Does your family ever eat seafood? Describe in your Science Journal seafood that you have eaten or have seen. Find out what water biome the plant or animal came from.

BACK HOME

Plants do not grow on the bottom of a deep lake because sunlight cannot reach the bottom. Fish, such as lake trout, live in deep lakes.

Fish are not the only animals that live in still fresh water. Frogs, newts, and turtles swim through lakes and ponds. Birds, such as ducks and loons, dive underwater to eat animals or plants that live there. Lakes and ponds are also home to beavers. The still water also provides a home for insects, worms, and tiny organisms called plankton.

Which part of the lake has the most plant life? Why?

How are you doing?

1. What is the main difference between freshwater and ocean-water biomes?
2. Why are you more likely to find river trout in a fast-moving stream than in a slow-moving stream?
3. **Think** How might a beaver's dam affect the living things in a stream?

What lives where salt water meets fresh water?

A view of Chesapeake Bay

One hundred and fifty freshwater rivers and streams flow toward the salty ocean where the coasts of Virginia and Maryland meet. From the shuttle, the land looks like a cracked sheet of glass. Each crack is a river. In the middle lies a giant crack. It is the Chesapeake Bay.

Chesapeake Bay is an **estuary** (es′tyo͞o er ē), a place where fresh water and salt water meet and mix. An estuary can be a bay, a sound, a marsh, or the mouth of a great river.

At high tide, salty ocean water pushes into the bay. During spring and autumn, heavy rains swell the rivers, and fresh water tumbles toward the sea. The saltiness of the water changes minute by minute, from one spot to another and from one depth to another. Special kinds of plants and animals can adjust to these changes.

One of these hardy creatures is the blue crab. In the spring, blue crabs dig out of the muddy and salty bottom of Chesapeake Bay. They head upstream where the water is less salty. There they hunt for food among clumps of grasses.

Far up in the estuary, where the water is not too salty, there are snails, mussels, and some catfish. Closer to the sea there are oysters, shrimp, and starfish.

Some animals can live in all parts of the estuary. Fish such as sturgeon, herring, and striped bass, can live in waters of different saltiness. Turtles, insects, and birds also live along the shores of the Chesapeake.

What lives near the seashore?

Florida's coast viewed from space

"Look, the seashore!" exclaims an astronaut aboard the space shuttle as she points to a white stripe separating the blue sea from the brown land. The living things in this water biome are adapted to the pounding waves and changing tides that are found where the sea meets the land.

Giant green sea anemones, goose barnacles, and starfish attach themselves to the rocks near the shore. Brightly colored fish swim against the waves and tides. Other animals, such as clams and crabs, dig into the sand.

On the shallow ocean bottom, swaying brown kelp is anchored to rocks. The kelp grows up towards the light near the top of the ocean. The shallow part of the ocean is full of plants and algae because sunlight is plentiful.

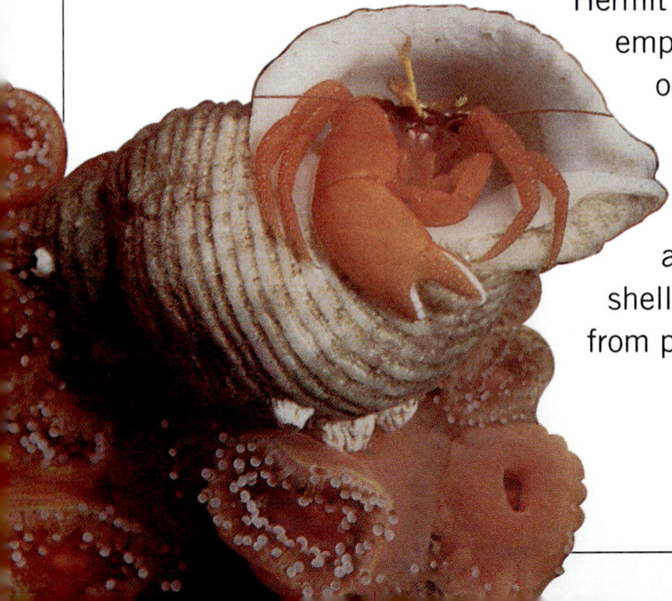

Hermit crabs live in the empty shells of dead ocean animals. When they grow too big for one shell, they leave it and find a larger one. The shells protect the crab from predators.

YOU CAN HELP

If you take shells from a beach, you may be leaving a hermit crab homeless! Leave living and nonliving parts of the environment alone. Animals and plants depend on both living and nonliving things to survive.

Fish, such as this seahorse, live near the shore.

Be a Scientist

Why is ocean water salty?

1. Mix equal amounts of sand and salt. Put the mixture inside a filter.
2. Hold the filter over an empty cup. Pour a cupful of water into the filter. Once the water has run through the filter, taste the water using a cotton swab.

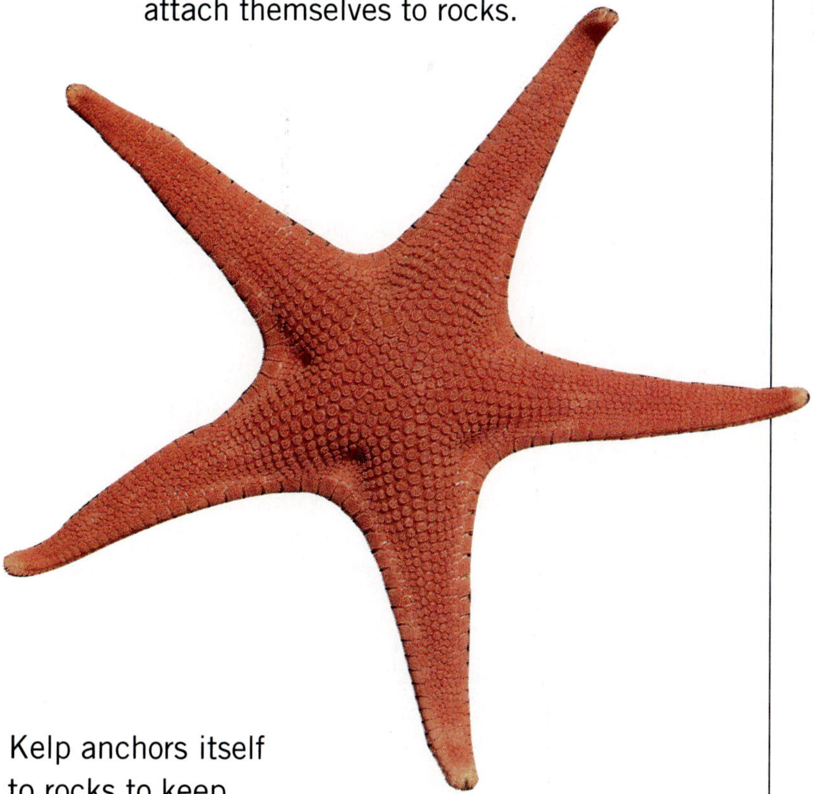

To hold themselves in place, starfish attach themselves to rocks.

Kelp anchors itself to rocks to keep from washing away with the tides and currents.

What lives in the open ocean?

The astronauts aboard the space shuttle cannot see below the ocean's surface. But scientists on the earth can explore the ocean bottom with the help of underwater vessels. Scientists can either travel down to the ocean floor in these submersible vessels or send cameras down in the vessels to take pictures of the ocean bottom.

Near the ocean's surface, small shrimp-like animals, called krill, bob in the waves. Thousands of krill will make a single meal for one of the largest animals ever to live on the earth—the blue whale. Whales, dolphin, sharks, tuna, and other marine animals live near the surface of the open ocean.

Sunlight can only reach 100 meters into the ocean. Below that, the ocean becomes colder and darker. Animals that live below 100 meters have adaptations to handle the pressure, temperature, and darkness.

Deep in the ocean, it is so dark that the powerful lights of the submersible vessel have to be turned on. Miles of water push against the walls of the vessel with a force equal to the thrust of the space shuttle engines. That's why the walls and windows of the vessel are thick and strong. Could anything possibly live down here?

There's a strange fish! A glow of light is coming from its open mouth. It is called a lantern fish. Attracted by the light, a smaller fish enters the gaping mouth for a closer look. Slam! The lantern fish's jaws snap shut. Other animals living in this dark world use light for protection or to attract mates.

Amazing!

The torpedo ray uses electricity to shock attackers. This fish makes enough electricity to power a TV set.

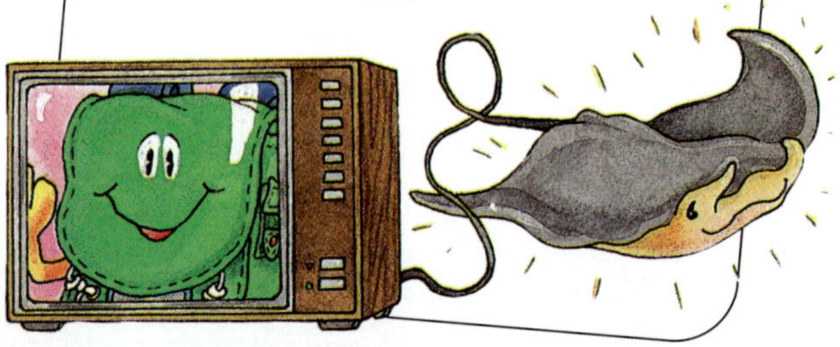

How are you doing?

1. What is an estuary?
2. Why can't plants grow in the deepest parts of the ocean?
3. **Think** Why are the organisms that live on or near the deep ocean floor different from those that live on or near the shallow ocean floor?

Looking Back

MINDS-ON ASSESSMENT

Words and Concepts

Match the item in Column A with the correct aquatic biome in Column B.

Column A

1. Is cold and dark
2. Contains plenty of oxygen
3. Has mixed salt and fresh water
4. Where ocean water meets land
5. Contains lots of green plants
6. Where kelp and seaweed are found

Column B

a. Shallow lake or pond
b. Estuary
c. Shoreline
d. Deep ocean water
e. Fast-moving stream
f. Shallow ocean water

Applied Thinking Skills

Answer the following questions. You can use words, drawings, and diagrams in your answers.

7. What are some differences between still fresh water and moving fresh water?
8. Describe the changes that occur as you travel deeper and deeper into the ocean.
9. What is an estuary? Why does it contain such a wide variety of plant and animal life?
10. **Your World** Describe how you might set up a small aquarium in your home.

Looking back on the earth

Show What You Know

How can you build a water biome?

Observe and Collect Data

1. ACTIVITY JOURNAL Design a model of part of the earth that has a river, a lake, an estuary, and an ocean. Draw your design in your Activity Journal.
2. Build your model using clay.
3. In your drawing, show which way the water flows and whether the biome is salty or fresh.

Draw Conclusions

1. List some of the plants and animals that live in each kind of water.
2. If you were to add a land biome to your model, what would it be? What would the physical conditions be?

Process Skills
Making models, Inferring

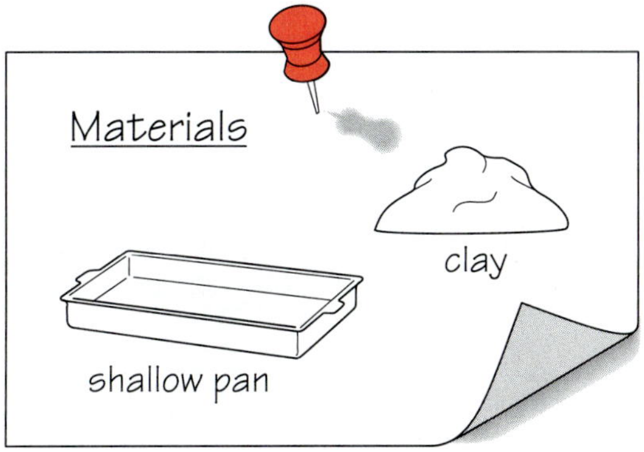

Biomes

Show what you know about biomes. Work by yourself, with a partner, or with a group. Select one activity.

Artist Make a painting or a sculpture of a biome. Include as many of the characteristics of the biome as you can. Display your piece of art for the class.

News Broadcaster You've been asked to produce a radio show to explain what a biome is. Write a script for your show. Use a tape recorder to produce the show. If you wish, include background music and sound effects. You can also use the voices of different people to tell your story.

Songwriter Write a song about biomes for people who can't see. You can write your own music or use the music of another song and write new words for it. Play or sing your song for the class.

Playwright Choose one of the biomes you have studied. Write a play about something that is harming this biome. The play should have a villain and a hero. The hero should do something to help the environment. Act out the play for your class.

Ecologist Keep a record of the daily changes in temperature and precipitation where you live. Find out how they affect the plants and animals. Report what you find.

Game Inventor Invent a biome board game. The game should take people to different biomes. The players can be rewarded for preserving the biome or understanding how it works.

Glossary

aquatic biome (ə kwat′ik bī′ōm′) An environment that consists of water. Aquatic biomes include marine (ocean) biomes and freshwater (lakes, ponds, and rivers) biomes. (page B44)

biome (bī′ōm′) A large area of the earth that has its own set of conditions and characteristic living things. (page B10)

climate (klī′mət) The average weather conditions of a place over a long period of time. (page B12)

climax plants (klī′maks′ plants) The most abundant plants in a biome. (page B10)

desert (dez′ərt) A biome that receives very little precipitation and has high daytime temperatures. (page B33)

estuary (es′tyo͞o er ē) A coastal region where fresh water and salt water mix. (page B52)

grassland (gras′land′) A biome, characterized by grasses, that does not have enough precipitation to support the growth of trees. (page B32)

precipitation (prē sip′ə tā′shən) Any form of water that falls from the sky, such as hail, rain, sleet, or snow. (page B12)

taiga (tī′gə) A biome with cool temperatures that is covered with many evergreen forests. (page B29)

temperate forest (tem′pər it fôr′ist) A biome with distinct seasonal changes and deciduous trees. (page B30)

tropical rain forest (träp′i kəl rān fôr′ist) A biome that receives a lot of precipitation and has high daytime temperatures. (page B34)

tundra (tun′drə) A treeless biome in which the soil beneath the surface is always frozen; the coldest of the earth's biomes. (page B28)

Unit B Index

Boldface numerals denote glossary terms. Italic numerals denote illustrations.

Credits

Photographs

1 NASA; 2–3 Mike Phillips/Peter Arnold, Inc.; 3R GHP Studio*; 4L NASA. Artwork by B. J. Storey; 4R NASA; 5 Ken Karp*; 6BL Tom Bean/DRK Photo; 6BR Greg Vaughn/Tom Stack & Associates; 6T Mary Clay/Tom Stack & Associates; 7 NASA; 8 GHP Studio*; 9 Elliott Smith*; 10 M. P. L. Fogden/Bruce Coleman Inc.; 11L Jim Brandenburg/Minden Pictures; 11R Michael P. Gadomski/Bruce Coleman Inc.; 12B Michael Ma Po Shum/Tony Stone Images; 12T Randa Bishop/Tony Stone Images; 13T Louis Goldman/Photo Researchers; 13B J. Lichter/Photo Researchers; 14–15T Steve Lissau/Rainbow; 14 NASA; 15 Brian Parker/Tom Stack & Associates; 16 NASA/Rainbow; 17 David Madison/Bruce Coleman Inc.; 18 GHP Studio*; 19B GHP Studio*; 19T Ken Karp*; 22 GHP Studio*; 23 Zig Leszczynski/Animals, Animals; 24–25 NASA; 25T NASA; 27 Elliott Smith*; 28 Tom Walker/Stock, Boston; 29B Leonard Lee Rue III/Stock, Boston; 29T Renee Lynn*; 30 Lynda Richardson/Peter Arnold, Inc.; 31 Stephen J. Krasemann/AllStock; 31(inset) Tom Bean/DRK Photo; 32 Jim Brandenburg/Minden Pictures; 33 Doug Sokell/Tom Stack & Associates; 34 Tim Davis/AllStock; 35 John M. Roberts/The Stock Market; 38B Joan Baron/The Stock Market; 38T NASA; 39 Renee Lynn/AllStock; 40C Fred Bruemmer/DRK Photo; 40T Ken Karp*; 41 GHP Studio*; 42 Stephen J. Krasemann/DRK Photo; 43 Elliott Smith*; 44B GHP Studio*; 44T NASA; 45 Wayne Lynch/DRK Photo; 47 Elliott Smith*; 48L NASA; 48R Breck P. Kent/Animals, Animals; 49B Bob Pool/Tom Stack & Associates; 49T Anne Dowie*; 50 NASA; 52 Nellaine Price/Bruce Coleman Inc.; 54BL F. Stuart Westmorland/AllStock; 54BR Ken Karp*; 54T NASA; 55BR R. N. Mariscal/Bruce Coleman Inc.; 55BL Stephen Frink/The Waterhouse; 55T Doug Perrine/DRK Photo; 56 Mark Kelley/Stock, Boston; 58 NASA; 59B Elliott Smith*

*Photographed expressly for Addison-Wesley Publishing Company, Inc.

Illustrations

Nea Bisek 8T, 26T, 41, 43, 46
Jane McCreary 8B, 26B, 47, 56
Mike Reed 20
Randy Vergoustraete 60–61
Pat Welch 16, 24, 28, 30, 32, 34, 35, 36, 37, 51, 52–53, 57

Text

1, 38 Sally Ride with Susan Okie, *To Space and Back.* (New York: Lothrop, Lee & Shepard Books, a div. of William Morrow & Co., Inc., 1986). Copyright © 1986 by Sally Ride and Susan Okie.

20–21 Francis Kalnay, *Chúcaro, Wild Pony of the Pampa.* Copyright © 1958 by Francis Kalnay, renewed. Reprinted with permission of Harcourt Brace & Company.

44 Edgar Mitchell (U.S. Astronaut) from *The Home Planet,* Kevin W. Kelley, ed. (Reading, MA: Addison-Wesley Publishing Co., 1988).

It's a pie, 

but it's
not for
dessert.

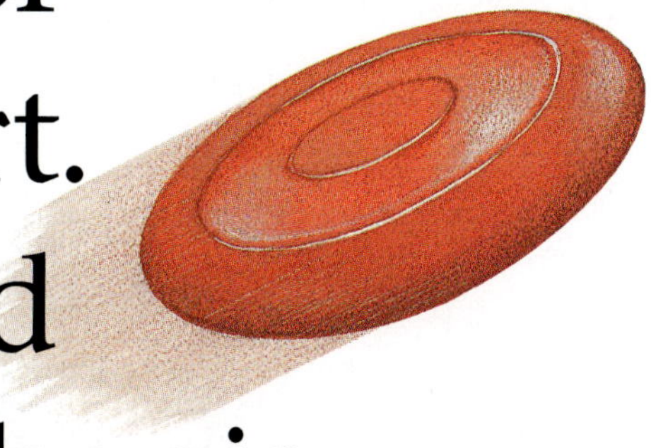

It gets tossed

into the air
and can fit
in a box.

It can be deep
or shallow. 

What is it?

Pizzeria

You notice the sweet smell of tomatoes when you walk in the door. Then you see it. It's a golden circle of cheese dotted with olives, mushrooms, pepperoni, and other toppings. At last you taste it. This meal was worth the trip!

The pizzeria is filled with different things. In the kitchen, tomato sauce simmers in a shiny copper pot, chefs toss pizza dough into the air, and spices, sauces, and other ingredients line every counter. People at the tables have pizzas, pastas, and salads spread before them. Food, furniture, people, even the air—everything in the pizzeria is made of matter.

- What are the building blocks of matter?
- How do the building blocks join together?
- How does matter mix?

FORMS OF MATTER

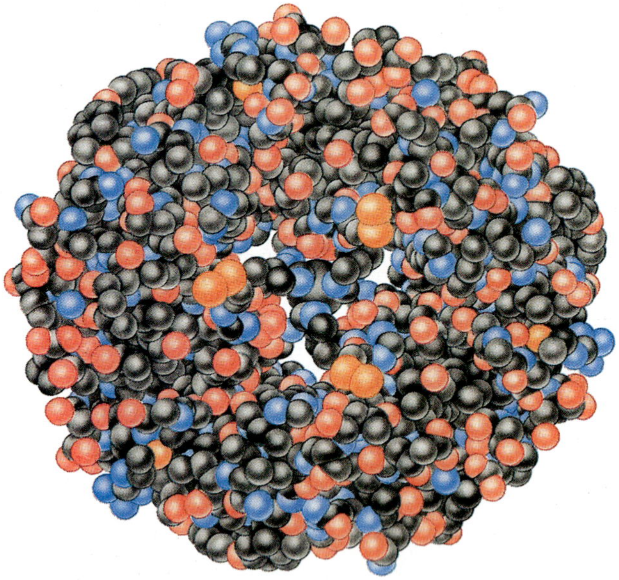

Activities

Features

Elements

Everything in the pizzeria is made of matter. The food is matter, the pots and pans are matter, even the people are matter! Matter is anything that has mass and takes up space. Matter can be solid like your table, liquid like your lemonade, or gas like the air.

Matter is made of basic parts, or building blocks. The building blocks of matter combine to produce all the different kinds of matter around you. To understand the many kinds of matter, you must first learn about the building blocks that make it up.

Compare the building blocks of matter with the building blocks that make up a pizzeria. The types of materials used during construction determine some characteristics of the finished building. A pizzeria built of bricks looks different from a pizzeria built of cinder blocks. The same thing is true for the building blocks of matter. The type of particle that a substance is made of affects the properties of that substance.

Another factor that can affect the properties of matter is the arrangement of the building blocks. The same kind of bricks can be used to make a skyscraper, a home, or a pizzeria. The basic parts of matter can also be arranged differently to form different substances.

SCIENCE JOURNAL Look around your home and your school. Do you see things that are made of smaller building blocks? Record your observations in your Science Journal.

Explore Activity

What's in the mystery box?

Process Skills
Observing, Inferring

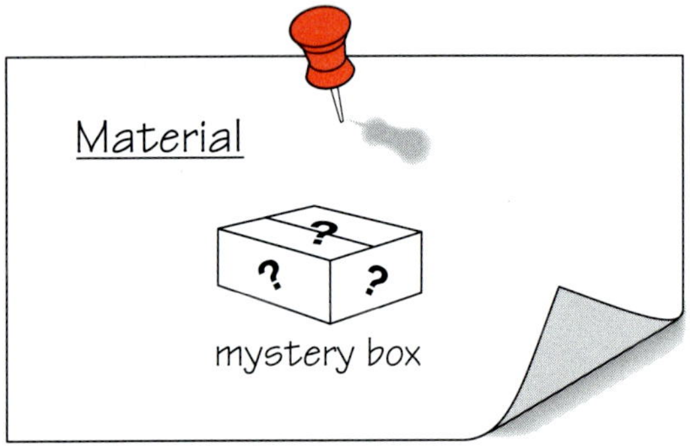

The scientists who study matter cannot see the tiny particles that make it up. Yet scientists have found ways to study the particles that they cannot see. Your teacher will give you a "mystery box." You will determine what is inside without opening it.

Observe and Collect Data

1. ACTIVITY JOURNAL Pick up the "mystery box." Tilt and turn it in different ways. What do you feel? What do you hear? Write your observations in your Activity Journal.
2. Continue to move the box around in your hands until you have a good idea of what the inside is like.
3. **Predict** what is inside the box. Draw a picture, or model, of what you believe the inside of the box looks like and what it contains.

Share Your Results

1. Discuss your observations with your classmates. Try to figure out together what is inside the box.
2. Exchange boxes with a classmate. Do you both think they look the same? Give a reason for your answer.

Draw Conclusions

1. Which senses did you use in this activity? What did you learn from each of the senses?
2. Which senses didn't you use in this activity?

Apply What You Know

How does this activity resemble the way scientists study the tiny particles that make up matter?

What are the building blocks of matter?

The chef tosses the dough for the crust, stretches it out on a sheet of aluminum foil, and covers it with sauce from a huge copper pot. The copper in the pot and the aluminum in the foil are examples of elements in the pizzeria. An **element** (el′ə mənt) is a substance that cannot be changed into a simpler substance.

You cannot change one element into another element in a chemical reaction. For example, you cannot change aluminum into copper. If you make a pot out of aluminum and paint it to look like copper, it will not have the properties of a copper pot. If you roll copper into foil and paint it silver, it will not have the properties of aluminum foil.

Each element has its own set of properties. An element's properties include:

- how it looks
- how hard it is
- how well it conducts electricity
- how it reacts with other elements

Elements are made of particles called **atoms.** An element is made of only one kind of atom. Atoms are the smallest unit of an element that can exist and still keep the element's properties. Atoms are so small that a million atoms are no bigger than a period.

HISTORY

SCIENCE TECHNOLOGY & SOCIETY

Alchemists

The first chemists, who practiced their art hundreds of years ago, were called alchemists (al′kə mists). They made medicines and poisons from plants and animals, but alchemists were best known for their attempts to change lead into gold. They did not realize that they could not change one element into another. Although they failed to turn lead into gold, they succeeded in learning much about the basic building blocks of matter.

What's inside an atom?

It is the structure of an atom that gives each element its properties. To understand how the atoms of elements differ, you must understand atoms.

We know about the building blocks of atoms because scientists have figured out a way of studying what they can't see. First, scientists cause a collision between an atom and another particle. This splits the atom. Then scientists can use special instruments to study the behavior of particles coming out of the collision.

Three kinds of particles that make up atoms are protons, neutrons, and electrons. The protons and neutrons are found in the center of an atom, in an area called the nucleus. The electrons are located around the nucleus in an area called the electron cloud.

Be a Scientist

HANDS-ON ACTIVITY

How can you model atoms of different elements?

1. Move to a large area. One member of your team should stand still in the center of the area. Another team member should run in circles around the first team member. This is a model of a hydrogen atom.

2. ACTIVITY JOURNAL Draw in your Activity Journal the arrangement you just acted out. Identify which student was the proton and which was the electron.

3. Repeat the activity with four in the center, two protons and two neutrons, and two people running in circles. This is a model of a helium atom.

4. In your Activity Journal, draw the arrangement you made for the helium atom model.

Amazing!

There is so much empty space in an atom that if an atom's nucleus were the size of your head, the electrons around it could be up to one hundred miles away!

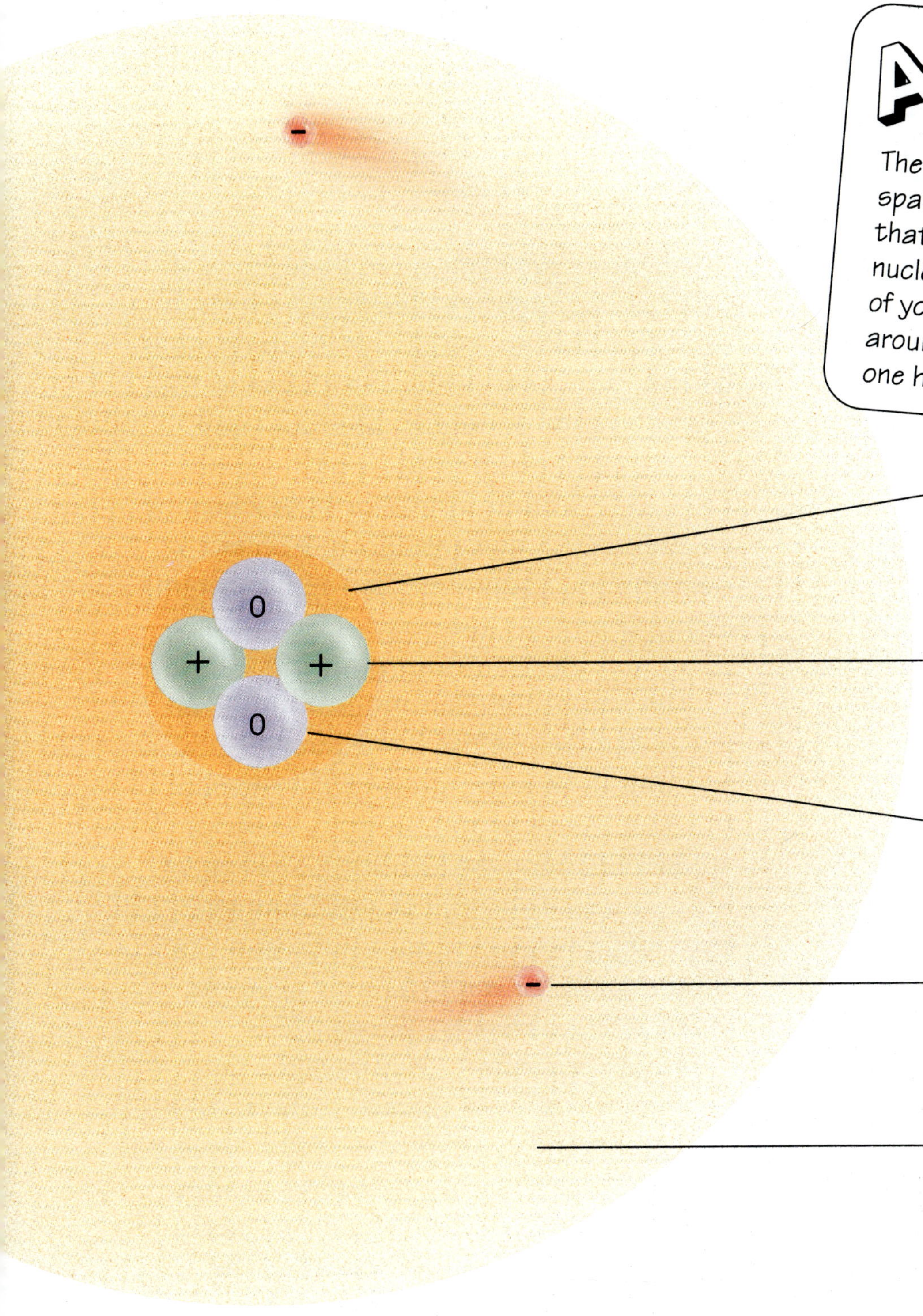

Nucleus
The dense center of an atom is called a **nucleus** (noo′kle əs). Most of the atom's mass is in the nucleus.

Proton
One of the particles in the nucleus is called a **proton** (prō′tän′). Protons have a positive charge.

Neutron
Another particle in the nucleus is called a **neutron** (noo′trän′). Neutrons have no charge.

Electron
An **electron** (ē lek′trän′) has a negative charge and is almost 2,000 times smaller than a proton or a neutron.

Electron Cloud
Electrons move so fast around a nucleus that their position is hard to pin down. The cloud in this picture shows where the electrons might be at any given moment. The volume, or size, of an atom is mostly made up of the electron cloud.

How do atoms differ from one another?

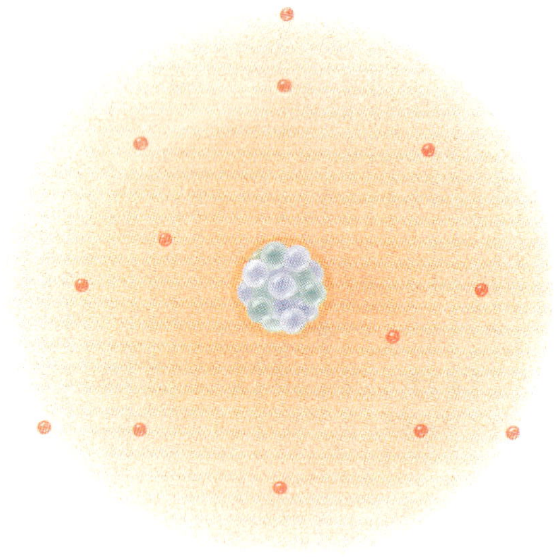

Each aluminum atom contains 13 protons.

All atoms are made up of three kinds of particles, yet there are many different kinds of atoms. The number of protons in an atom determines which element that atom is. For example, each aluminum atom contains 13 protons. If an atom contains one more proton, 14 protons instead of 13, it would be an atom of the element silicon. If an atom contains one less proton than an aluminum atom, 12 protons instead of 13, it would be an atom of the element magnesium.

The number of neutrons in atoms of different elements can vary. The number of electrons in an atom can vary in a chemical reaction. Neutrons and electrons, however, do not determine the identity of an element. For example, if an atom of aluminum loses electrons, it will still remain aluminum. Some aluminum atoms might have 14 neutrons, others might have 13 neutrons.

Atoms are neutral. They have the same number of positively charged particles as they do negatively charged particles. Since electrons have a negative charge, an atom that gains an electron will have a negative charge. How do you think the charge would change if an atom lost an electron?

DILEMMA

Nuclear Power

When the nucleus of an atom is split in a nuclear (noo′klē ər) reactor, heat is given off. This heat can be used to make electricity.

Some people say that nuclear power plants are better than power plants that burn fuels like coal or oil. Burning fuels pollutes the air and uses resources that are limited.

Other people point out that there are dangers in using nuclear power. Accidents have occurred at nuclear reactors. Radioactive material has leaked from the reactors into the environment. The radioactive waste products of nuclear power plants are health hazards.

Think About It Make a list of the pros and cons of nuclear power. Mark each item as very important, important, or not important. Do you think the benefits of using nuclear power outweigh the risks? Explain your answer.

Each iron atom contains 26 protons.

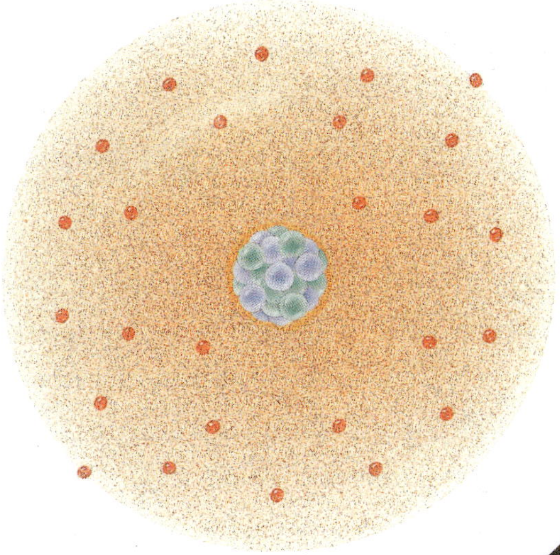

How are you doing?

1. What particles are there in an atom? What charge does each particle have?
2. How are the atoms of one element different from the atoms of another element?
3. **Think** If an atom of the element iron lost a proton, would it still be iron? If it lost an electron, would it still be iron? Explain your answer.

Lesson 2 Classifying Elements

What are the different elements?

In the pizzeria, you've seen some examples of elements, including aluminum, copper, and iron. These are only three of the 109 known elements. All of the known elements are listed in a table called the **periodic table.** The periodic table is shown on pages C18–C19.

Only 92 of the 109 elements occur naturally. The other elements, which are shown in pink in the periodic table, have been made by scientists. Elements can be classified into groups—metals, semimetals, and nonmetals. Metals are good conductors: heat and electricity flow through them easily. Metals are also usually shiny. Copper, aluminum, and iron are three examples of metals. Semimetals have some properties of metals and some properties of nonmetals.

YOU CAN HELP

Aluminum and iron are elements that are used to make cans. Help conserve the earth's supply of these metals by recycling cans.

The element helium fills this balloon.

Each element has an abbreviation or symbol. Sometimes these symbols come from the English name for the element. The symbol for aluminum, for example, is Al. Other times the symbol for an element comes from its Latin name. For example, the Latin name for iron is *ferrum*. The symbol for iron in the periodic table is Fe.

Each box of the periodic table includes an element's **atomic number.** The atomic number tells how many protons are in each atom of that element. As you can see from the box shown below, the atomic number of helium is 2. Helium has two protons.

Be a Scientist

HANDS-ON ACTIVITY

Does cereal contain iron?

1. Crush cereal in a bag until it is broken into tiny crumbs. Place the cereal and a magnet in a plastic container. Close the container and shake it for about fifteen minutes.
2. ACTIVITY JOURNAL Open the container and remove the magnet. Record in your Activity Journal your observations of the magnet. Repeat the activity with objects that are not magnetic.
3. Read the ingredients on the cereal box. What do you think was sticking to the magnet?

Atomic number
The atomic number shows how many protons are in one atom of an element.

Symbol
An element's symbol is an abbreviation of its English or Latin name.

Element name

The Periodic Table of the Elements

In the periodic table, elements are listed by atomic number. As you read across each row, you can see that the atomic number increases from left to right. Elements are also grouped into columns. Elements in

1 H Hydrogen								
3 Li Lithium	4 Be Beryllium							
11 Na Sodium	12 Mg Magnesium							
19 K Potassium	20 Ca Calcium	21 Sc Scandium	22 Ti Titanium	23 V Vanadium	24 Cr Chromium	25 Mn Manganese	26 Fe Iron	27 Co Cobalt
37 Rb Rubidium	38 Sr Strontium	39 Y Yttrium	40 Zr Zirconium	41 Nb Niobium	42 Mo Molybdenum	43 Tc Technetium	44 Ru Ruthenium	45 Rh Rhodium
55 Cs Cesium	56 Ba Barium	57 to 71 See below	72 Hf Hafnium	73 Ta Tantalum	74 W Tungsten	75 Re Rhenium	76 Os Osmium	77 Ir Iridium
87 Fr Francium	88 Ra Radium	89 to 103 See below	104 Unq Unnilquadium	105 Unp Unnilpentium	106 Unh Unnilhexium	107 Uns Unnilseptium	108 Uno Unniloctium	109 Une Unnilennium
			57 La Lanthanum	58 Ce Cerium	59 Pr Praseodymium	60 Nd Neodymium	61 Pm Promethium	62 Sm Samarium
			89 Ac Actinium	90 Th Thorium	91 Pa Protactinium	92 U Uranium	93 Np Neptunium	94 Pu Plutonium

- Metal
- Semimetal
- Nonmetal
- Made artificially

each column have many of the same properties. For example, the elements in the far right-hand column are all gases that do not usually react with other elements.

								2 He Helium
			5 B Boron	6 C Carbon	7 N Nitrogen	8 O Oxygen	9 F Fluorine	10 Ne Neon
			13 Al Aluminum	14 Si Silicon	15 P Phosphorus	16 S Sulfur	17 Cl Chlorine	18 Ar Argon
28 Ni Nickel	29 Cu Copper	30 Zn Zinc	31 Ga Gallium	32 Ge Geranium	33 As Arsenic	34 Se Selenium	35 Br Bromine	36 Kr Krypton
46 Pd Palladium	47 Ag Silver	48 Cd Cadmium	49 In Indium	50 Sn Tin	51 Sb Antimony	52 Te Tellurium	53 I Iodine	54 Xe Xenon
78 Pt Platinum	79 Au Gold	80 Hg Mercury	81 Tl Thallium	82 Pb Lead	83 Bi Bismuth	84 Po Polonium	85 At Astatine	86 Rn Radon

63 Eu Europium	64 Gd Gadolinium	65 Tb Terbium	66 Dy Dysprosium	67 Ho Holmium	68 Er Erbium	69 Tm Thulium	70 Yb Ytterbium	71 Lu Lutetium
95 Am Americium	96 Cm Curium	97 Bk Berkelium	98 Cf Californium	99 Es Einsteinium	100 Fm Fermium	101 Md Mendelevium	102 No Nobelium	103 Lr Lawrencium

What are some of the most common elements?

Although there are 109 known elements on earth, most things are made of only a handful of elements. They are found in many different combinations. These elements are combined with other elements, forming different substances.

Iron

Iron is found in many foods, such as the spinach in your salad. Iron is a metal.

Calcium

Calcium (kal′ sē əm) is part of your bones and teeth. It is also in cheese and milk. Calcium is also in shells and rocks.

Potassium

The tomato sauce on your pizza is one of the many foods that contain potassium (pō tas′ē əm). Potassium also exists in the earth's soil and rocks.

Aluminum

Aluminum is a metal that is used to make many things, like juice cans and pizza pans.

Sodium

Sodium (sō′dē əm) is one of the elements in salt. You can find salt in the shaker on your table and in ocean water.

Oxygen

Oxygen (äks′i jən) is the earth's most common element. It is in the air you breathe. Oxygen is also a part of water and part of most rocks on the earth's surface.

Hydrogen

Hydrogen (hī′drə jən) is the other element in water. Hydrogen is also in the air you breathe.

Silicon

Silicon (sil′i kän′) is the second most common element in the earth's crust. Silicon and oxygen combine to form sand particles. Silicon is also part of glass.

How are you doing?

1. List five of the most common elements and their atomic numbers.
2. What does the atomic number tell you about an element?
3. **Think** The number of protons equals the number of electrons in an atom. How many electrons does hydrogen have? Explain your answer.

VIEWPOINT

Iron

When you think of the element iron, what do you imagine? A metalworker thinks of a substance that can be formed into different shapes for making parts of buildings, automobiles, or pieces of art.

To a doctor, iron is an element that the body needs. Iron is a part of your blood, and it helps the blood carry oxygen to all parts of your body. Without enough iron, a person is anemic.

What properties of iron would you have to know about to work with iron the way the metalworker does? What properties of iron would you have to know about to use iron to take care of someone who is anemic?

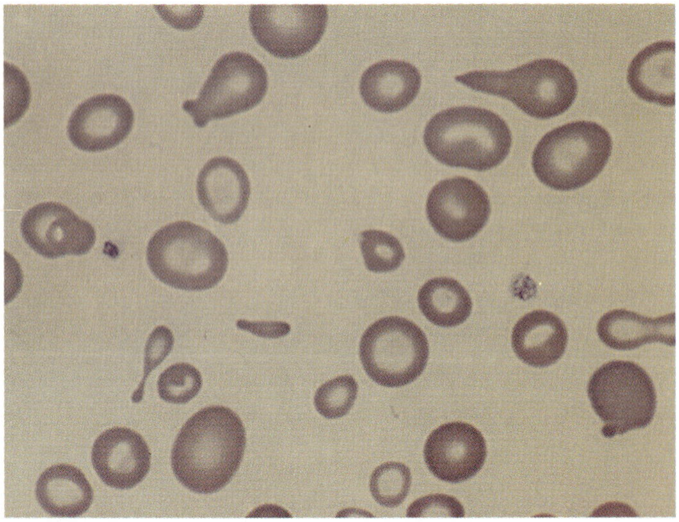

Red blood cells that do not have enough iron are smaller and paler than healthy red blood cells.

Data Collection and Analysis

MATH CONNECTION

How much iron do you eat?

Observe and Collect Data

1. ACTIVITY JOURNAL You need 10 to 18 milligrams (mg) of iron a day to stay healthy. Study the chart below. Look at the labels on food containers. Make a list of other foods that contain iron in your Activity Journal.
2. Create a meal plan for one day that will give you 10 mg of iron. Be sure to include a variety of foods.

Materials

food containers with content labels

Food	Amount of Iron (mg) in One Serving
1 serving broccoli	2.1
1 piece of chicken	0.9
1 orange	0.1
1 apple	0.4
1 piece of fish	1.0
1 carrot	0.4
1 slice of roast beef	2.0
1 egg	0.7
1 serving soybeans	4.9
1 slice of cheese	0.2
1 slice of bread	0.9

Draw Conclusions

1. What foods are the best sources of iron?
2. If you decided not to eat chicken, fish, or beef, what would your meal plan include?

Looking Back

MINDS-ON ASSESSMENT

Words and Concepts

Complete the following statements.

1. Most of an atom's mass is in the ________.
2. Every ________ has its own kind of atom.
3. In an atom, electrons are in the ________.
4. A(n) ________ is a particle in the nucleus that has a positive charge.
5. A particle is located outside the nucleus of an atom is the ________.
6. The ________ is a particle in the nucleus that has no electrical charge.
7. The ________ is the number of protons in the atoms of an element.

Applied Thinking Skills

Answer the following questions. You can use words, drawings, and diagrams in your answers.

8. The pizza shown on this page is a model of a helium atom. Which toppings represent the protons, neutrons, and electrons? How is this model like an atom? How is it different?
9. What properties do the metals in the jewelry shown on this page share? What properties make them different?
10. **Your World** Choose an element you see in your home or school. Write a description of this element.

Show What You Know

What do atoms look like?

Observe and Collect Data

1. ACTIVITY JOURNAL Use the materials listed or other art materials to build a model of an atom. Draw your model and label its parts in your Activity Journal.
2. Compare your model with those of your classmates.

Draw Conclusions

1. Which element did you make a model of?
2. How did you determine the number of protons and electrons to include in your model?
3. In what ways is your model like an atom? In what ways is it not like an atom?

Process Skills
Making models,
Defining operationally

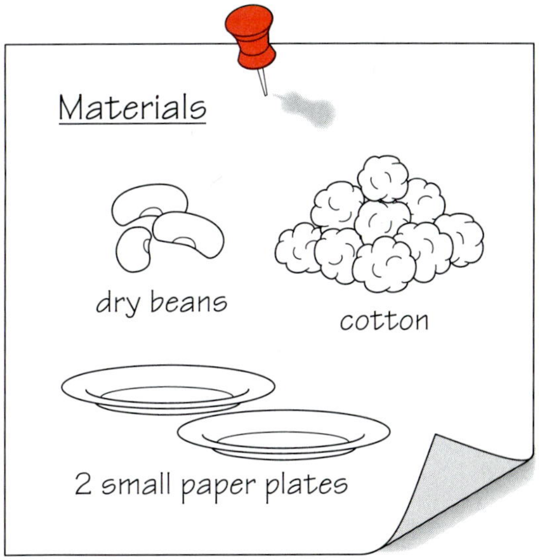

Chapter 2

Compounds

When the pizza chef has finished putting together the ingredients for a pizza, he puts the pizza in the oven. When it comes out of the oven it looks different from when it went into the oven. The crust has risen and looks brown.

What happened in the oven was a chemical change. The heat in the oven changed the ingredients that the cook mixed together into a different substance. The product had different properties than the ingredients.

Elements cannot be changed into different elements in a chemical reaction, but elements are often combined with other elements to make compounds. Substances made of two or more elements that are combined in a chemical reaction are called **compounds.** A chemical change often produces a compound. Compounds have properties that are different from the properties of the elements that make them up.

Many of the ingredients the cook uses at the pizzeria are compounds. Water, sugar, and salt are three examples of compounds the cook uses to make a pizza crust. The compounds in the pizza crust are rearranged when the cook bakes it.

SCIENCE JOURNAL

If you had a set of building blocks, you could build different structures by rearranging the blocks. In your Science Journal, draw or write about something you have seen that could be changed by rearranging the pieces from which it was made.

MONTAGUE
MONTAGUE

Explore Activity

How do elements combine?

Process Skills
Making models,
Defining operationally

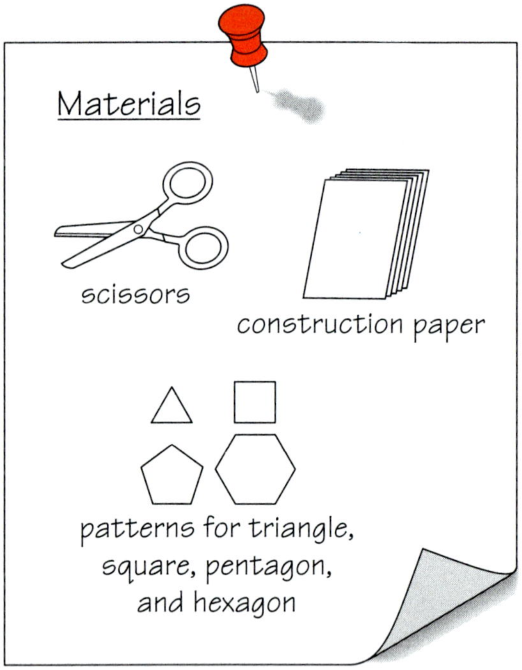

Observe and Collect Data

1. Trace the pattern for each shape on construction paper. Then cut out eight copies of each shape. Each shape represents and atom.
2. ACTIVITY JOURNAL Construct a model of an element by arranging groups of cutouts of the same shape. Put them together so there is little or no space between each piece. In your Activity Journal, draw the arrangements you made.
3. Repeat step 2 using cutouts of all of the different shapes. Draw your new arrangements.

Share Your Results

Compare your drawings with those of your classmates. How many of your drawings were like those of your classmates? How many were different?

Draw Conclusions

1. Which arrangements represent elements? compounds? Explain.
2. How are the compounds different from the patterns, or atoms, you used to make them?

Apply What You Know

How might the shape of different atoms affect which compounds they form?

What happens when elements combine?

Elements may combine chemically to form a compound. The elements in a compound are held together by chemical bonds. When a chemical reaction occurs, you may see some of the following changes:

- a new gas is produced
- heat or light is given off
- a new solid substance is produced
- there is a color change

If you combine two substances and see any of these four changes, you know that you have made a compound that is different from what you started with.

You can tell that a chemical change occurs when baking soda is added to vinegar because a gas is produced.

Heat and light are given off when the charcoal in this oven burns.

When chemists combine lead nitrate and potassium iodide, a chemical change produces a solid substance called lead iodide.

A chemical change causes a tomato to ripen. You can tell a chemical change has occurred because the color of the tomato changes from green to red.

Be a Scientist

Can you make a chemical change?

1. Use lemon juice and a small paint-brush to write a secret message on a piece of white paper.
2. Put the paper with your secret message in the sun for thirty minutes.
3. Record your observations in your Activity Journal. Is this a chemical reaction? How do you know?

The properties of a compound are different from the properties of the elements that make it. The compound carbon dioxide, for example, is quite different from the elements carbon and oxygen. Carbon dioxide is a gas you breathe out. The element carbon can be in the form of charcoal, a diamond, or the graphite in your pencil. The element oxygen is a gas you breathe in. When these elements combine, a new and different substance is formed.

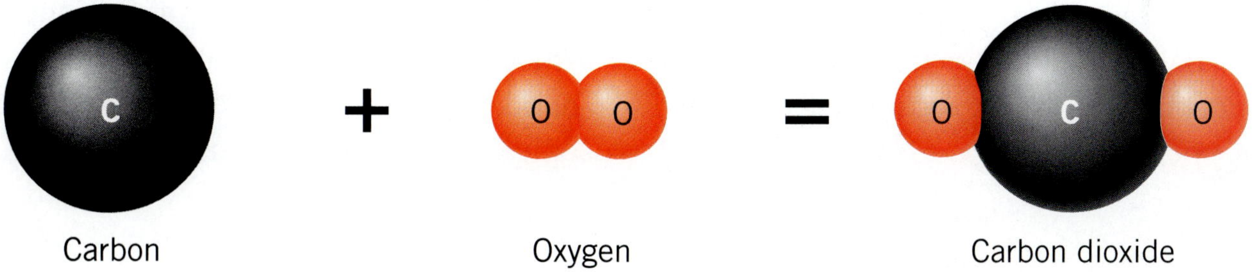

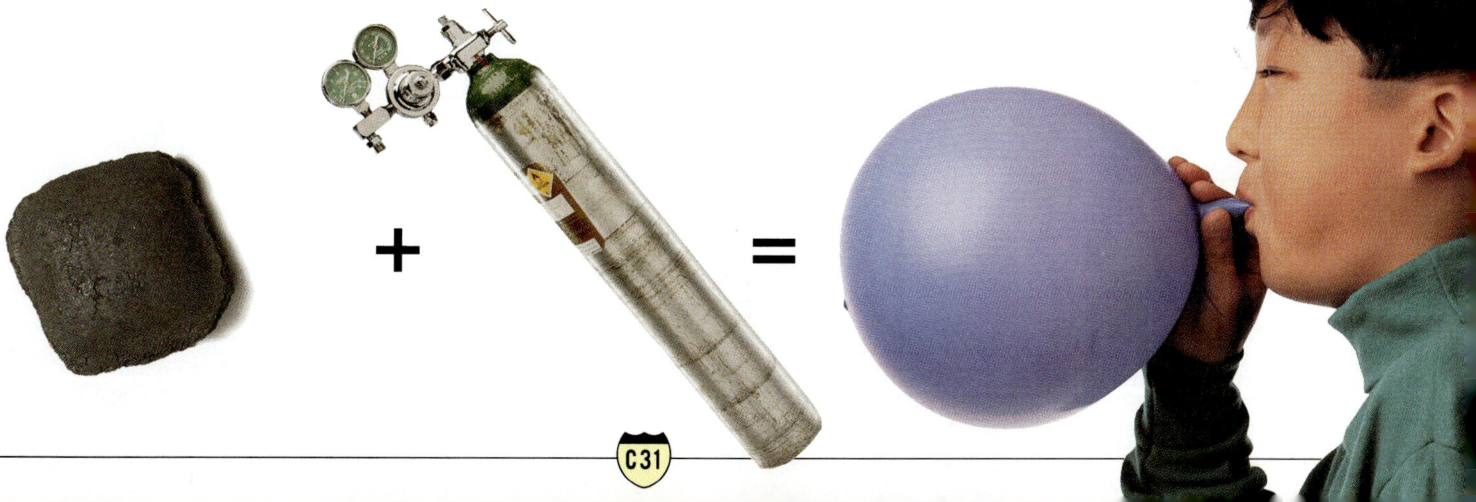

How do compounds differ?

There are several basic factors that account for differences between compounds. The first factor is the elements that make up the compound. Compare a compound to a pizza crust. Pizza crusts that contain different ingredients taste different. Imagine substituting chocolate for flour when making a pizza. Your crust would certainly taste different!

Compounds that are made of different elements are also different. For example, carbon dioxide is very different from silicon dioxide. Carbon and oxygen combine to form a gas you exhale. Silicon and oxygen make a compound that is found in sand.

A second factor that accounts for the difference between compounds is the number of atoms there are in each element. Compare compounds to a pizza crust again. Pizza crusts with different amounts of ingredients taste different. If you made two pizza crusts and added 1 teaspoon of salt to one and 5 teaspoons of salt to the other, the two crusts would taste very different.

Compounds containing different amounts of the same elements also have different properties. Sugar and olive oil, for example, are both made from the elements carbon, oxygen, and hydrogen. Table sugar has 12 atoms of carbon, 22 atoms of hydrogen, and 11 atoms of oxygen. Olive oil, on the other hand, has 18 atoms of carbon, 34 atoms of hydrogen, and 2 atoms of oxygen.

A pizza recipe has a definite ratio of ingredients. A compound has a definite ratio of elements, no matter how much of the compound there is. This is called the law of constant proportions.

SIDE TRIP

A Meadow

Imagine that you are walking through a field of flowers on a perfect spring day. The first flowers you see are blue cornflowers. Then you see bright red poppies. These two brilliant, but very different, flower colors result from a difference of just one hydrogen atom in the compound that gives the flowers their colors!

What holds compounds together?

The salt on your table at the pizzeria is a compound called sodium chloride. When you reach for the salt shaker, you can be sure that sodium chloride will come out. You'd be surprised if one day you found that the compound salt had split apart. If this happened, you'd have poisonous sodium metal in your salt shaker and poisonous chlorine gas floating around the room.

Elements join together by forming chemical bonds. A bond is something that holds two or more things together. Chemical bonds involve the electrons of atoms. Some atoms bond by gaining or losing electrons, and some atoms bond by sharing electrons.

Table salt is a compound formed by transferring electrons. A sodium atom gives up one electron to a nearby chlorine atom. Because the sodium atom has lost an electron, it has one more proton than electron. The sodium atom is now an **ion** (ī′ən), a particle that has a charge. The sodium ion has a positive charge and is written Na+.

Because the chlorine atom gains an electron from the sodium atom, it has a negative charge. It is, therefore, a chlorine ion, and is written Cl-. Because opposite charges attract, the two atoms are held together by an electrical attraction. A bond between ions is called an ionic (ī än′ik) bond.

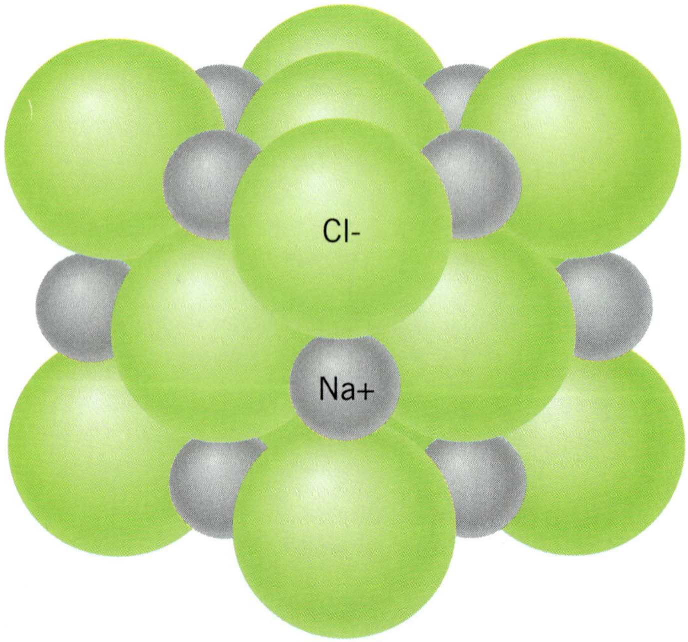

Ionic bond
An electron from the sodium (Na) atom moves to the chlorine (Cl) atom. The sodium ion (Na+) has a positive charge. The chlorine ion (Cl-) has a negative charge. They are held together by electrical attraction.

Another type of chemical bond is a covalent (kō′vā′lənt) bond. Ammonia is an example of a compound that forms covalent bonds. The compound ammonia is made of one nitrogen atom and three hydrogen atoms. The hydrogen and nitrogen atoms share electrons. Many compounds, such as sugar, are formed by covalent bonds.

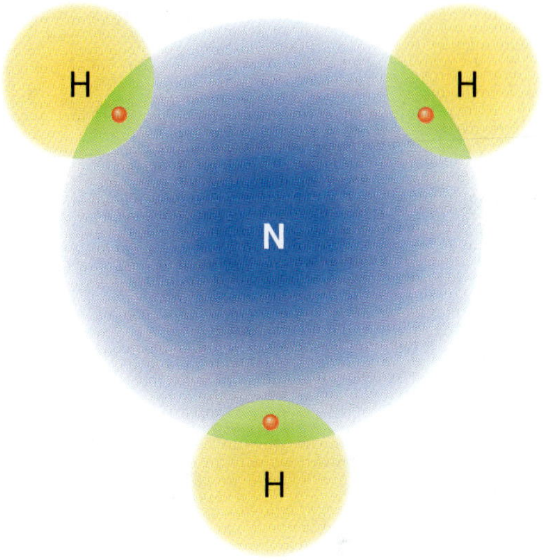

Ammonia (NH_3)

Covalent bond

An electron from each hydrogen (H) atom is shared with the nitrogen (N) atom. This sharing of electrons holds the atoms together.

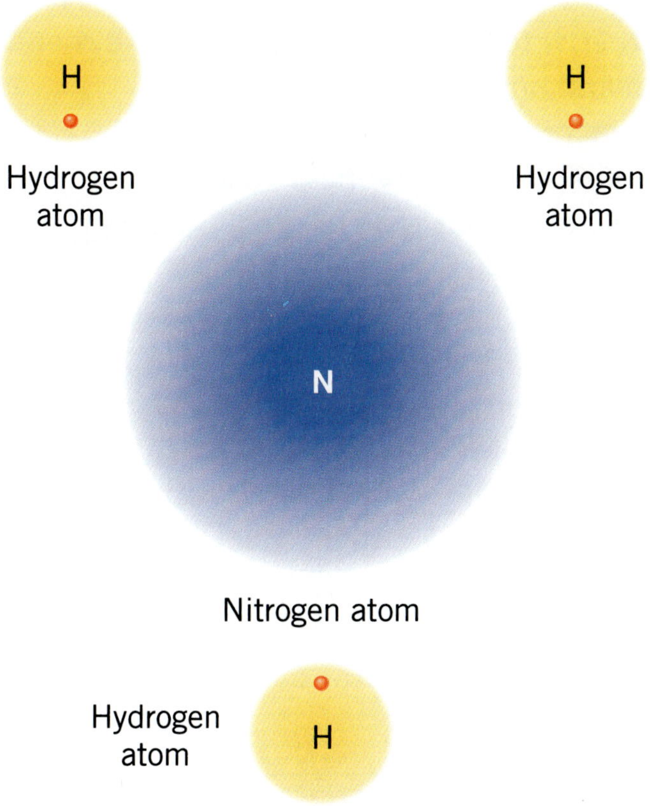

How are you doing?

1. What is a compound?
2. Compare and contrast ionic and covalent bonds.
3. **Think** You just spilled chlorine bleach on your jeans. Now they are covered with pale spots. What has happened? How can you tell?

How do you write a chemical formula?

A pizza chef has a list of ingredients that make up the pizza. Chemists also make lists of the ingredients that make up compounds. The names of ingredients that chemists use are abbreviated, or shortened. As you've learned, element names can be abbreviated with atomic symbols. The names of compounds can also be abbreviated with chemical formulas.

A chemical formula tells you the number and kind of each atom that makes up a compound. The formula for salt, for example, is NaCl. The atomic symbols for sodium (Na) and chlorine (Cl) can be found on the periodic table. When the two symbols, Na and Cl, are written together, it tells you that salt, or NaCl, has one sodium atom and one chlorine atom.

The formula for water is H_2O. The two after the H tells you that one molecule of water has two atoms of hydrogen. When only one atom of an element is present in a compound, scientists do not include the number one. In the formula for water, for example, oxygen does not have a number because there is only one atom of oxygen.

Have you ever seen a rusty object? Rust is formed when there is a chemical reaction between iron and oxygen. The compound that is formed, iron oxide, is the reddish brown substance that covers the iron object. Look at the formula for rust on the next page. What does the symbol Fe tell you? What does the number 2 after the Fe symbol tell you? How many atoms of oxygen are in rust?

The letters in a chemical formula tell you what elements are in the compound.

Water

=

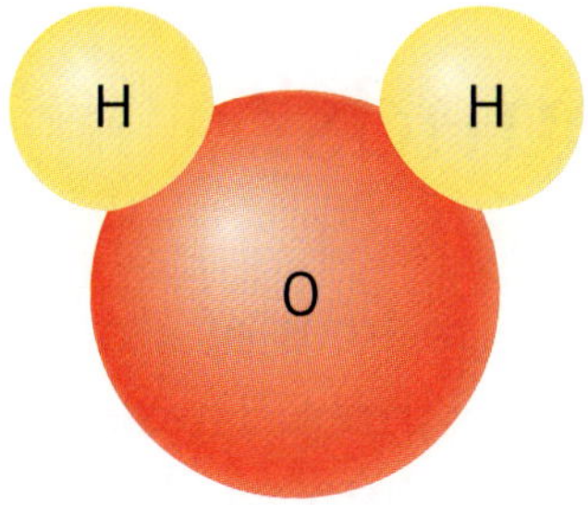

= H_2O

The numbers in a chemical formula tell you how many atoms of each element there are. If there is no number, there is only one atom of that element.

Rust

=

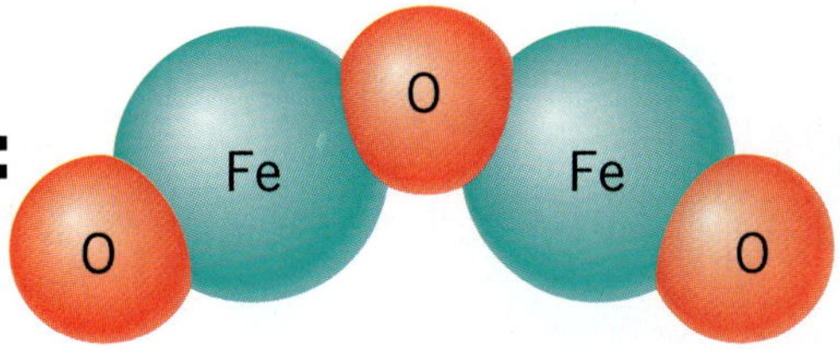

= Fe_2O_3

Be a Scientist

HANDS-ON ACTIVITY

How can you write a chemical formula?

1. ACTIVITY JOURNAL Choose symbols of one or two letters to stand for the bolts, nuts, and washers your teacher provides. Draw each object and write its symbol in your Activity Journal.
2. Put the nuts, bolts, and washers together in as many different ways as possible. Use your symbols to write a formula for each arrangement. Record this in your Activity Journal.
3. Exchange lists of symbols and formulas with a classmate. How do your formulas compare?

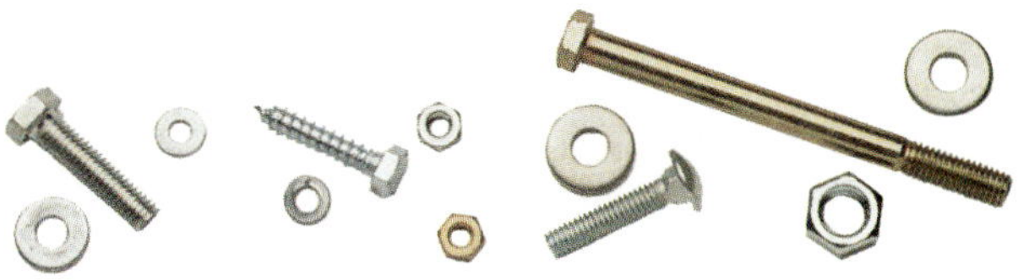

What are some common compounds?

Some compounds are made of hundreds of atoms while others are made of only two or three. These pictures show just a few of the compounds in your world.

The chemical formula for chalk is $CaCO_3$.

Glucose is a kind of sugar. The chemical formula for glucose is $C_6H_{12}O_6$.

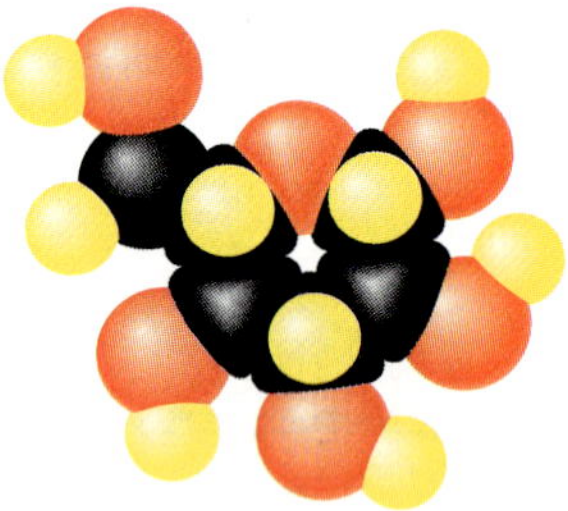

Have you ever been bitten by an ant? Some ants use formic acid to defend themselves and to communicate with other ants. The chemical formula for formic acid is CH_2O_2.

Career Corner

Chef

Do you use chemistry when you cook? My name is Martha Moreles and I am a pizza chef. I use my knowledge of chemistry every day when I'm preparing pizzas. For example, I must know how long to knead the pizza dough. If I knead it too long, the pizza crust ends up rubbery.

I also know how much yeast to mix into the dough. Yeast makes a gas that makes the dough rise. A lot of yeast makes light crust because more gas is produced. Too little makes a heavy crust. My knowledge of chemistry can make the difference between a good pizza and a great pizza.

This huge compound is called insulin (in′se lin). Insulin is a protein in your body that balances the amount of sugar in your blood.

How are you doing?

1. Baking soda's chemical formula is $NaHCO_3$. What elements are in baking soda?
2. Write a chemical formula for a compound with one atom of nitrogen and two atoms of oxygen.
3. **Think** What is the minimum number of atoms needed to form a compound? Is there a maximum?

Science & Literature Connection

A COOL DRINK ON A HOT DAY

by John Ciardi

This poem is from a book called *You Read to Me, I'll Read to You* by John Ciardi.

The Hoo-hah and the Rinky-dink
    And the Automatic Chugg
Were sitting around—in a fog, I think—
Mixing chocolate mud and lemon ink
To make themselves a good cool drink
    Inside a cider jug.

They had tons and tons and tons of ice
    And plenty of mud, do you see?
But the ink ran low, and once or twice
The Rinky-dink stopped to ask for advice
From the Automatic Chugg. "Use spice,
    If we're out of ink," said he.

"There's pepper and mustard and garlic, too.
    And plenty of dynamite dust.
And some rocket fuel. If that won't do,
All I can say is, it's up to you.
Or, if you're desperate, ask the Hoo."
    "Ask," said the Hoo, "if you must."

"Well, then, I must," said the Rinky-dink.
"Hah!" said the Hoo, "you're a fool!
Why should you bother to ask what I think?
I never did care for lemon ink.
The one thing to think about mixing a drink
Is simply to make it cool."

"If you can't make it cool, don't stand there and bawl,"
Said the Hoo-hah, nibbling his mug.
"Your tears are too salty. Just look at them fall!
Well, if you insist, I suggest that you call
For some worthless advice from the best of us all,
Which, such as it is, is the Chugg."

But the Chugg, though he spoke, had nothing to say
Except, "My, the fog's getting thick.
I really believe that's enough for today.
What I suggest is you throw it away.
Besides, if we drink it, I half think we may
Discover the stuff makes us sick."

So the Chugg and the Hoo and the Rinky-dink,
As nearly as I recall,
Had little to eat and nothing to drink.
They would have gone home rather thirsty, I think.
Except that the fog had grown darker than ink
And they couldn't go home at all.

Think About Your Reading

1. What do you infer is the main purpose of this poem?
2. Use what you know about chemistry. Were the characters in this poem making a compound? Explain your answer.

Communicating Write a recipe for a cool drink on a hot day. Describe any chemical changes that take place when you make your cool drink.

Where to Read More

Vivian Grey, *The Chemist Who Lost His Head: The Story of Antoine Larent Lavoisier* (Coward, McCann, and Geoghegan, 1982)
Antoine Lavoisier made a mistake when he agreed to help collect taxes for a French king.

Looking Back

Words and Concepts

Match the description in Column A with the word or chemical formula in Column B.

Column A

1. An atom that has lost an electron.
2. Water is a compound made of two hydrogen atoms and one oxygen atom.
3. Carbon dioxide is a gas made of a carbon atom and two oxygen atoms.
4. Table salt contains one atom of sodium and one atom of chlorine.
5. A chemical bond in which electrons are shared.
6. Rust is a compound of two atoms of iron and three atoms of oxygen.

Column B

a. CO_2
b. NaCl
c. Covalent bond
d. Fe_2O_3
e. Ion
f. H_2O

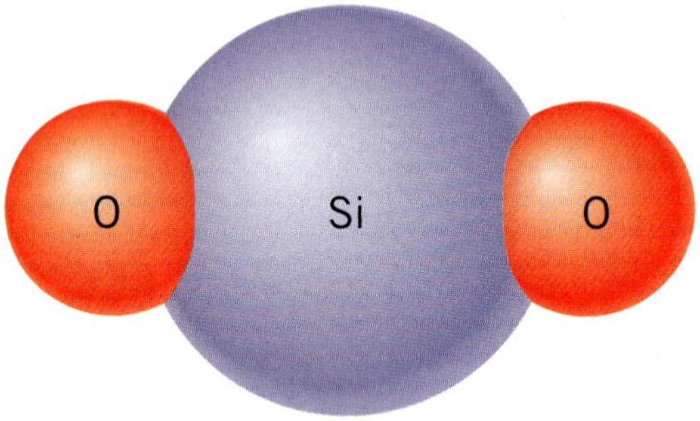

Applied Thinking Skills

Answer the following questions. You can use words, drawings, and diagrams in your answers.

7. Why do atoms in a compound formed by ionic bonding have an electrical attraction for each other?
8. What elements make up the compound shown on this page? Write the formula for this compound.
9. Flour, like sugar, is made of carbon, hydrogen, and oxygen. What factor might account for the differences between sugar and flour?
10. **Your World** List evidence of five chemical changes that happen at home or at school.

Show What You Know

How do compounds form?

Each color of gumdrop stands for a different kind of atom. The toothpicks stand for the bonds between atoms. Each kind of atom can form a different number of bonds.

Process Skills
Making models, Inferring

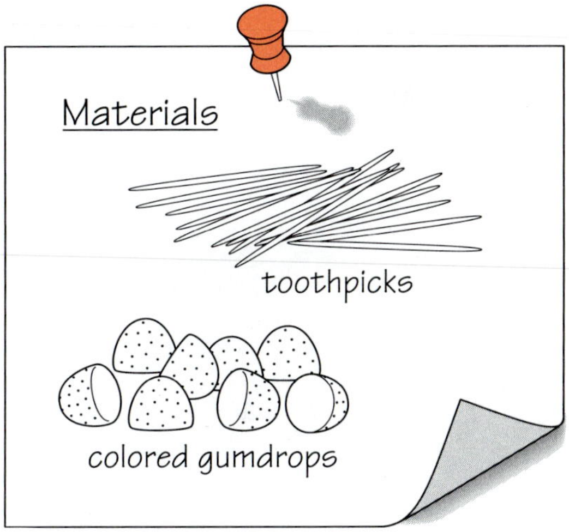

Observe and Collect Data

1. Use the rules of bonding shown in the table below to make compounds of ammonia (NH_3), water (H_2O), and methane (CH_4).
2. In your Activity Journal, draw the models you made. Write the formula of each compound.

Draw Conclusions

How does the number of bonds an element can make affect the compounds it forms?

Element	Symbol	Number of Bonds	Gumdrop Color
Hydrogen	H	1 	yellow
Oxygen	O	2 	red
Nitrogen	N	3 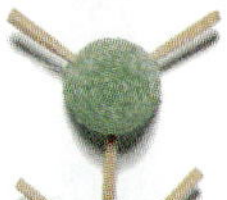	green
Carbon	C	4 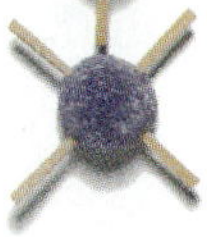	purple

Chapter 3

Mixtures

There is an amazing assortment of things to eat at the pizzeria. You can order pasta with pesto sauce, marinara sauce, or cream sauce. You can also order different-colored pastas. Would you like some green spaghetti? It is made by mixing spinach into the pasta dough.

There is also an assortment of toppings for the pizzas. You can get anything from pepperoni and mushroom to ham and pineapple! When you visit the salad bar, you can mix together your favorite vegetables. The salad bar is also stocked with different kinds of salad dressings.

Each dressing contains a mixture of herbs, spices, oils, and vinegars.

A **mixture** contains two or more different substances that are not chemically joined. Mixtures are a result of physical changes, not chemical changes. Though they may be mixed together, each substance in a mixture remains chemically unchanged.

In a salad, for example, the atoms of lettuce do not combine with the atoms of the tomato. The lettuce still looks and tastes like lettuce, and the tomato still looks and tastes like a tomato. If a reaction had occurred, your salad would be a compound instead of a mixture.

SCIENCE JOURNAL

In your Science Journal, write a recipe for a salad. How do the properties of your salad mixture relate to the properties of the ingredients that make it up? Compare and contrast your salad recipe with a classmate's recipe.

Explore Activity

How can mixtures be separated?

Process Skills
Collecting data, Classifying, Predicting

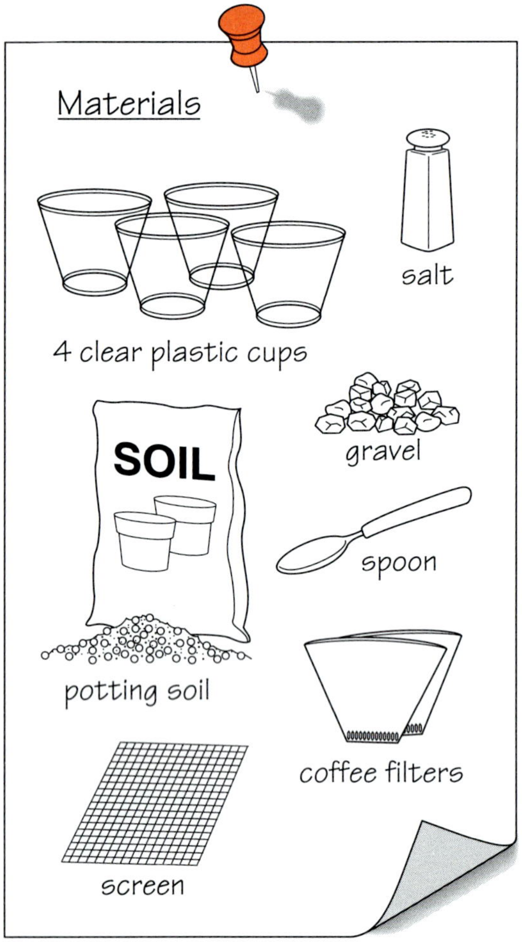

Observe and Collect Data

ACTIVITY JOURNAL

Fill a cup with one teaspoon each of salt, gravel, water, and potting soil. Stir well. **Predict** which tool, the filter or the screen, will separate the mixture. Record your prediction in your Activity Journal.

2. Use the filter and screen to try to separate this mixture. Describe what happened.
3. Fill three more cups halfway with water. To one cup add a teaspoon of salt. To the second cup add a teaspoon of gravel. To the third cup add a teaspoon of potting soil. Stir each mixture well. **Predict** which tool will separate these mixtures. Record your predictions in your Activity Journal.
4. Try to separate each mixture using either the filter or the screen. Record your results.

Share Your Results

Compare how you and your classmates separated the mixtures. Did someone try a way you didn't think of? How did it work?

Draw Conclusions

1. Compare your predictions and your results.
2. Was there any mixture you could not separate? Think of a reason why it could not be separated.

Apply What You Know

Suppose you were going to start a garden or grow potted plants indoors. How might you separate sand and pebbles from the soil you plan to use?

What are the properties of mixtures?

This salad is a mixture of lettuce, cucumbers, cabbage, tomatoes, and carrots.

The pizzeria is full of mixtures of all kinds. A mixture is a combination of substances that are not chemically bonded. Because the substances in a mixture are not linked together by chemical bonds, they can be separated without a chemical reaction. This is one way that mixtures and compounds differ.

Another difference between mixtures and compounds is that the makeup of compounds is always the same, while the makeup of mixtures can vary. A mixture can contain substances in any proportion. Spaghetti and sauce is a mixture. When you make spaghetti, you can use a little more sauce or fewer noodles in your mixture and still get spaghetti. Although you can change the makeup of a mixture, you can't change the makeup of a compound. For example, if you took one atom of oxygen out of carbon dioxide, you would have a different compound, a poisonous gas called carbon monoxide.

The properties of mixtures depend upon the properties of the substances that make up the mixtures. If tomatoes are added to a salad, the salad will look different. It will taste different too. A mixture changes according to the amount of each substance present.

SCIENCE JOURNAL

Choose a mixture that you have eaten. In your Science Journal, describe the properties of the substances that make up the mixture. Describe the properties of the mixture. Can the amount of the foods that make up this mixture vary?

BACK HOME

This lemonade is a mixture of lemon juice, sugar, and water.

Tomato sauce is a mixture of tomatoes, herbs, mushrooms, and spices.

What is a solution?

The sugar in lemonade is dissolved in the liquid. This means that the sugar particles are evenly mixed throughout the liquid at all times, and they do not settle out. This type of mixture is called a **solution.** A solution is a mixture in which particles spread evenly throughout.

Making a solution does not involve a chemical change. It does, however, involve a physical change. When you put a spoonful of sugar into a glass of lemonade, the sugar crystals seem to vanish. The sugar has undergone a physical change. The sugar crystals have broken up into sugar particles that are so small you can't see them as they mix with the lemonade. Although they are too small to see, the sugar crystals have not undergone a chemical change. They are still sugar crystals.

In order to mix evenly, substances that dissolve must separate into molecules or ions. Molecules are a type of compound. When the sugar is added to the lemonade, the sugar crystals separate into sugar molecules. The sugar molecules are small enough to mix evenly among the water molecules.

Most solutions contain two types of substances. The substance that there is more of is called the **solvent** (säl′vənt). For example, the lemonade is a solvent. The substance that there is less of is called the **solute** (säl′yo͞ot′). The sugar you added to the lemonade is a solute. In solutions, the tiny molecules or ions of the solute are mixed with the solvent.

Changing the amount of solute you add to a solution changes the concentration (kän′sən trā′shən) of the solution. The concentration of a solution tells you how much solute is dissolved. A solution with a lot of solute is called a concentrated solution. A solution with a small amount of solute is called a dilute solution. When a solvent contains as much solute as it can hold, it is called a saturated solution. No more solute will dissolve into a saturated solution.

Solutions can involve solids, liquids, and gases. The air that you breathe, for example, is a solution. It contains different gases, such as nitrogen, oxygen, and water vapor. If you were to examine a sample of air, you would find that these gases are evenly mixed throughout. The chart on this page shows the solutes and solvents in some solutions.

Solute	Solvent	Solution
Water droplets (liquid)	Air (gas)	 Steam
Carbon dioxide (gas)	Water (liquid)	 Soda water
Salt (solid)	Water (liquid)	 Ocean water
Copper (solid)	Zinc (solid)	 Brass

What is a suspension?

Have you ever read "Shake well before using" on a bottle of salad dressing or lotion? By shaking the bottle, you mix together the contents of the bottle. You need to do this because the bottle contains a suspension.

A **suspension** (sə spen′shen) is a kind of mixture that separates if it is left alone for some time. In a suspension, some of the particles sink to the bottom. They are no longer evenly mixed throughout. A suspension must be shaken to remain mixed.

The salad dressing at the pizzeria is a good example of a suspension. The oil and vinegar in the container remain mixed for a short time. If you do not shake them, the oil will stay at the top of the jar and the vinegar will settle to the bottom.

Suspensions can be made with solids, liquids, and gases. A liquid suspended in a liquid is an emulsion. The salad dressing is an example of an emulsion. Milk is another example of an emulsion. A solid or liquid suspended in a gas is called an aerosol. Many spray cans contain aerosols. A gel, such as jelly, is a solid suspended in a liquid. A foam, such as whipped cream, is a gas suspended in a liquid.

One factor that makes suspensions different from solutions is the size of the particles that make up the solutions. The particles in a solution are tiny ions or molecules. The particles in suspensions are much larger. Because they are larger, the particles in a suspension do not dissolve.

Be a Scientist

How can you make a suspension?

ACTIVITY JOURNAL

Make your own suspension. You can use liquids or solids. In your Activity Journal, list the ingredients you use. **Predict** how many layers will form when your suspension settles. Have your teacher check your list. Then write or draw how many layers actually formed.

◀ The oil and vinegar salad dressing in the pizzeria is a suspension. If it sits for a while, the lighter oil and the denser vinegar will separate.

How are you doing?

1. What is a mixture?
2. What is the difference between a solution and a suspension?
3. **Think** The pulp settles to the bottom of a glass of orange juice. The juice stays at the top of the glass. Is this a solution or a suspension? How do you know?

How can mixtures be separated?

Most mixtures can be easily separated into the substances that make them. Since no chemical bonds are formed, the substances are not linked together. The method you use to separate a mixture depends on the size of the pieces that make up that mixture.

Some mixtures can be separated with filters. For example, pasta and water can be separated with a colander. The size of the filter you need to use depends on the size of the particles in the mixture. Most suspensions can be separated with filters.

Some mixtures, such as the mixture of socks in this laundry basket, are made of large pieces. You can separate these mixtures by hand. What are other mixtures you can separate by hand?

Be a Scientist

What is in the mystery solution?

1. Cut a filter into strips. Place 2 drops of the mystery solution about 1.5 cm from the bottom of the strip.
2. Place a straw across the top of a container. Attach the strip to the straw so that the bottom of the strip dips into the water but the mystery solution does not.
3. ACTIVITY JOURNAL In your Activity Journal, describe what you see as the mystery solution moves up the filter strip.

One way to separate liquid solutions is to let the solvent evaporate until all you have left is the solute. If you boil salt water, the water will evaporate, leaving salt crystals behind.

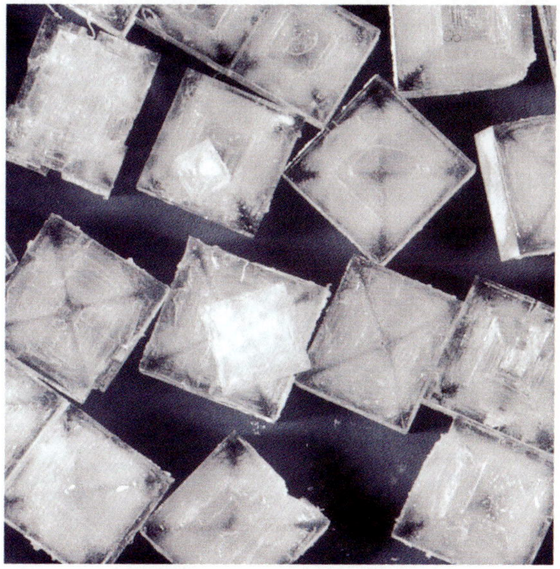

When the solvent is evaporated, many solutes form crystals (kris′təlz). Crystals are solid matter whose particles are arranged in a certain shape. Crystals can be in many shapes, including cubes, needles, and diamonds. You might be familiar with crystals such as salt or rock candy.

What are acids and bases?

The lemonade you ordered at the pizzeria tastes sour. Sour taste is a property of an **acid.** A substance called citric (si′trik) acid makes lemonade taste sour. Another kind of solution is called a **base.** A base is very different from an acid. Bases taste bitter and feel slippery.

Many solutions are neutral, which means that they are neither acids nor bases. Pure water, for example, is a neutral substance. When acids and bases are mixed together, they produce a neutral solution.

Many foods and drinks are weak acids or bases. Strong acids and bases can be harmful. You should not taste or touch solutions to find out if they are acids or bases. Scientists use dyes called indicators to safely test different solutions.

Indicators tell you if a solution is an acid or a base. Most indicators do this by changing color. For example, one kind of litmus (lit′məs) turns blue in a base and another turns red in an acid. Tea and beet juice also change color in acids or bases.

The pH scale is used to measure the strength of acids and bases. The smaller the pH number is, the stronger the acid is. The larger the pH number is, the stronger the base is. The pH of any neutral substance, such as water, is 7.0.

There is a relationship between the strengths of acids and bases and how hazardous they are. A strong acid, such as hydrochloric acid, will burn your skin. A weak acid, such as vinegar, will not burn you.

Be a Scientist

HANDS-ON ACTIVITY

How can you identify acids and bases?

1. Get several small cups of indicator. The indicator will turn pink in an acid and greenish blue in a base.

2. ACTIVITY JOURNAL Get several solutions and describe them in your Activity Journal.

3. Put a teaspoon of each solution into a separate cup of indicator. Use a different spoon for each solution. Record your observations and whether each solution is an acid or whether it is a base.

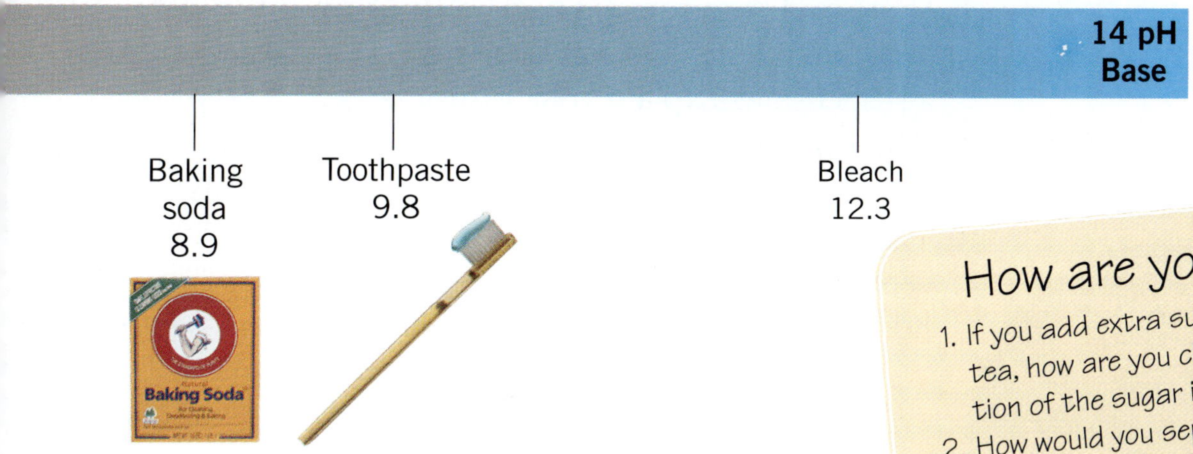

How are you doing?

1. If you add extra sugar to a glass of iced tea, how are you changing the concentration of the sugar in this solution?
2. How would you separate a mixture of sugar and water? Sand and water?
3. **Think** Predict whether soap is an acid or a base. How might you test soap to find out if your prediction was correct?

Looking Back

MINDS-ON ASSESSMENT

Words and Concepts

Match the example in Column A with the word in Column B.

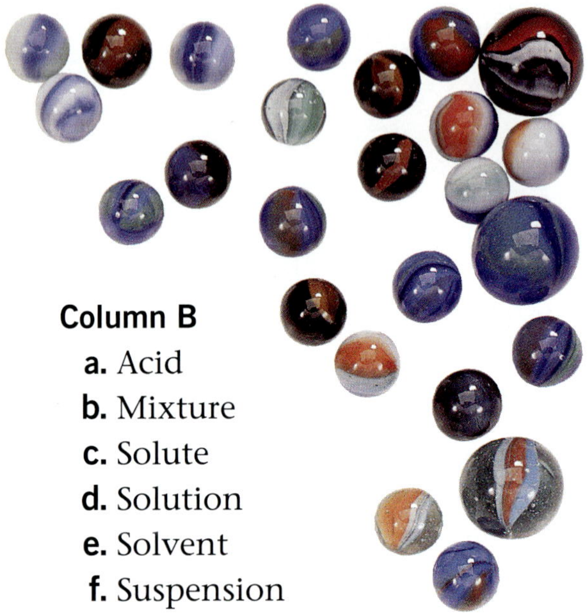

Column A

1. The water in a glass of lemonade
2. The powdered drink mix to make lemonade
3. Oil-and-vinegar salad dressing
4. A group of differently colored marbles
5. Salt water
6. A solution with a pH of 3

Column B

a. Acid
b. Mixture
c. Solute
d. Solution
e. Solvent
f. Suspension

Applied Thinking Skills

Answer the following questions. You can use words, drawings, and diagrams in your answers.

7. Compare and contrast compounds and mixtures.
8. Some tea leaves come in bags while others are loose. Which kind of tea makes a solution? Which makes a suspension? Explain your answer.
9. Water is often called the "universal solvent." Write a few sentences telling what you think this means.
10. **Your World** Describe some of the mixtures, such as cereals, soups, and dressings, in your kitchen at home. How would you separate these mixtures?

Show What You Know

How do you classify mixtures?

Observe and Collect Data

1. 

Add a spoonful of juice mix to a cup of water and stir. Describe this mixture in your Activity Journal.
2. Put two spoonfuls of dry beans and two spoonfuls of flour into a jar filled with water. Screw the lid on tightly. Shake the jar until the materials are thoroughly mixed. Describe the contents of the jar in your Activity Journal.
3. Let the two mixtures stand undisturbed for about twenty minutes. In your Activity Journal, describe how both mixtures look after twenty minutes.

Draw Conclusions

1. Compare and contrast the two mixtures you made. What kind of mixtures are they?
2. What methods would you use to separate these two mixtures?

Process Skills
Observing, Classifying

Forms of Matter

You have learned about basic chemistry (and a little bit about pizza) in this unit. Work on your own or with classmates on one activity described below.

Yearbook Editor Work with classmates. Each student chooses an element. The yearbook should include the element's name, symbol, and atomic number. It should also include a picture that shows what the element is like or how it is used.

Director Create a show based on elements, compounds, and mixtures. Get together with other students to create songs, poems, essays, or other works of art about what you learned in this unit. Present your show to the rest of the class.

Choreographer Make up a dance with classmates showing how elements combine in compounds and different kinds of mixtures. Characters can include protons, neutrons, and electrons, or they can be different elements.

Nutritionist Find out about the contents of different foods. Report on the elements and compounds that make up the foods. State whether each food is a compound, a solution, or a suspension.

Game Designer Make a game about elements, compounds, and mixtures. You can create a board game or an active game.

Artist Make a model of atoms, compounds, or mixtures. You might want to make a mobile, a sculpture, or a collage.

Glossary

acid (as′id) A solution that tastes sour and has a low pH, from 0–7. (page C56)

atomic number (ə täm′ik num′bər) Each element has a different atomic number. It tells you how many protons are found in atoms of that element. (page C17)

atom (at′əm) The smallest particle of an element that can exist and keep the element's chemical properties. (page C11)

base (bās) A solution that tastes bitter, is slippery, and has a high pH, from 7–14. (page C56)

compound (käm′pound′) A substance that is made up of two or more elements that are combined chemically. (page C26)

electron (ē lek′trän′) A particle with a negative charge that is found in a cloud around the nucleus. (page C13)

element (el′ə mənt) A substance that cannot be changed into a simpler substance. (page C10)

ion (ī′ən) A charged particle formed when an atom gains or loses electrons. (page C34)

mixture (miks′chər) A combination of substances that are not chemically bonded. (page C45)

neutron (no͞o′trän′) A particle with no charge that is found in the nucleus of an atom. (page C13)

nucleus (noo′klē əs) The dense center of an atom. The nucleus contains protons and neutrons. (page C13)

periodic table (pir′ē äd′ik tā′bəl) A chart that lists all elements arranged in order from lowest atomic number to highest atomic number. It shows the name, symbol, and atomic number of each element. (page C16)

proton (prō′tän′) A particle with a positive charge that is found in the nucleus of an atom. (page C13)

solute (säl′yo͞ot′) Dissolved particles in a solution. (page C51)

solution (sə lo͞o′shən) A mixture in which the substances stay mixed together evenly. (page C50)

solvent (säl′vənt) The dissolving medium in a solution. (page C51)

suspension (sə spen′shən) A kind of mixture that partially separates if left standing for a period of time. (page C53)

Unit C Index

Boldface numerals denote glossary terms. Italic numerals denote illustrations.

Credits

Photographs

11T Culver Pictures; 19T Randy Wells/AllStock; 22B G.W. Willis, MC/Biological Photo Service; 24L Jerry Jacka; 30RC Lincoln Russel/Stock, Boston; 33R Hans Reinhard/OKAPIA/Photo Researchers; 38BR J.H. Robinson/Photo Researchers; 51BC W. Bertsch/Bruce Coleman Inc.; 55B Dr. E.R. Degginger/Earth Scenes; 55T Michael Dalton/Fundamental Photographs; Tim Davis* 2–3, 6–7; Anne Dowie* 26–27, 33B, 39; GHP Studio* 4R, 18, 19C, 20–21, 21BR, 21TL, 22C, 30B, 30T, 31C, 31L, 32, 36, 37, 38C, 38T, 43L, 48, 49, 51B, 51T, 51TC, 53, 54T, 56CL, 56CR, 56R, 57, 58; Ken Karp* 5, 16L, 22T, 23, 30L; Ken Lax* 16R, 31R, 50, 52, 54B; Renee Lynn* 56L; Elliott Smith* 9, 25, 28, 29, 43R, 46, 47, 59; Nikolay Zurek* 4L, 10–11, 14, 15, 20, 21TR, 24R, 44–45

Special thanks to Malcolm X Elementary School, Berkeley; California; Franklin Year-Round School, Oakland, California; Carl B. Munck Elementary School, Oakland, California; Hintil Ku Ka Child Care Center, Oakland, California.

* Photographed expressly for Addison-Wesley Publishing Company, Inc.

Illustrations

Nea Bisek 8T, 23, 25, 28, 43, 46, 59
Rolin Graphics 4, 12–13, 14, 15, 31, 34, 35, 37, 38, 39, 42, 47
Jane McCreary 8B, 13R, 29, 47
Randy Vergoustraete 60–61
Pat Welch 1

Text

23 United States Department of Agriculture, Human Nutrition Information Service, Home and Garden Bulletin Number 72, *Nutritive Value of Foods,* June 1991, pages 10–11, 18–19, 22–23, 28–29, 40–41, 48–49, 54–55, 56–57.

40–41 John Ciardi, "A Cool Drink on a Hot Day," from John Ciardi, *You Read to Me, I'll Read to You* (New York: Harper, 1962). Copyright ©1962 by John Ciardi. Reprinted with the permission of HarperCollins Publishers.

Thousands of tiny lights twinkle below you,
like a mirror of the sky overhead.
You soar over towns and cities.
Buildings, houses, and cars look like tiny toys,
but you know they're real.
This is flight.

PASSPORT
United States
of America
UNITED

Airport

It's your first trip on an airplane and you are amazed by all the sights and sounds around you. You hear people talking, engines humming, and air vents hissing. When you look out the airplane window, you see the city lights below you and the moon above. Inside the plane, you see pictures on the movie screen and the airplane lights. As you listen to your radio, you realize there are other forms of energy, too.

Light, sound, and other kinds of energy travel in waves. You may have seen waves in a large body of water or across a field of grass. Invisible energy waves behave like the ones you can see.

- What is sound energy?
- What is light energy?
- What are other forms of wave energy?

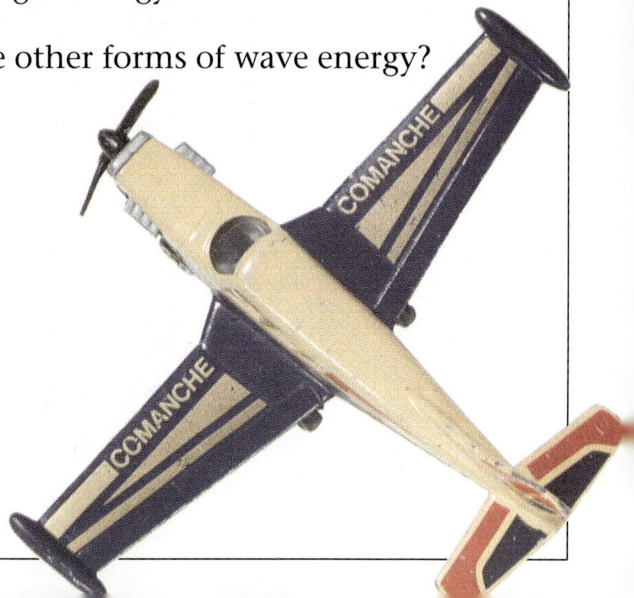

Unit D

SOUND AND LIGHT

Activities

Features

Sound Energy

"Ladies and gentlemen, prepare for landing," the flight attendant announces. Your face is pressed against the airplane window as it approaches the ground. You hear a slight whirring sound as the flaps of the plane come out from the wings. You can feel the window shake slightly back and forth. A thump signals that the landing gear is lowered and locked into place.

You were able to detect these events, from the flight attendant's message to the locking of the landing gear, by feeling and hearing vibrations. Vibrations (vī brā′shənz) are rapid back and forth movements. Sounds are vibrations that you can hear. Sound is a form of energy that is produced by and transferred by vibrating matter.

There are many kinds of sound, but all sounds are produced in the same way—by vibrations. For example, the vibrations of a bee's wings cause the buzzing sound you hear when a bee is near. When the wind moves the leaves of a tree back and forth, you hear a rustling sound. Many people can hear the sound of vibrations that move back and forth from 20 times a second to 20,000 times a second. Close your eyes. What sounds can you hear?

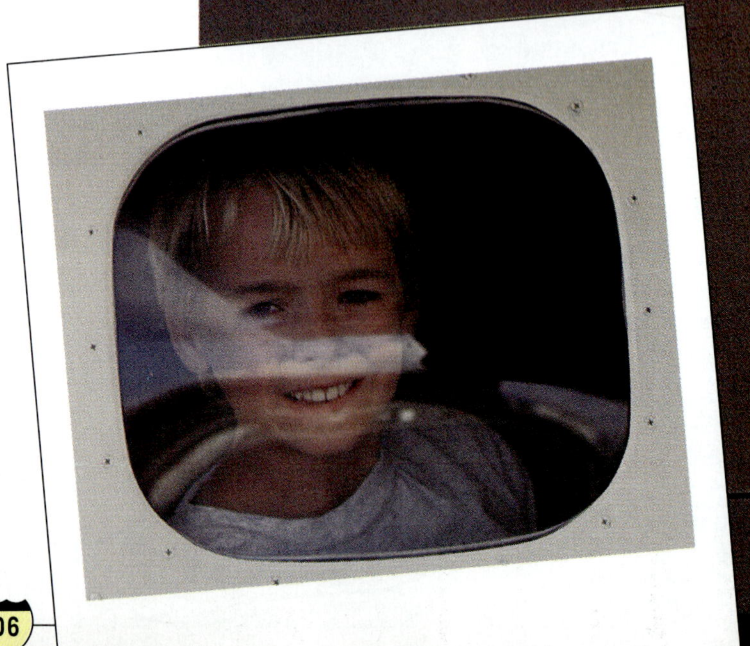

Put your hand on your throat and make a sound. Can you feel your throat vibrate? Does the vibration in your throat change when you make different sounds? Describe what you feel in your Science Journal.

Explore Activity

What makes sound?

Process Skills

Inferring, Making models

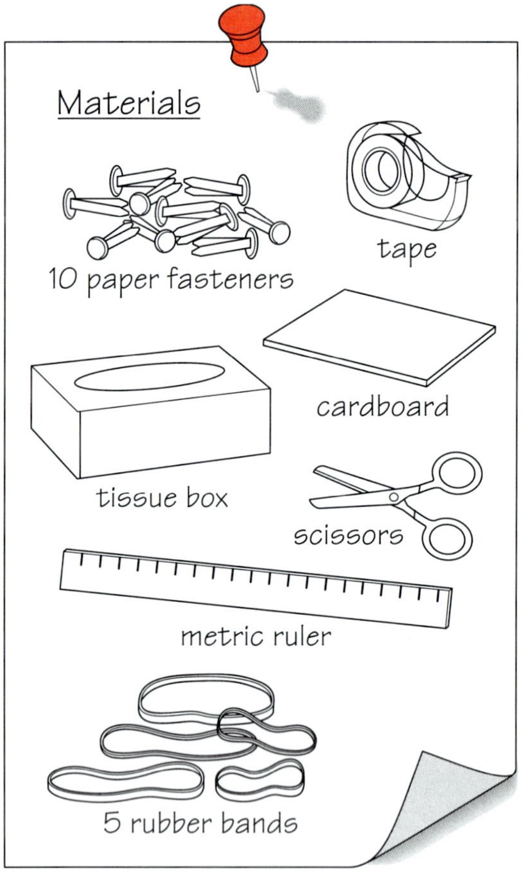

Observe and Collect Data

1. Punch five holes at each end of the tissue box. Place the fasteners in the holes. Open the prongs of the fasteners to hold them in place.
2. Cut the rubber bands to make five strings. Knot one end of each string around each fastener on one end of the box. Loop the other end of each string around the opposite fastener, but do not tie it.
3. Cut two cardboard rectangles 6 cm by 15 cm. Fold the rectangles to make two triangular bridges. Slide these under and across the strings. Tape the bridges to the box.
4. ACTIVITY JOURNAL Tune your instrument by tightening or loosening the ends of the strings. When you have found the right tension for each string, wrap the loose end two times around its fastener. Pluck the strings with one hand while touching the top edge of the box with the other hand. In your Activity Journal, draw or describe your instrument.

Share Your Results

Compare the sounds of your instrument and those of other groups' instruments. How are they similar? How are they different?

Draw Conclusions

1. What did you feel while you were plucking the strings? What does this tell you about sound?
2. How does the force you use to pluck the strings affect the sound that the instrument makes? How does the force affect the way the box feels when you touch it?
3. How did the tightness of the strings affect the sound the instrument makes?

Apply What You Know

Suppose you made another instrument, using the same length strings and a larger box. **Predict** how the sounds of this new instrument would differ from the sounds of the first instrument you made.

What is a sound wave?

You feel a thud when the wheels of the plane touch ground. A flight attendant's voice comes over the speaker again. "Please remain in your seats," the voice cautions.

You can hear the flight attendant's voice because of sound energy. Energy (en′ər jē) is the ability to cause a change in matter. **Sound energy** is the ability of sound to make something vibrate.

In order to make a sound, bands, called vocal cords, in the flight attendant's throat vibrate. The air between you and the flight attendant is made of tiny particles. The vibrations of the flight attendant's vocal cords cause the particles in the air to start moving back and forth. Each vibration produces a sound wave, a surge of sound energy that travels through matter.

This picture shows how air particles are loosely scattered when there is no sound.

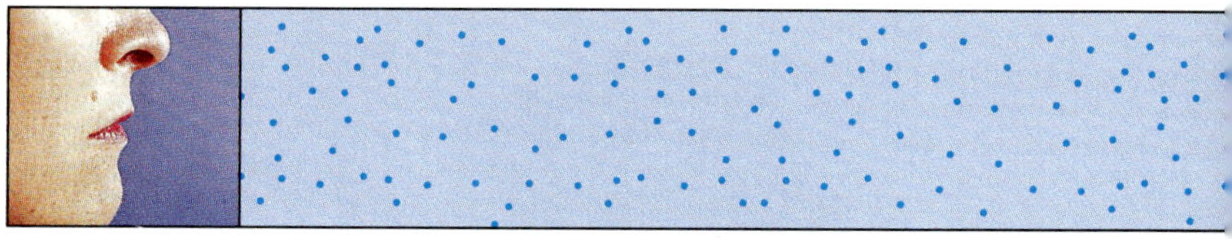

This picture shows how air particles are pushed together when sound vibrations move the air particles back and forth.

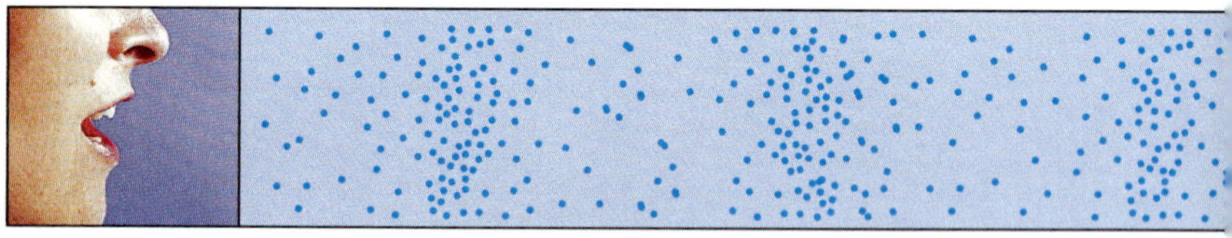

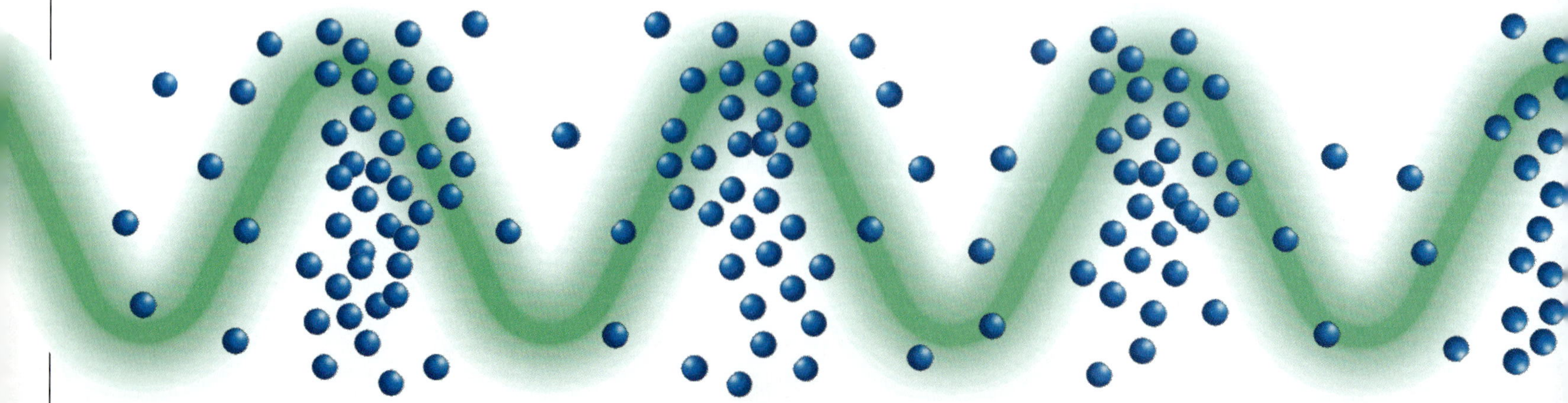

In a sound wave the air particles themselves do not travel very far. It is the wave energy that moves through the air to your ear. The vibrations of the particles are caused by the sound wave.

Wavelength is one way to measure sound waves. A **wavelength** is the distance between a point on one wave to the same point on the next wave.

Be a Scientist

HANDS-ON ACTIVITY

How can you model a sound wave?

1. Tie one end of a spring toy to the top of one leg of a chair or table. Pull the spring toy out so that the coils are one or two cm apart.
2. Hold the first eight or nine coils tightly together. Then let go of all but the first coil. Repeat the experiment three times.
3. ACTIVITY JOURNAL Draw or describe your observations in your Activity Journal.

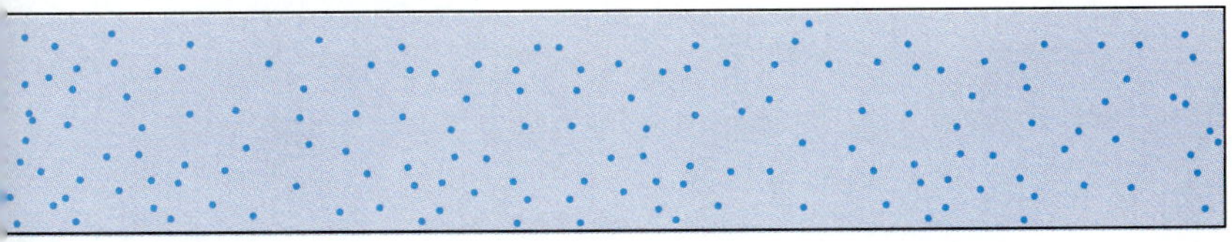

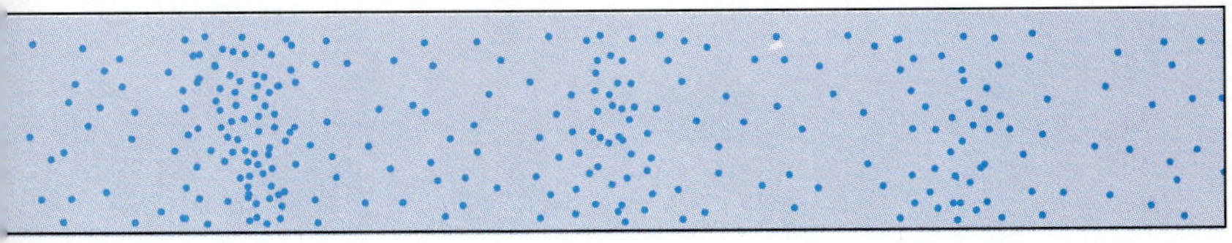

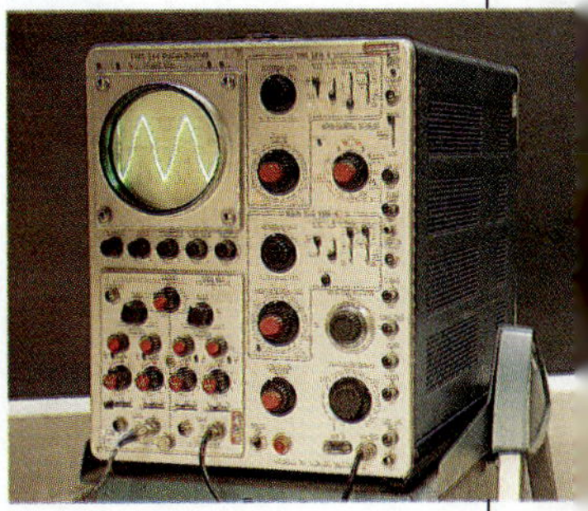

Sound waves are studied with an instrument called an oscilloscope (ə sil′ə skōp′).

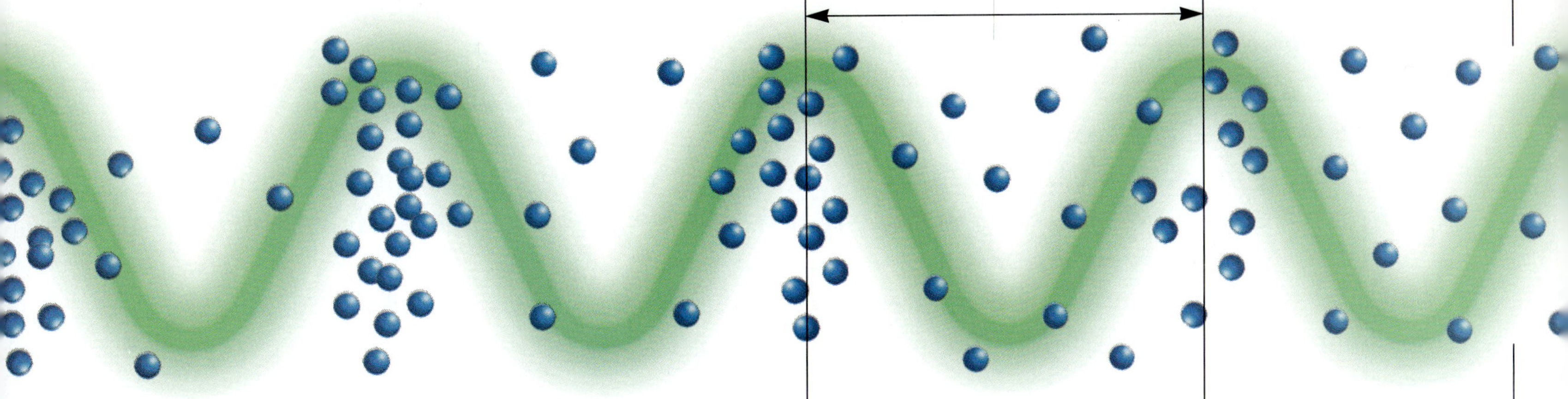

How do sounds vary?

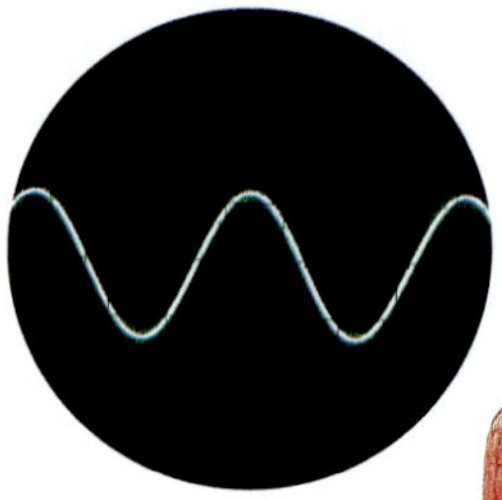

Once the plane lands, sounds continue to surround you. Near you a girl is talking to her father. You notice that the man's voice sounds low and the girl's voice sounds high. This difference in sound is called pitch.

The pitch of a sound is related to its frequency (frē′kwən sē). **Frequency** is the number of times the sound source vibrates in one second. The faster the sound vibrations, the higher the pitch of the sound. Some sound waves have frequencies that are too high or too low for our ears to pick up.

The girl's vocal cords vibrate with a higher frequency than the man's. This is why the girl's voice has a higher pitch. Sounds with low frequencies have a low pitch. The man's vocal cords vibrate slowly, making a low pitch.

The oscilloscope pictures show a simplified version of what the sound waves produced by the people on the plane might look like.

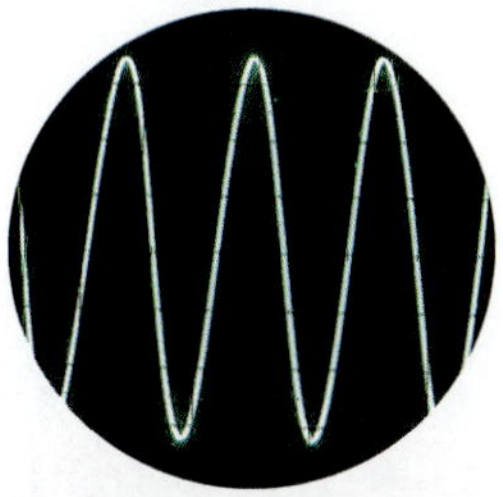

See how low and how high you can make your voice. In your family, whose voice has the lowest pitch? Whose voice has the highest pitch? Compare and contrast the frequencies of low and high voices.

You hear a loud sound from a child nearby. Loudness is another difference between sounds. Although some conversations near you are quiet, the child's voice is loud. The child is putting more energy into making noise than the other passengers. This energy is what makes the sound louder.

The height of a wave is called **amplitude** (am′plə tood′). Loud sounds have high amplitudes. The amplitude of the child's cry is higher than that of the other passengers. Make a soft sound and a loud sound. Which sound took more energy?

How do loud sounds affect your hearing?

The airline worker protects her ears from the noise of jet engines.

As the plane pulls up to the gate, you notice a worker on the ground wearing ear protection motioning the pilot where to steer the plane. The ground worker wears ear protection to shield her hearing from the loud noises of planes taking off and landing. Loud noises damage your hearing. The worker's ear protection blocks loud sounds so that they do not harm her ears.

A **decibel** (des′ə bəl′) is a unit used to measure the loudness of sound. You can barely hear sounds that measure 0 decibels. When you whisper, the sound you produce measures about 20 decibels. Your normal speaking voice measures about 60 decibels. Your hearing can be damaged by a single exposure to a sound louder than 150 decibels. Repeated exposure to sounds over 85 decibels can also cause damage to your hearing.

People are constantly exposed to noises they cannot control. Jackhammers, ambulance sirens, trucks, and

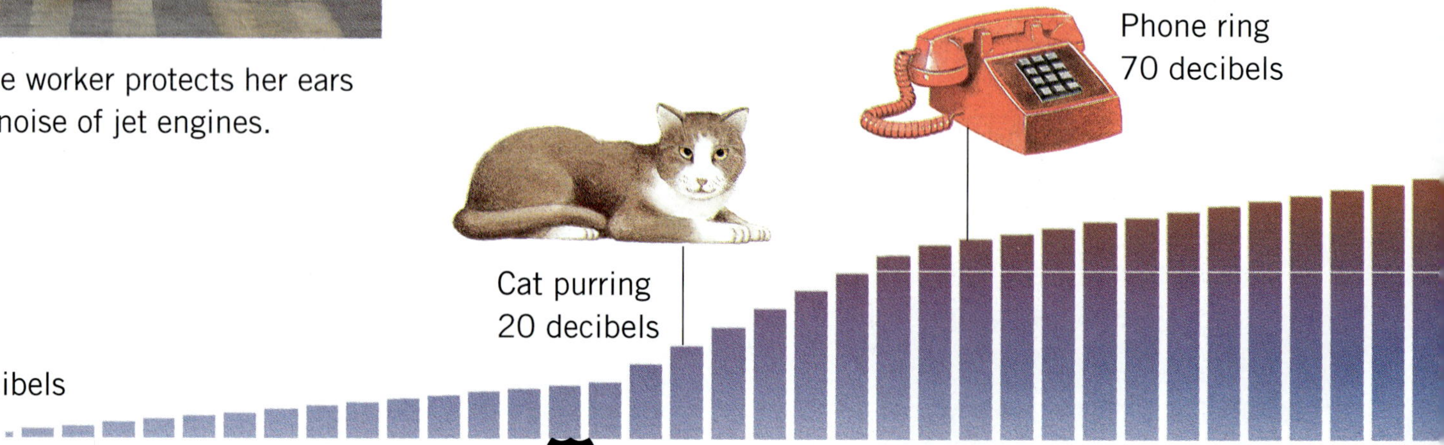

trains are a few sources of noise pollution. Some noises are within our control. It is important to remember that when you listen to music that is loud, the sound vibrations can damage your hearing.

SCIENCE JOURNAL In your Science Journal, make a personal decibel chart of the loudest and quietest sounds you have ever experienced and the loudest and softest sounds you have heard today.

DILEMMA

SCIENCE TECHNOLOGY & SOCIETY

Noise Pollution

The noise of airplanes taking off and landing bothers the people who live near airports. Airports aren't the only areas where people complain about noise pollution. Although the noise is unpleasant, many of the things that produce a lot of noise are necessary. We need road construction so we can drive, sirens are necessary so emergencies can get a response, and we use airplanes to get from place to place.

Think About It Choose an example of noise pollution in your area. Describe how you would handle complaints about the noise in a fair way.

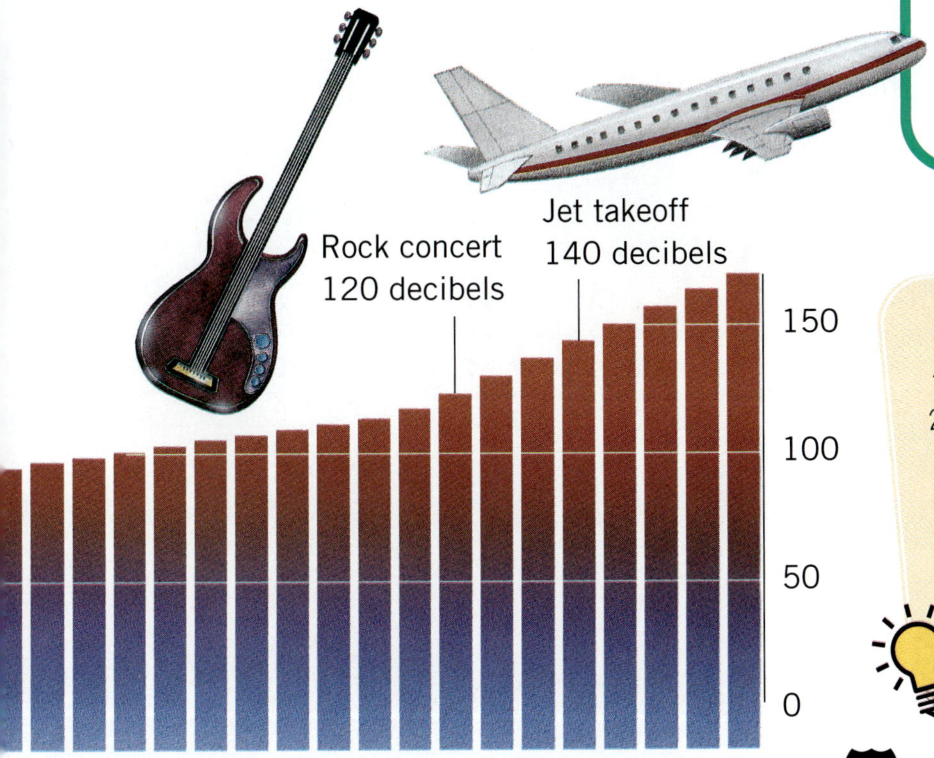

How are you doing?

1. Describe how sound waves are formed.
2. How does increasing the frequency of a sound wave affect the sound?
3. **Think** Compare the amplitude of a sound wave produced by a siren with the amplitude of a sound wave produced by a whisper.

What affects sound waves?

As you and the other passengers walk from the plane to the terminal, you stop to rest against the wall of the walkway, or jetway. As your ear rests against the wall, the sounds of the airport suddenly become louder.

Sound vibrations make waves by pushing the particles in the air. Sound vibrations can also make waves in solids and in liquids. Since the particles in solids and liquids are closer together than are the particles of air, sound travels better through many solids and liquids than it does through the air. The runway noise becomes louder when you put your ear next to the wall because sound waves travel better through the wall, which is a solid, than they do through air, which is a gas.

Tap your pencil on your desk. Put your ear against the desktop and tap it again. How did the material through which the sound wave passed affect the sound?

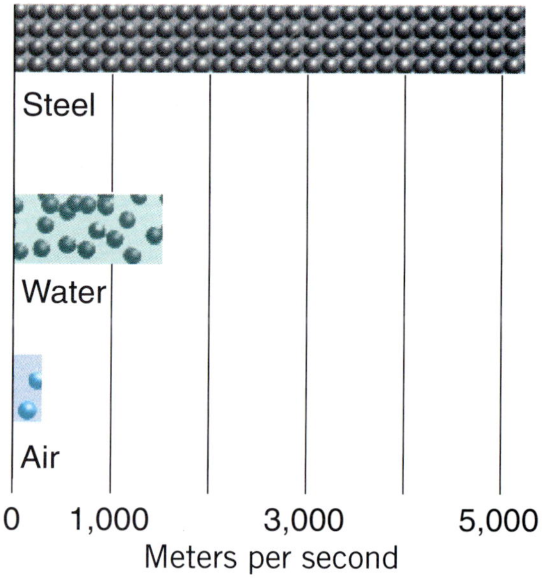

This chart shows the speed of sound as it passes through a solid, a liquid, and a gas.

SCIENCE JOURNAL

Listen to noises with your ear near a wall, then a window, and then a door at home. Now put your ear against these objects. How are the sounds different? Make a chart in your Science Journal to record how well different materials transmit sound.

BACK HOME

As you continue toward the terminal, you hear someone call you. It's a flight attendant. You've forgotten your backpack. To hear her call above the sounds of the airport, you cup your hand behind your ear.

The outside part of your ear collects sound waves. You cup your hand to increase the number of sound waves your ear can collect. Like humans, other animals have hearing membranes. Some animals, such as frogs and grasshoppers, have hearing membranes on the outside of their bodies. Look at the different animals pictured here. How do their ears compare? What does the shape of their ears tell you about how well they hear? What other adaptations do their ears have?

Be a Scientist

HANDS-ON ACTIVITY

How can you focus sound?

1. Make a device that will collect sound waves and aim them at your ear.
2. Test your device on different sounds at different distances.
3. ACTIVITY JOURNAL Draw your device and record your results in your Activity Journal.

How can you control sound?

You walk through the carpeted terminal to the main lobby. The lobby is louder than the terminal. The furnishings in the two areas contribute to this difference.

When a sound wave encounters an object, it either passes through that object, is absorbed by the object, or bounces back from the object. When a wave bounces back, it is called reflection. **Reflection** (ri flek′shən) is the change in direction of waves after they bounce off of a surface.

When a sound wave is reflected, you often hear an echo. If you stand in a large, empty room and shout, you may hear an echo. This is because the sound waves your shout produces reflect off the walls, ceiling, and floor. In the airport lobby, sound waves bounce many times from surface to surface before fading away. That is why the lobby seems louder than the terminal.

The terminal does not seem as loud because more sound waves are absorbed there. Things that are soft or filled with small air holes absorb sound waves. The carpeting and furniture in the terminal are all sound absorbers. If the terminal had bare floors and no furniture, how would you expect the noise level to be different?

Which of these areas inside the airport do you think is more likely to absorb sound?

SIDE TRIP

The Music Store

Musical instrument makers are experts in controlling sound. The music store has a variety of instruments. Drums occupy one section of the music store. Huge Japanese *taiko,* bongo drums, American Indian drums, and orchestral timpani are for sale.

The body shapes of these drums affect the sounds that they make. The drumheads on many drums can also be tightened or loosened to vary the pitch of sounds the drums produce.

How are you doing?

1. Compare and contrast the speed of sound through solids, liquids, and gases.
2. Why do you think people often hear echoes in a gymnasium?
3. **Think** Would the sound of a motor boat reach your ear faster if you were above water or under water?

Using Your Senses

There are many lights and sounds in an airport. How do you suppose a person who is visually impaired or hearing impaired would experience a visit to an airport? Think about times you have sensed sound in some way besides hearing it. What other senses would you have to use to get around without sight?

SCIENCE JOURNAL In your Science Journal, describe an airport visit from the perspective of a person your age who is visually or hearing impaired. Before writing, ask yourself: Might visually impaired people use their sense of hearing differently from sighted people? Can a person perceive a sound without hearing it?

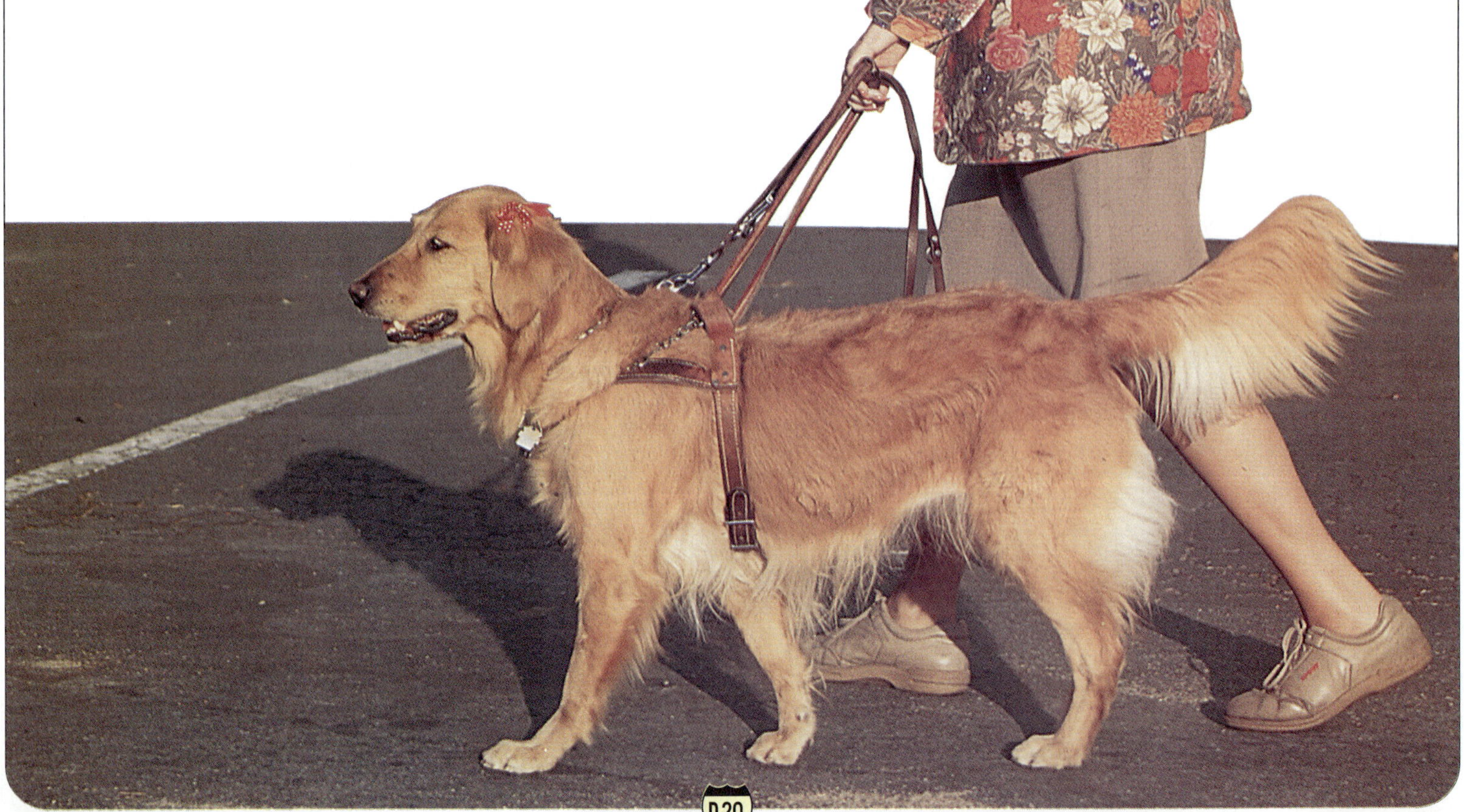

MATH CONNECTION

Where is the storm?

Lightning and thunder occur at the same time during a storm, but you see lightning before you hear thunder. This happens because light travels faster than sound travels. You can figure out how far away a storm is by counting the seconds between seeing lightning and hearing thunder. You can then multiply the number of seconds by the speed of sound.

Observe and Collect Data

1. ACTIVITY JOURNAL Calculate the distance of the storm by multiplying the time lapse by the speed of sound (330m/sec). Record the data in your Activity Journal.
2. The storm moves from west to east. Make a map that shows the storm's progress.

Lightning Flash	Time Lapse	Distance
first	10 seconds	3,300 meters
second	7 seconds	
third	5 seconds	
fourth	2 seconds	
fifth	1 second	
sixth	3 seconds	
seventh	4 seconds	
eighth	8 seconds	
ninth	9 seconds	
tenth	11 seconds	

Draw Conclusions

1. What can you learn about a storm by timing the lightning and thunder?
2. What information cannot be determined from lightning and thunder data? Why?

Looking Back

Words and Concepts

Match the description in Column A with the word or words in Column B.

Column A

1. Height of a wave
2. Surges of sound energy that travel through matter
3. Rapid back and forth motions
4. Number of times a wave vibrates in one second
5. How high or low a sound is
6. Unit for measuring the loudness of sound

Column B

a. Vibrations
b. Frequency
c. Decibel
d. Pitch
e. Sound waves
f. Amplitude

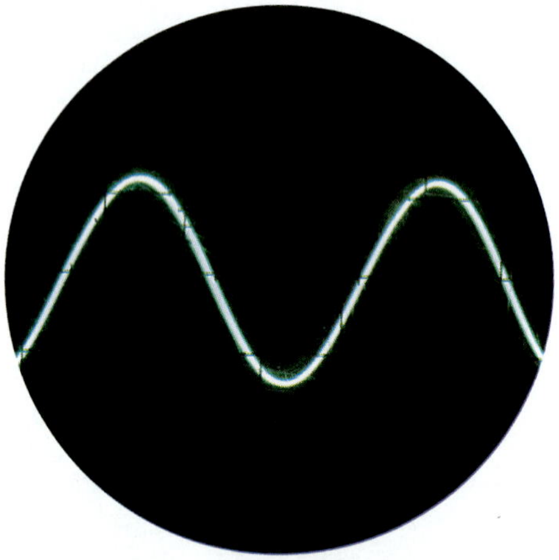

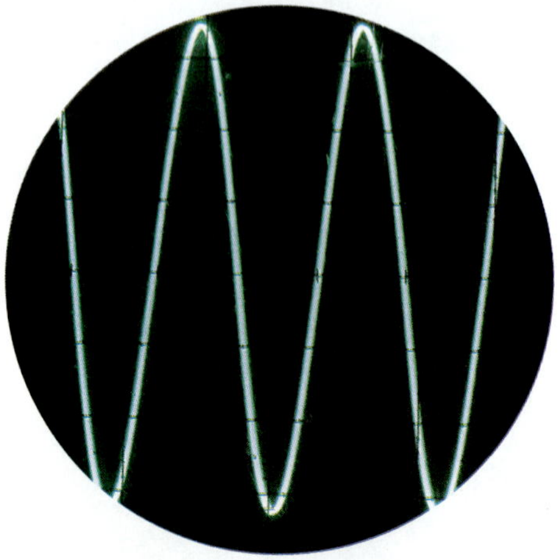

Applied Thinking Skills

Answer the following questions. You can use words, drawings, and diagrams in your answers.

7. Give evidence to support the statement, "Sound is a form of energy."
8. Describe what must happen to make a sound.
9. Look at the sound waves pictured on the page. Which sound has a lower pitch? Which sound is louder? Compare and contrast the frequencies and amplitudes of the waves.
10. **Your World** Describe two different sounds you have experienced recently. Compare and contrast the decibels, frequencies, and amplitudes of the sounds.

Show What You Know

How can you absorb sound?

Observe and Collect Data

1. In your Activity Journal, draw a design for a soundproofing device that can reduce the sound of beans shaking in a container. The device should fit inside a shoe box.
2. Construct your device. Test the device with your partner. Measure the distance at which the beans can no longer be heard shaking.
3. Compare your results with those of your classmates.

Draw Conclusions

What qualities made some materials muffle sound better than others?

Process Skills
Predicting, Measuring

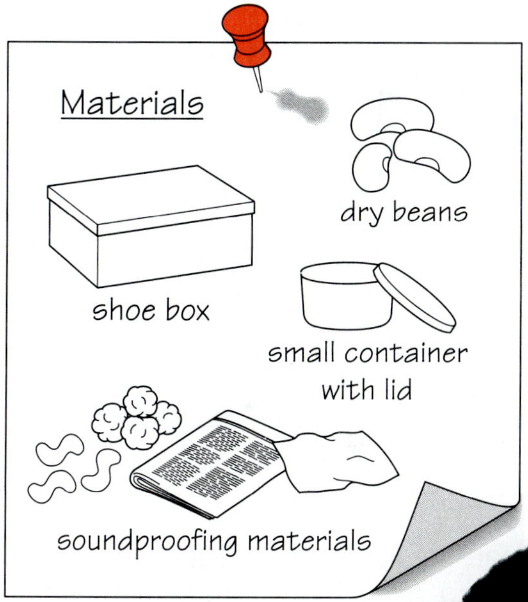

Chapter 2

Light Energy

Have you ever been to an airport at night? If you have, you probably saw many different lights. Inside the terminal, baggage claim areas, gates, ticket counters, shops, and restaurants are all brightly lit. Television screens show the gates and times of flight departures and arrivals.

Outside the terminal, white and red approach lights on the runway show pilots where to touch down. Blue lights on the taxiways guide aircraft to and from the runways. Red lights point out obstacles or dangers. There are also lights on both the insides and the outsides of the planes themselves.

SCIENCE JOURNAL

Some objects, such as light bulbs, produce light. Most objects, such as the plane, the buildings, and the people, do not produce light. You see these things because light reflects off, or bounces off, these objects. In your Science Journal, write about the sources of light in your home.

Explore Activity

How can you predict the path of light?

Process Skills
Observing, Predicting

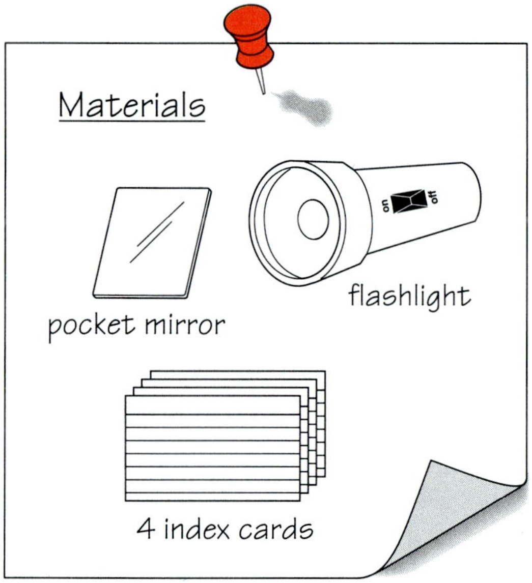

Observe and Collect Data

1. Punch a hole with your pencil in each of the four index cards. Bend about 2 cm of one end of each card so that the card will stand on its edge.
2. Have your partner shine the light through the hole in one of the cards.
3. ACTIVITY JOURNAL Move two other index cards so you can still see the light through all three holes. Draw or describe in your Activity Journal the arrangement of the cards and the path of light.
4. Place the fourth card on the desk, to one side of the others. **Predict** where you would have to place a mirror to make the light shine through the first three cards and then through the fourth card. In your Activity Journal, make a drawing of your plan.
5. Use a mirror to test your plan. If it did not work, move the mirror around until light shines through the fourth card. If you had to move the mirror, make a drawing of the arrangement that worked.

Share Your Results

1. Trade drawings with another group. Test the other group's plan. Did it work?
2. How are other plans different from yours?

Draw Conclusions

1. Describe the path of light from the flashlight through the holes in the index cards.
2. Draw or describe what happened when the light hit the mirror.

Apply What You Know

Suppose you look into a pond or swimming pool and you see yourself reflected in the water. Using what you learned in this activity, explain what is happening.

Where does light come from?

As you learned, energy is the ability to cause change in matter. **Light energy** is the ability of light to cause changes, such as heating matter. You can feel light energy change to heat energy when the sun warms you up.

There are many sources of light. Light comes from two kinds of sources—natural and artificial.

Some animals, such as this fish, have chemicals in their bodies that produce light.

YOU CAN HELP

You can save energy by turning off lights when you don't need them.

The most important source of natural light is the sun.

Firelight or candlelight is produced by a chemical reaction.

In a typical electric light bulb, electricity heats a wire until it gets hot enough to glow. In a neon light, electricity passes through neon gas, making the gas glow.

What happens when light hits an object?

Light energy travels in waves. Light waves travel at a speed of about 300,000 kilometers per second. If an airplane went this fast, it could fly around the world more than seven times in one second. Light usually travels in a straight line until it hits an object. What happens then depends on the kind of object the light hits.

Light passes through some objects. You can see through the windows of the terminal because light passes through them. Materials that let the most light pass through are described as **transparent** (trans per′ənt).

There are other materials, such as window shades or some plastics, that let only some of the light that strikes them pass through them. You can't see clearly through these materials. These materials are described as **translucent** (trans lo͞o′sənt).

You can't see through the metal beams in the terminal because they do not let any light pass through them. Materials that don't let any light through are described as **opaque** (ō pāk′). When light hits an opaque object, it is either reflected by the object or absorbed by the object.

TECHNOLOGY

SCIENCE TECHNOLOGY & SOCIETY

Lasers

Lasers produce light energy that is used to do many kinds of work. High-powered lasers produce so much heat that they can cut materials as strong as steel. Factory workers use lasers to cut steel plates used in building automobiles. Surgeons use a concentrated beam of laser light in delicate operations.

The clear glass in this picture is transparent, the frosted glass is translucent, and the metal beams are opaque.

How are you doing?

1. Give examples of two natural and two artificial light sources.
2. What happens when light strikes matter?
3. **Think** Explain the difference between light hitting solid margarine and light hitting melted margarine. Is margarine transparent, translucent, or opaque?

What happens when light bounces back?

Light rays reflecting off a mirror

Light rays reflecting off an uneven surface

Many objects in the airport reflect light. As you walk through the terminal, you see your reflection in the windows, the floor, and other shiny surfaces. Surfaces that are not shiny, such as the carpets, the people, and the luggage, also reflect light.

Reflected light acts like a bouncing ball. If you throw a ball at a smooth wall, it bounces off at the same angle you threw it. If the wall is uneven, the ball can bounce off in any direction.

When light waves hit a smooth surface, such as a mirror, they are reflected at a predictable angle. When light strikes an uneven surface, it scatters. This is why images do not reflect well from uneven surfaces such as the floor of the airport terminal.

When you stand directly in front of a mirror, you see your reflection because the light bounces directly back to you. When you look at a mirror from the side, you do not always see yourself reflected because the light bounces away from you. Look at the way light from the flashlight reflects off the mirror shown on this page. This shows that the angle of the light and the angle of reflection are the same. What you see in a mirror, or any reflective surface, depends on where you are when you look at the mirror.

Be a Scientist

How does a mirror reflect light?

1. Shine a flashlight at a mirror. Notice the angle at which the light bounces off the mirror.
2. Change the angle at which you hold the flashlight. How does the angle of reflected light change?
3. ACTIVITY JOURNAL Experiment by holding the flashlight at different angles. In your Activity Journal, draw your observations of how a mirror reflects light.

Compare the reflections from the floor pictured here to the reflection you see in a mirror.

How do curves in a mirror affect the reflections you see?

When you look into a flat mirror, you see an image of yourself. But when you look at yourself in a silver balloon in the airport gift shop, you look strange!

Unlike flat mirrors, which give an accurate image in reverse, curved mirrors change or distort the images we see. When you look at your reflection in a spoon, the reflection looks different on each side. A mirror that curves inward, such as the inside of a spoon, is a **concave** (kän kāv′) mirror. A mirror that bulges outward, like the underside of a spoon, is a **convex** (kän veks′) mirror.

Objects that are reflected in convex mirrors appear smaller than they really are. A convex mirror can show a larger area than a flat mirror. Stores, such as the airport gift shop, use convex mirrors so workers can see a large part of the store. The silver balloon in the airport gift shop is also a convex mirror.

An object that is placed near a concave mirror will appear larger than it really is. Makeup mirrors are often concave. Look at mirrors on cars and buses in your area. Are they flat, concave, or convex? Why?

Be a Scientist

HANDS-ON ACTIVITY

How do spoons reflect light?

1. Look at both sides of the bowl of a shiny metal spoon. Hold the spoon at various distances from your face.
2. ACTIVITY JOURNAL In your Activity Journal, draw or describe the reflections in the spoon. Which side is concave? Which side is convex?

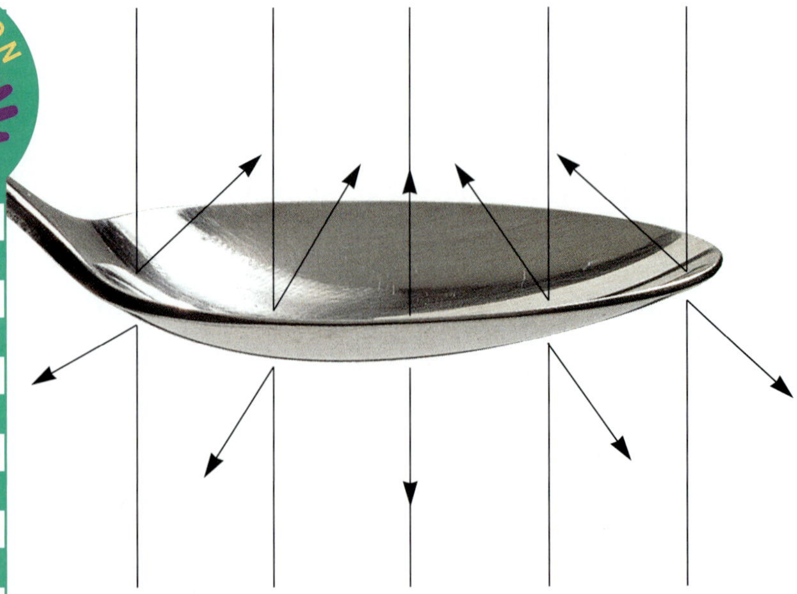

These arrows show how light reflects off a spoon.

The Mylar balloon acts as a convex mirror, distorting the girl's reflection.

How are you doing?

1. Draw what happens when light strikes a smooth, flat reflective surface.
2. Draw a bowl and label which side is convex and which side is concave.
3. **Think** How are the reflections you see in a flat mirror different from those you see in a curved mirror?

What causes light to bend?

The stem seems to bend at the water line. In fact, it is the light that bends as it travels from water to air.

In the airport gift shop you see a flower in a vase. When you look at the flower, it looks like the stem is broken. But when you take the flower out of the vase, the stem is whole. What makes it look broken?

As you've learned, light travels in straight lines. This general rule, however, has an exception. When light passes from one kind of material, such as water, to another kind of material, such as air, it bends.

The bending of light is called **refraction** (ri frak′shən). Refraction is caused by a change in the speed of light as it passes through different transparent materials. Since water is more dense than air, light travels more slowly in water than it does in air. Glass is also more dense than air. Like water, glass causes refraction.

Refraction explains why the flower stem you see in the gift shop looks broken. The light that is reflected from the part of the stem that is above the water travels through glass and air. The light that is reflected from the part of the stem under water travels through water, glass, and air. As it passes from one material to the next, the light is bent.

Refraction creates an optical illusion. It makes an object appear to be somewhere it's not. The bending of light makes the flower stem look as though it is broken. If you look at a fish in a fish tank, refraction will make the fish appear to be higher in the water than it really is.

Be a Scientist

How can you show refraction?

1. Place a coin in the bottom of a bowl. Bend down until you can no longer see the coin. Keep your head in that position.

2. ACTIVITY JOURNAL Have your partner slowly add water to the dish. Record your observations in your Activity Journal.

This picture shows how the bending of light can fool you. Here, refraction makes the goldfish appear to be where it isn't.

How does bending light help us see?

A magnifying glass makes objects look bigger than they really are.

Lenses are curved pieces of glass or transparent material that refract or bend light in a particular way. Lenses are used in cameras, telescopes, eyeglasses, and many other objects. There are also lenses in your eyes. The shape of a lens determines how it refracts light. Light always bends toward the thickest part of the lens.

A lens that is thinnest at the center is called a concave lens. A concave lens bends light away from the center. Concave lenses make objects appear to be smaller than they actually are.

A lens that is thickest at the center is a convex lens. A convex lens bends light rays together. After the light that passes through a convex lens is bent together, it crosses and spreads apart.

SCIENCE JOURNAL

In your Science Journal, make a list of people you know who wear eyeglasses. Interview three people on the list. Ask them how things look with and without their glasses. Record their answers in your Science Journal.

BACK HOME

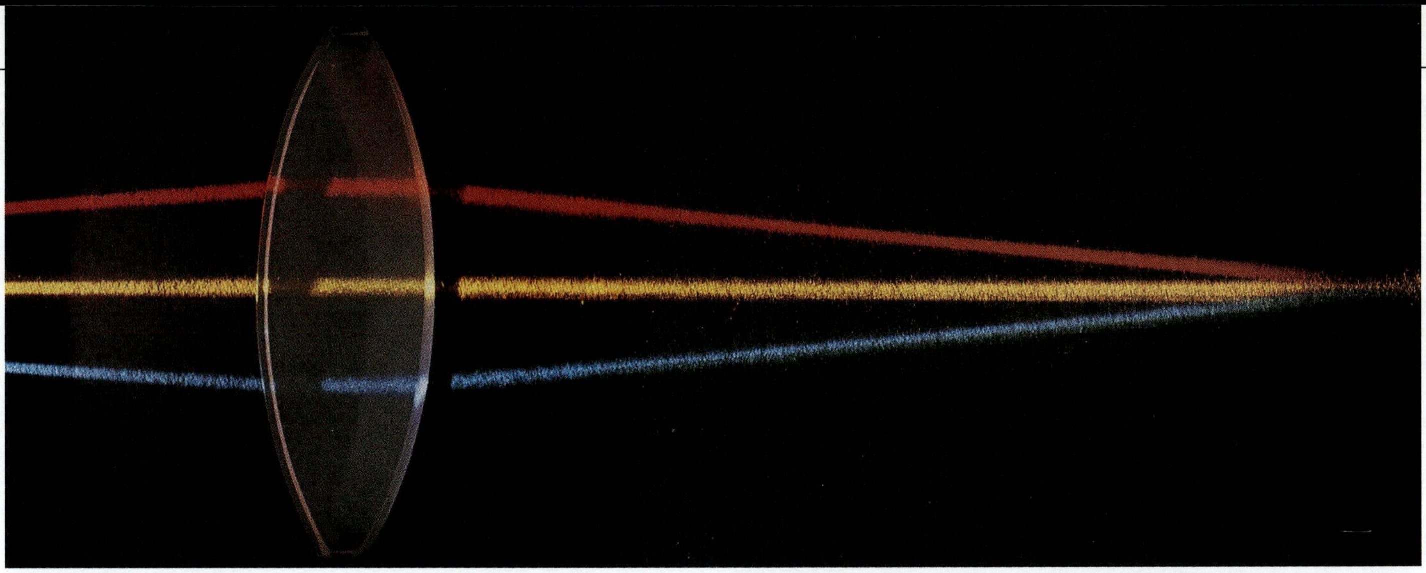

A convex lens brings light rays together.

A concave lens spreads light rays apart.

Each of your eyes contains a convex lens. Muscles in your eyes adjust the shape of the lens so you can focus on objects. Your eye muscles contract, making the lens thicker, when you look at an object up close. When you look at a distant object, the muscles relax, which makes the lens thinner.

Sometimes the lenses in people's eyes do not bend light enough or bend it too much. When that happens, people wear additional lenses to help them see. The kind of lens used in eyeglasses or contact lenses depends on the condition the lens helps correct. A nearsighted person has a hard time seeing objects that are far away. Concave lenses can help nearsighted people see clearly. A farsighted person has a hard time seeing objects that are very close. Farsighted people usually wear convex lenses.

Think about what it was like for people who had poor eyesight before eyeglasses were invented. It must have been very difficult for them to see.

How are you doing?

1. Under what conditions does light refract? What happens to the speed of light when refraction occurs?
2. How are convex and concave lenses different? How do they bend light?
3. **Think** Make a drawing that shows how light refracts when it passes from air into a pond.

Science &
Literature
Connection

a wrinkle in time

by Madeleine L'Engle

In this excerpt from a science fiction book, Meg has landed on a strange, dark planet.

"Why is it so dark in here?" Meg asked. She tried to look around, but all she could see was shadows. Nevertheless there was a sense of openness, a feel of a gentle breeze moving lightly about, that kept the darkness from being oppressive.

Perplexity came to her from the beast. "What is this dark? What is this light? We do not understand. Your father and the boy, Calvin, have asked this, too. They say that it is night now on our planet, and that they cannot see. They have told us that our atmosphere is what they call opaque, so that the stars are not visible, and then they were surprised that we know stars, that we know their music and the movements of their dance far better than beings like you who spend hours studying them through what you call telescopes. We do not understand what this means, *to see.*"

"Well, it's what things look like," Meg said helplessly.

"We do not know what things *look* like, as you say," the beast said. "We know what things *are* like. It must be a very limited thing, this seeing."

"Oh no!" Meg cried. "It's—it's the most wonderful thing in the world!"

"What a very strange world yours must be!" the beast said, "that such a peculiar-sounding thing should be of such importance. Try to tell me, what is this thing called light that you are able to do so little without?"

"Well, we can't see without it," Meg said, realizing that she was completely unable to explain vision and light and dark. How can you explain sight on a world where no one had ever seen and there is no need of eyes?

Think About Your Reading

1. Compare and contrast life on Earth and what life might be like on a dark planet like the one in the excerpt.
2. Try to help Meg out. Use what you already know about light. Try to write a description to help the beast understand it.

Inferring The beast seems to have a sense other than sight that helps it understand the world around it. Talk with a classmate about what this imaginary sense might be like. Name it and write a paragraph about it.

Where to Read More

Roy A. Gallant, *Rainbows, Mirages and Sundogs: The Sky as a Source of Wonder* (Macmillan Publishing Company, 1987) Learn about why stars twinkle, how the Northern lights dance, and what makes a sun halo.

Looking Back

MINDS-ON ASSESSMENT

Words and Concepts

Match each question in Column A with a word or phrase in Column B.

Column A

1. Which is a natural source of light?
2. How does light usually travel?
3. Which material is transparent?
4. Which material is translucent?
5. Which mirror curves inward?
6. What makes a straw in a glass of water seem to bend at the water's surface?

Column B

a. Convex lens
b. Refraction
c. In a straight line
d. Concave mirror
e. Wax paper
f. The sun

Applied Thinking Skills

Answer the following questions. You can use words, drawings, and diagrams in your answers.

7. Compare and contrast concave and convex lenses. How do they bend light?
8. Which mirror in the picture is convex? Which is concave? How can you tell?
9. A driver positions her rear view mirror so that she can see the light of the headlights of the car behind her. Draw a diagram showing the path of light from the headlights to the driver's eyes.
10. **Your World** What kind of materials would be best to use for building a clubhouse if you did not want people to see inside it?

Show What You Know

How can you make a periscope?

A periscope is a device that lets you see around corners or over people or objects that are taller than you.

Process Skills
Making models

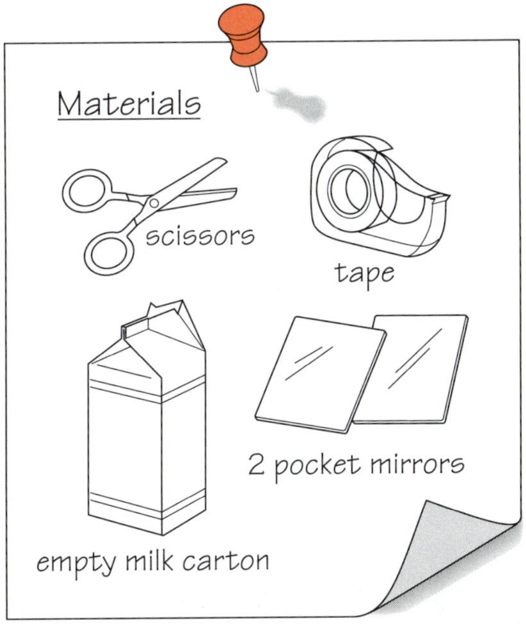

Observe and Collect Data

1. Cut a hole in one side of the carton near the top. Cut a similar hole on the opposite side of the carton near the bottom.
2. Cut slots on opposite sides of each end of the carton.
3. Slide the mirrors into the slots. The shiny side of the mirror in the top slot should face down. The bottom mirror should be inserted with the shiny side up. Tape them onto the outside of the carton.

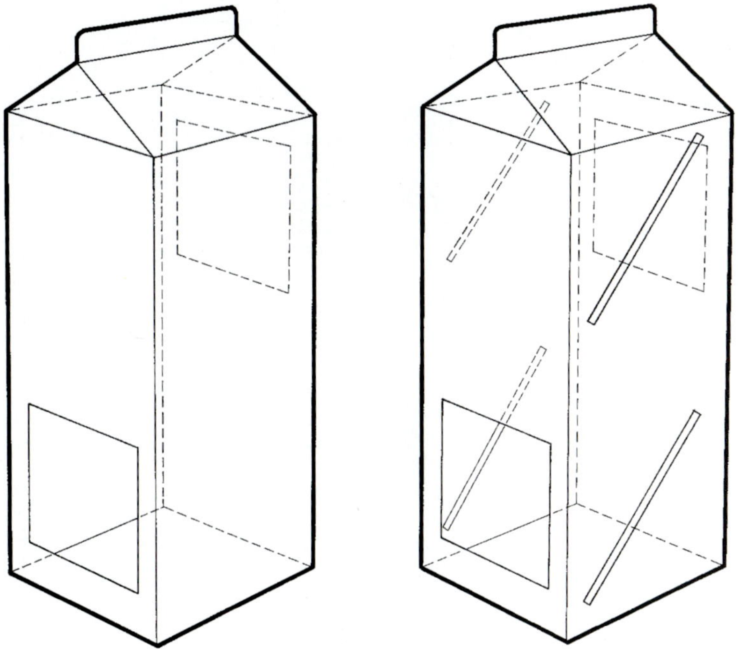

Draw Conclusions

ACTIVITY JOURNAL

In your Activity Journal, make a drawing that shows the path of light through your periscope.

2. Design a device that you can use to look behind you.

Electromagnetic Waves

You head back toward the departure gate. It's almost time to board your plane. Before entering the passenger terminal, your backpack is passed through an X-ray machine. This machine shows the airport employees what is inside your backpack without opening it. X-rays are a form of energy that you cannot see, although you can see the pictures that they make.

The pilot is in communication with the control tower. This communication occurs through another form of energy that you cannot see—radio waves. Radio waves, X-rays, and some other invisible forms of wave energy that you will study in this chapter are part of the electromagnetic spectrum (ē lek′trō mag net′ik spek′trəm). The **electromagnetic spectrum** is a band of energy waves, including visible light waves, that vibrate at different frequencies.

SCIENCE JOURNAL

Compare radio waves and X-rays. Describe in your Science Journal other places where radio waves or X-rays are helpful.

How does a prism affect light?

HANDS-ON ACTIVITY

Process Skills
Observing, Inferring

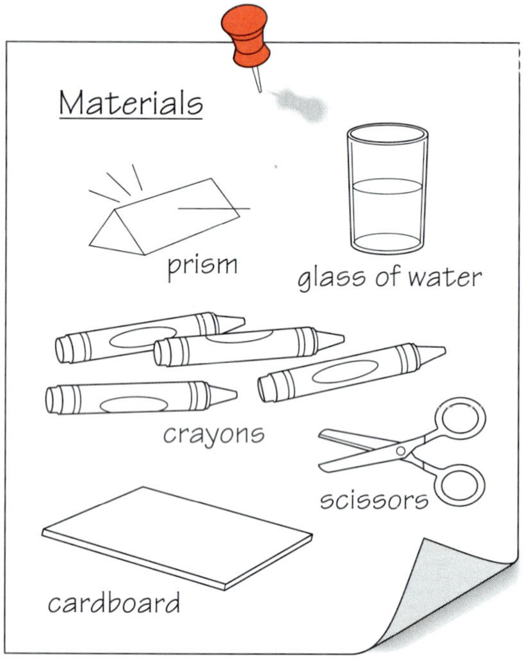

Observe and Collect Data

1. Place a piece of white paper in front of a sunny window. Position the prism between the window and paper.
2. ACTIVITY JOURNAL Observe what happens on the white paper when sunlight passes through the prism. In your Activity Journal, use the crayons to draw what you see.
3. Cut a slit about 1 cm wide in the cardboard. Place the glass of water on the white paper. Hold the cardboard between the window and the glass.
4. Observe what happens on the white paper when sunlight passes through the slit and then the water. Draw what you observe.

Share Your Results

Compare your observations with those of other groups. How were your observations alike? How did they differ?

Draw Conclusions

1. What happened when light passed through the prism?
2. What happened when light passed through the glass of water?
3. What colors make up white light?

Apply What You Know

What happens when sunlight shines while it is raining? Write a hypothesis explaining why this occurs.

What makes up the light you see?

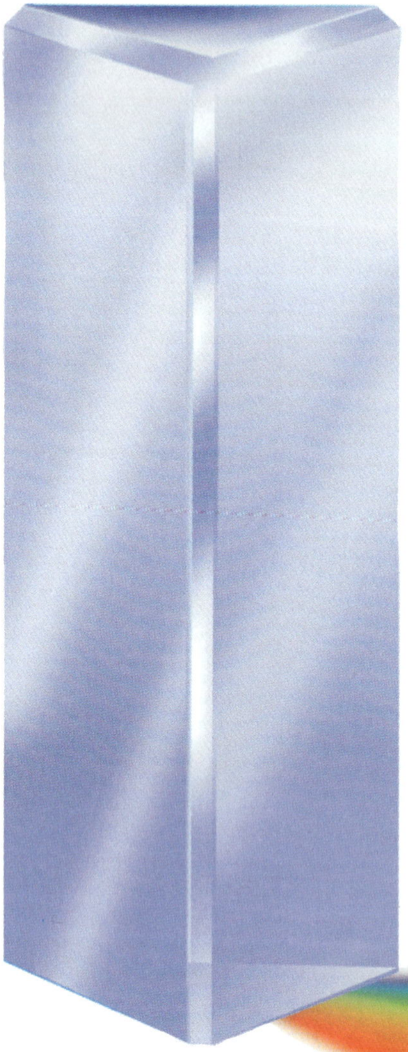

As you wait to board your plane, you notice a rainbow on the floor. A woman has bought a prism from the gift shop and is holding it to the window. Sunlight passing through the prism is split into a band, or spectrum, of colors. This spectrum includes the colors of the **visible** (viz′ə bəl) **spectrum,** light that you can see.

Light waves do not need a material through which to travel. Light waves can travel through empty space. All light waves travel through space at the same speed—300,000 kilometers per second.

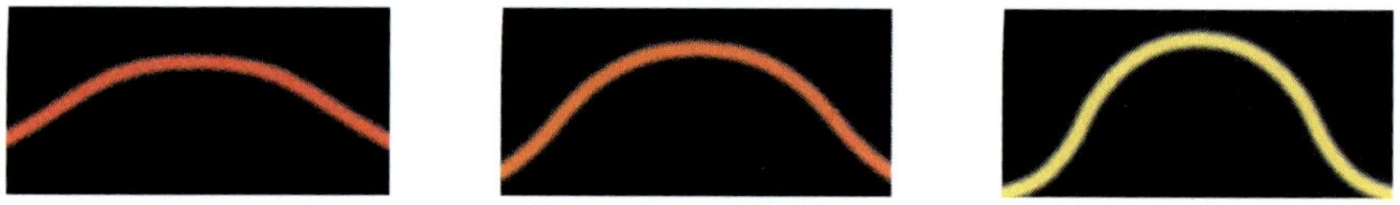

Red Orange Yellow

As you have learned, scientists call the distance between a point on one wave and the same point on the next wave a wavelength. The wavelength of a light wave determines the color of the light. Wavelength is also related to the amount of energy the light has. Longer light waves are less energetic. Red light has the longest wavelength in the visible spectrum. Red light has less energy than orange, yellow, green, blue, or violet waves. Which color has the shortest wavelength? Which color has the most energy?

Amazing!

The sky looks blue because small particles of air scatter, or reflect, violet and blue light more than the other wavelengths of light.

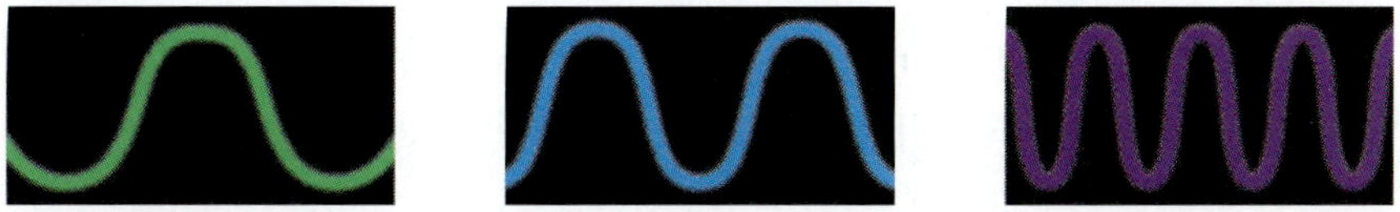

Green Blue Violet

Why do you see different colors?

The stripes on the plane reflect some wavelengths of light and absorb some wavelengths of light.

From the terminal window you watch your airplane pull up to the gate. When you look outside at your plane, you notice different colored stripes on the plane's nose.

When light strikes an object, the light passes through, is reflected by, or is absorbed by the object. Different colors of light have different wavelengths. Color vision is the ability to distinguish between the different wavelengths of light.

Color is associated with objects you see, but the objects themselves are not what you see. You see the light that is reflected off the object. You see a color when one or more wavelengths of light is reflected.

When white light strikes colored objects, some wavelengths are absorbed and some are reflected. The color that you see is the wavelength of light that is reflected.

When you look at the plane, you see a red stripe. When white light hits red paint on the plane, most wavelengths are absorbed except red. The red wavelength of light is reflected from the plane to your eye. That is how you see the color red.

There are three primary colors of light—red, blue, and green. Other colors, such as yellow and magenta, are produced when a combination of primary colors is reflected. For example, mixing green light with red light makes yellow light. A lemon actually reflects a combination of green and red light.

Mixing all three primary colors of light makes white light. The white part of the plane reflects all colors. If all the colors of light are absorbed, an object appears black. When you read this page, you are really seeing the white light that surrounds the black letters. The black letters reflect no light to your eyes.

Since color determines how many wavelengths of light are absorbed and reflected, the color of your clothes can affect how hot you get. Black absorbs more wavelengths of light. Absorbing more light energy means black objects absorb more heat. Things that look white, on the other hand, don't get as hot because they reflect more light energy. What color would you wear if you were flying to somewhere hot?

Be a Scientist

MINDS-ON ACTIVITY

What colors of light do plants use?

1. To determine what colors of light plants use, think about the pigments in plants. Plant pigments are mainly green, though they can include yellow and red.
2. The colors of light that a plant reflects are the colors that it doesn't use. The colors of light that a plant absorbs are the colors it does use.
3. ACTIVITY JOURNAL Look for plants inside and outside your school. In your Activity Journal, tell which colors are used by the plants you find.

How are you doing?

1. Which light has more energy, green light or violet light? Explain your answer.
2. Which wavelengths do a red apple, green grass, and a blue shirt reflect?
3. **Think** Which color would you wear to keep warm on a sunny winter day? Explain your answer.

What is the electromagnetic spectrum?

As you walk through the airport and the plane, you are walking through a sea of waves. Some of these waves are sound waves and light waves. There are other kinds of waves, too. Waves of energy make the radios, televisions, microwave ovens, and other machines in the airport work. These waves are part of the electromagnetic spectrum.

Light waves are only one small part of a large band of energy called the electromagnetic spectrum. All electromagnetic waves travel at the same speed, but you cannot see most of the electromagnetic spectrum because the waves are too small or too large for your senses to register.

All kinds of waves behave the same way. They can all be reflected, absorbed, or refracted. All waves have a frequency, amplitude, and wavelength. The measurement of a wave tells you how much energy the wave has.

Radio waves have the least energy of all waves in the electromagnetic spectrum. They

TV

Microwave

Radio

Radar

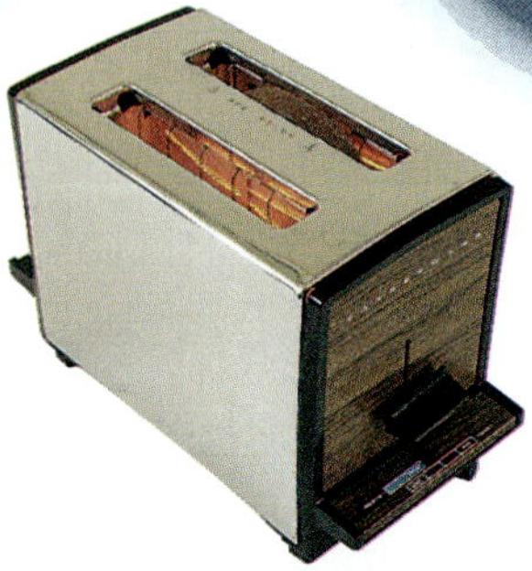

Infrared

also have the longest wavelength. The wavelength of radio waves can be longer than a football field. Gamma rays have the most energy and the shortest wavelength. A gamma ray's wavelength is shorter than the width of an atom.

Visible light waves are longer than gamma rays and shorter than radio waves. How do you think the amount of energy light has compares with the amount of energy in radio waves and gamma rays?

Be a Scientist

HANDS-ON ACTIVITY

What do electromagnetic waves look like?

1. Hold one end of a rope while your partner holds the other. Take turns shaking the rope at one end. Make waves of different sizes and speeds.
2. ACTIVITY JOURNAL In your Activity Journal, compare the motion of the rope as waves traveled through it with the motion of the spring you experimented with in Chapter 1.

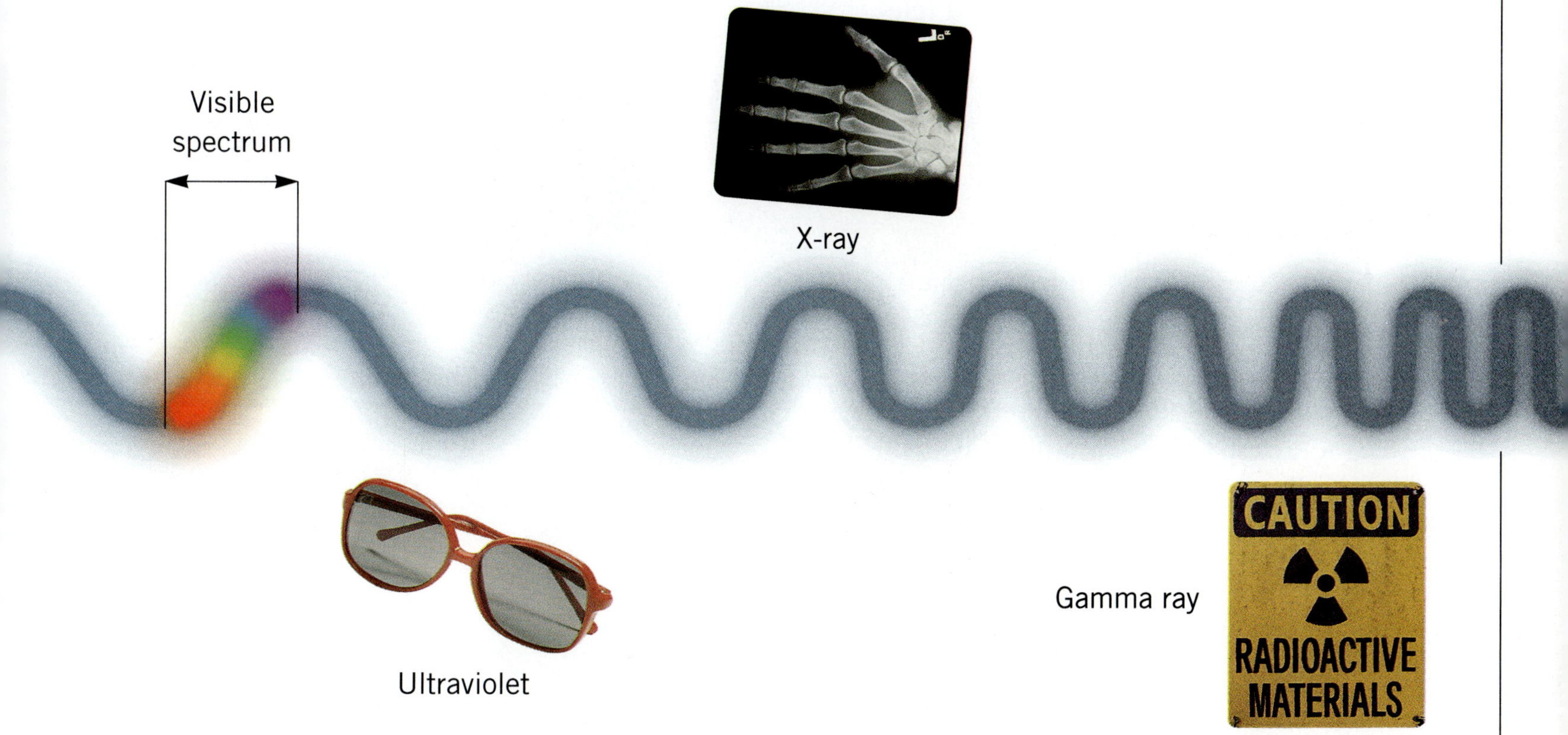

How are radio waves used?

After boarding the plane, you are invited to the cockpit. The cockpit is filled with screens, knobs, and dials. You can hear voices from the air traffic control tower on a radio. You can also see blips on a colorful computer screen. The pilot tells you that the screen is part of a radar system and the blips show where there are clouds.

Radar systems and radios both use electromagnetic waves. Radio waves are used to transmit sounds over long distances. In addition to radar and radios, electromagnetic waves are used to send television and telephone signals.

Radar uses radio waves to locate distant objects. Radar works like an echo. It sends out waves, and when the waves strike an object, they bounce back. The direction they bounce back and the time it takes for them to bounce back tell where the object is. While pilots use radar to monitor weather conditions, air traffic controllers use radar to locate planes.

Just as with other waves, radio waves can have different frequencies and amplitudes. FM radio stations send radio waves of different frequencies than AM radio stations.

Career Corner

Air Traffic Controller

My name is Zane Watts and I'm an air traffic controller. I rely heavily on radar to do my job. I decide on and tell pilots and ground workers the exact route that each aircraft will take through the airport. Some air traffic controllers, like me, work at the airports. Others work in central offices that keep track of every plane in the sky.

YOU CAN HELP

Reduce noise pollution by playing your radio at a low volume.

Flight instruments, which use radio and radar waves, allow pilots to fly and land planes safely, even when poor weather conditions prevent them from seeing the ground below.

What are other uses of electromagnetic waves?

As these pages show, electromagnetic waves are remarkably useful forms of energy. You rely on them every day.

Microwaves
are used in navigation and communication. They are also used for cooking. Microwave ovens heat and cook food quickly with electromagnetic waves.

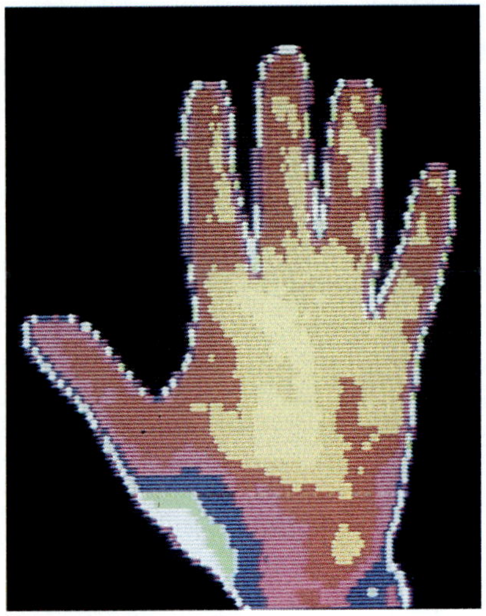

Infrared waves
create the warmth you feel when you sit in the sun. Airports use infrared energy to keep food warm. This photo shows infared waves. Warmer areas appear red.

SCIENCE JOURNAL Interview members of your household about their experiences with X-rays. Record their experiences in your Science Journal.

BACK HOME

X-rays

have enough energy to pass through some parts of your body, and they are used to look at your bones. Airports also use X-rays to check the contents of baggage.

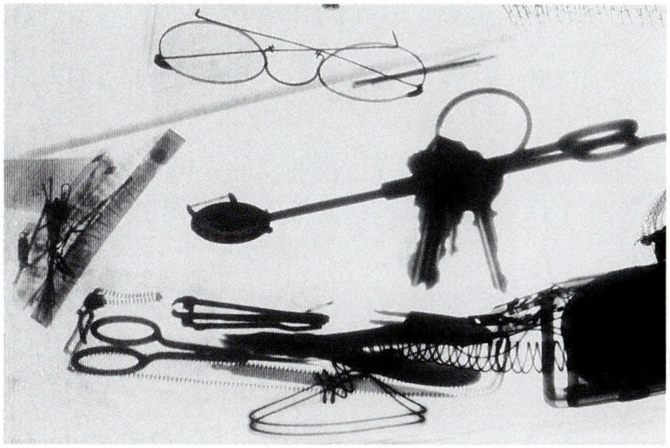

Gamma rays

are produced by radioactive elements. Gamma rays are very short and have a huge amount of energy. Gamma rays can destroy cells. Doctors use gamma rays to destroy harmful cells, such as cancer cells.

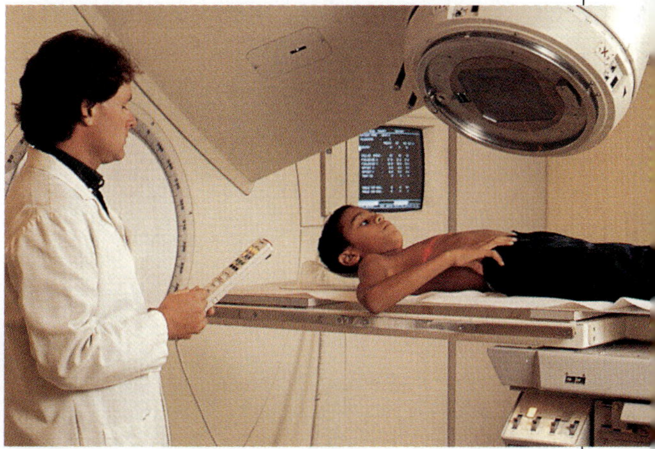

Ultraviolet waves

have shorter wavelengths and more energy than visible or infrared waves. The energy in ultraviolet light can damage your skin. Hats and sunscreen can help protect you from ultraviolet light.

How are you doing?

1. What is radar, and how does it work?
2. Compare the amount of energy and the wavelengths of radio waves, visible light waves, ultraviolet rays, and X-rays.
3. **Think** X-rays can take pictures of the bones inside your body, but visible rays cannot. Explain why.

Looking Back

Words and Concepts

Complete the following statements.

1. Visible light and other parts of the electromagnetic spectrum travel in ________.
2. ________ have the most energy in the electromagnetic spectrum.
3. White light can be separated into different colors using a ________.
4. ________ waves have the least energy in the electromagnetic spectrum.
5. The ________ that are reflected by an object are those that your eyes see.
6. Radio waves, microwaves, and gamma rays are all part of the ________.

Applied Thinking Skills

Answer the following questions. You can use words, drawings, and diagrams in your answers.

7. Which flame is hotter, a blue flame or a yellow flame? Explain your answer.
8. When you see a green leaf, which wavelengths of light are being reflected? Which are being absorbed?
9. Does the existence of a form of energy depend on our ability to see it? Explain your answer.
10. **Your World** Choose one part of the electromagnetic spectrum and explain how it affects your daily life.

Show What You Know

How can colors change?

Observe and Collect Data

1. Draw a circle 10 centimeters in diameter on a piece of white cardboard. Cut out the circle.
2. Measure and mark three equal sections of the circle on both sides of the cardboard. Color them red, green, and blue.
3. Make two small holes near the center of the circle and pass the string through them. Tie the ends of the string together.
4. Have a friend hold the string tightly as you wind the circle until the string is twisted many times. Let go. Observe the circle.

Process Skills
Observing, Inferring

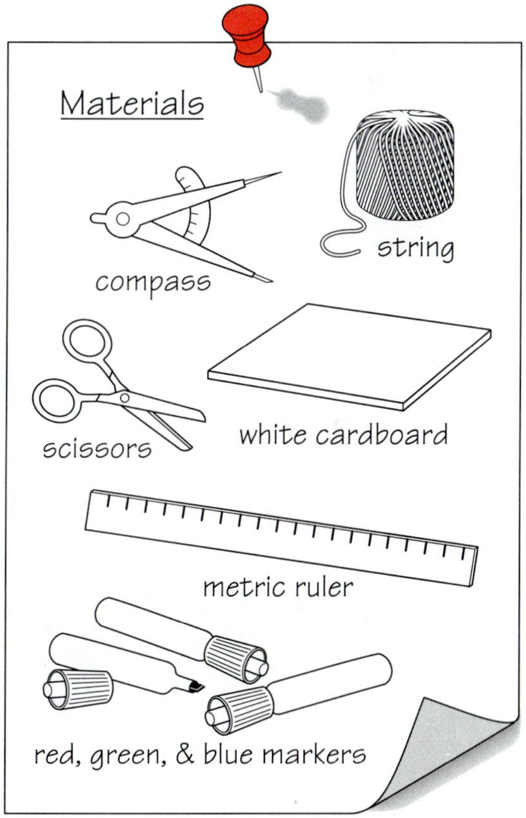

Draw Conclusions

1. What do you see when the wheel turns slowly?
2. Why does the wheel look almost white when it is turning fast?

Sound and Light

Show what you know about sound, light, and the electromagnetic spectrum. Work by yourself, with a partner, or in a group. Select one activity.

Choreographer Create a dance that shows how light or sound reacts to various materials or to other light or sound.

Cartoonist Create a comic strip that has sound, light, or another part of the electromagnetic spectrum.

Sculptor Create a piece of art that uses light or sound. Make your sculpture interactive, so that people have to do something with it to get its full effect.

Science-Fiction Writer Imagine that you can see part of the electromagnetic spectrum that other people can't see, or that you can hear sounds that others can't hear. Write a story describing your experiences with these additional senses.

Puzzle Maker Create a game or puzzle in which the pieces act as sound waves and/or electromagnetic waves.

Naturalist Find out about how other species hear and see things in the world. Write a report or story to share this information with the class.

Glossary

amplitude (am′plə to͞od′) The height of any kind of wave. (page D13)

concave (kän kāv′) A surface that curves inward, such as a mirror, or a lens that is thinnest at the center. (page D34)

convex (kän veks′) A surface that bulges outward, such as a mirror, or a lens that is thickest at the center. (page D34)

decibel (des′ə bəl′) A unit that is used to measure the loudness of a sound. (page D14)

electromagnetic spectrum (ē lek′trō-mag net′ik spek′trəm) Bands of energy waves that vibrate at different frequencies. It includes light waves and wave frequencies we cannot see. (page D44)

frequency (frē′kwən sē) The number of times a wave vibrates in one second. (page D12)

light energy (līt en′ər jē) The ability of light to cause change, such as heating an object. (page D28)

opaque (ō pāk′) A material that lets no light pass through it. (page D30)

reflection (ri flek′shən) The change in direction of waves after they bounce off of a surface. (page D18)

refraction (ri frak′shən) The bending of waves as they travel at an angle from one medium to another. (page D36)

sound energy (sound en′ər jē) The ability of sound to cause change in matter. (page D10)

translucent (trans lo͞o′sənt) A material that lets only some light waves pass through it. (page D30)

transparent (trans per′ənt) A material that lets most light waves pass through it. (page D30)

visible spectrum (viz′ə bəl spek′trəm) The band of light waves of different colors in the electromagnetic spectrum that vibrate at frequencies our eyes can detect. (page D48)

wavelength (wāv′leŋkth′) The distance between a point on one wave to the same point on the next wave. (page D11)

Unit D Index

Boldface numerals denote glossary terms. Italic numerals denote illustrations.

Credits

Photographs

1 Bill Ross/Westlight; 2–3 Lawrence Manning/Westlight; 2TL GHP Studio*; 3BR GHP Studio*; 4L C J Allen/Stock, Boston; 4R Mike Mazzaschi/Stock, Boston; 5 Ken Karp*; 6–7 Joe Towers/Check Six; 6L Tim Davis*; 9 Ken Karp*; 10 Tim Davis*; 11R Tim Davis*; 12B Ken Karp*; 12T Tim Davis*; 13B Ken Karp*; 13T Tim Davis*; 14 Ron Watts/Westlight; 16 Wolfgang Kaehler; 17BC Roger & Donna Aitkinhead/Animals, Animals; 17BL Kevin Schafer & Martha Hill/AllStock; 17BR Tim Davis*; 17T Tom McHugh/AllStock; 18–19 Jimmy Rudnick/The Stock Market; 19L Carl Purcell/Photo Researchers; 19R Ken Karp; 20B Tim Davis*; 20T Ken Karp*; 21 Harold Pfeiffer/AllStock; 22 Tim Davis*; 23 Nick Pavloff*; 24–25 Michael Ventura/Bruce Coleman Inc; 24L Lawrence Manning/Westlight; 27 Elliott Smith*; 28–29 Lindsay Hebberd/Woodfin Camp & Associates; 28BL Ken Karp*; 28BR Ken Karp*; 28TL Larry Lipsky/Bruce Coleman Inc; 29BR GHP Studio*; 29T Joe Towers/Check Six; 30 Chuck O'Rear/Woodfin Camp & Associates; 31 Bill Ross/Westlight; 32L GHP Studio*; 33 Mike Mazzaschi/Stock, Boston; 34 GHP Studio*; 35 Tim Davis*; 36–38 Ken Karp*; 39 Richard Megna/Fundamental Photographs; 42 Bill Ross/Westlight; 44–45 Doug Milner/DRK Photo; 44L Chuck Fishman/Woodfin Camp & Associates; 47 Elliott Smith*; 50 Terry Farmer/Tony Stone Images; 52BC Jon Feingersh/Tom Stack & Associates; 52BL C J Allen/Stock, Boston; 52BR Tim Davis*; 52TL Ken Karp*; 52TR Bill Horsman/Stock, Boston; 53BL GHP Studio*; 53BR Jose Fernandez/Woodfin Camp & Associates; 53T Stuart L Craig Jr/Bruce Coleman Inc; 54 Anne Dowie*; 55L Joe Towers/The Stock Market; 55R Ken Karp*; 56L Bill Horsman/Stock, Boston; 56TR E R Degginger/Earth Scenes; 56–57 Ken Karp*; 57R David Pollack/The Stock Market; 57TL Courtesy Dr Paul Fisher; 58B Janice Sheldon*; 58T Richard Fukuhara/Westlight; 59 Nick Pavloff*

Special thanks to Malcolm X Elementary School, Berkeley, California; Franklin Year-Round School, Oakland, California; Carl B. Munck Elementary School, Oakland, California; Hintil Ku Ka Child Care Center, Oakland, California.

*Photographed expressly for Addison-Wesley Publishing Company, Inc.

Illustrations

Carey Austin 40
Nea Bisek 8, 23, 26, 43T, 46T, 59
Jane McCreary 9, 27, 46B, 49T
Randy Verougstraete 60–61
Pat Welch 10–11, 14–15, 16, 32, 43B, 48–49B, 52–53

Text

40–41 Madeleine L'Engle, *A Wrinkle In Time* (New York: Farrar, Straus & Giroux, Inc.). Copyright ©1962 and copyright renewed ©1990 by Crosswicks Ltd. Reprinted with permission of Farrar, Straus & Giroux, Inc.

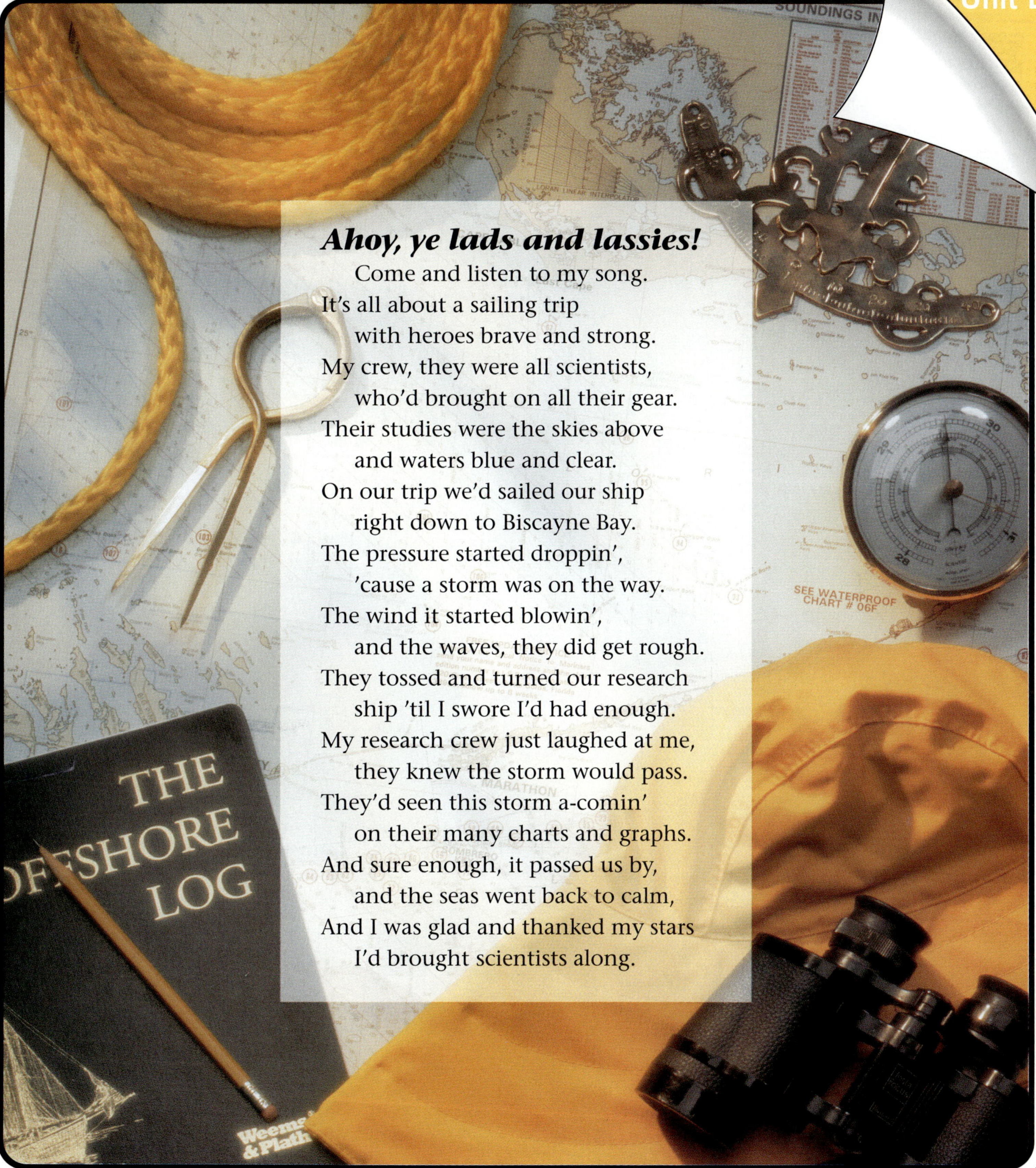

Ahoy, ye lads and lassies!

Come and listen to my song.
It's all about a sailing trip
with heroes brave and strong.
My crew, they were all scientists,
who'd brought on all their gear.
Their studies were the skies above
and waters blue and clear.
On our trip we'd sailed our ship
right down to Biscayne Bay.
The pressure started droppin',
'cause a storm was on the way.
The wind it started blowin',
and the waves, they did get rough.
They tossed and turned our research
ship 'til I swore I'd had enough.
My research crew just laughed at me,
they knew the storm would pass.
They'd seen this storm a-comin'
on their many charts and graphs.
And sure enough, it passed us by,
and the seas went back to calm,
And I was glad and thanked my stars
I'd brought scientists along.

Florida Keys

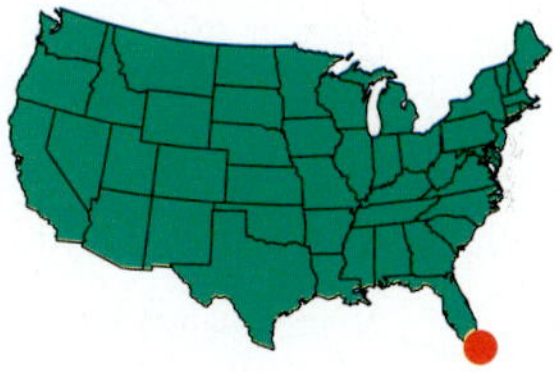

Welcome aboard the ocean research vessel *Destination*. We're about to set sail for the Florida Keys. After exploring the shallow reefs near the Keys, we'll set our course for the open ocean. We're not searching for gold in a sunken ship, but we will find many of the treasures in the ocean. Hurry up, the captain's calling, "All aboard!"

Hold onto your hat! The wind is strong here. Is this wind going to continue? How can you predict what the weather will be?

As you step onto the ship, you feel a little unsteady. You're not the one swaying—the ship is swaying. The waves below rock the ship back and forth. How do waves form? Are there other kinds of ocean motion?

You peer over the railing into the blue water. What's underneath the water? How can you find out what's down there?

- How can you predict the weather?
- How and why do oceans move?
- What lies beneath the waves?

AIR AND WATER

FLORIDA KEYS

Activities

Features

Chapter 1

The Air

The crew has boarded the research vessel, and you are ready to set sail. Before you sail out of the harbor, however, you should find out what the weather is going to be like on your trip. Weather is the condition of the air at a given time and place.

Bad weather can be dangerous, especially at sea. Rain can swamp a small boat. Wind can turn it over. Before you set sail, you have to know what weather you'll encounter so you can be prepared.

Have you seen the weather forecast on television or in the newspaper? Some forecasts show you pictures taken from weather satellites to predict what kind of weather is moving into your area.

You won't have a TV or daily newspaper on the research ship. But you can learn how to predict the weather yourself by using a few instruments that give you information about the air. The characteristics of air determine what weather will be like. There are several different characteristics you need information about in order to predict the weather: moisture, temperature, wind, and air pressure.

Write a sample weather forecast in your Science Journal. Include information about precipitation, wind, temperature, and cloudiness. Also describe how the weather forecast affects your daily decisions. For instance, how does weather affect what you do or what you wear?

29
30
Change
RAIN
FAIR
28
31
Airguide
27

Explore Activity

What are some characteristics of air?

Process Skills
Observing, Predicting

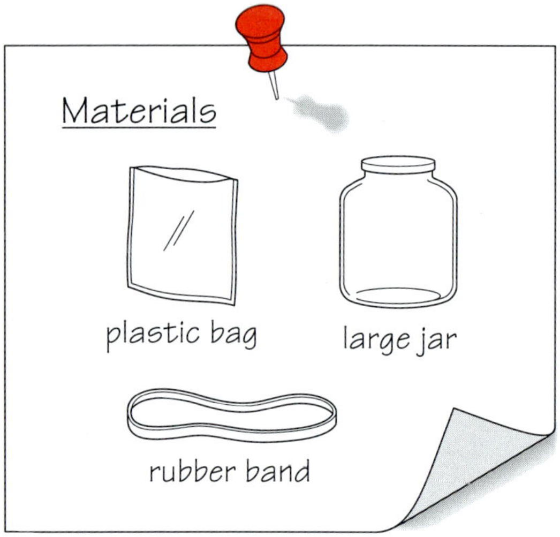

Observe and Collect Data

1. Inspect the bag to make sure it has no holes. Fill the plastic bag with air by blowing in it or by pulling it through the air.
2. ACTIVITY JOURNAL Attach the air-filled bag to the top of the jar with the rubber band. Make sure a tight seal is formed so no air can escape from the bag. **Predict** what will happen when you try to push the bag into the jar. Record your prediction in your Activity Journal.
3. Without popping it, try to push the bag into the jar. Record your observations in your Activity Journal.
4. Remove the rubber band and the bag. Hang the bag inside the jar and reattach it with the rubber band. **Predict** what will happen when you try to pull the bag out of the jar. Record your prediction in your Activity Journal.
5. Try to pull the bag out of the jar. Record your observations.

Share Your Results

Compare your predictions and observations with those your classmates made. Does the size of the bag or the jar affect the results?

Draw Conclusions

1. How did air affect your ability to push the bag into the jar or pull the bag out of the jar?
2. Does air take up space? Does it weigh anything? Explain your answers.

Apply What You Know

1. **Predict** what would happen if there was a hole in the bag. Explain your prediction.
2. Imagine you could bring your jar with a bag full of air into space, where there is no air. How do you think your results would differ in space?

What is in the air?

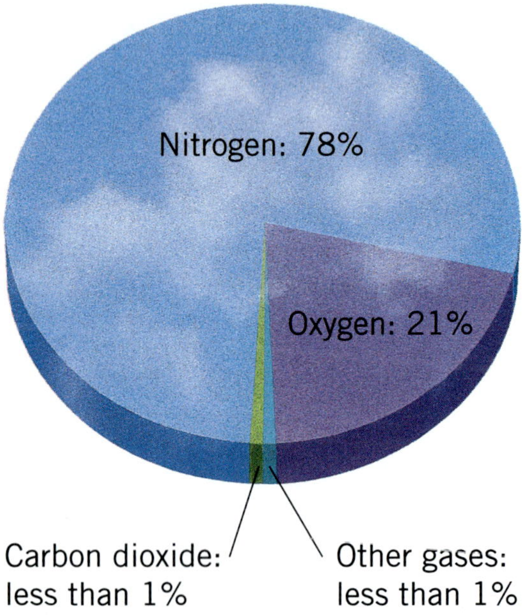

Air is a mixture of many tiny particles. Some of the particles are gases. These include oxygen, which you need to survive, and carbon dioxide, which plants use to make sugar. Other air particles, such as dust and pollen, are solids.

On the research vessel, you are surrounded by water. There is water in the ocean below you and in puddles on the deck. There is also water vapor in the air. The amount of water vapor in the air is known as **humidity** (hyo͞o mid′ə tē). Water moves between the earth and the air in a pattern called the water cycle.

Be a Scientist

HANDS-ON ACTIVITY

How much water is in the air?

1. Build the device shown in the picture. Use enough clay to balance with the blotter paper.
2. ⚠ Place your device near a pan of hot water. Be careful not to touch the water.
3. Cover the device and the water with a large glass jar. Record your observations.

Evaporation
When the sun heats water, it evaporates, or turns into a gas called water vapor.

Condensation
As water vapor rises, it reaches cooler air and condenses into tiny water droplets.

Cloud formation
Clouds form when water droplets come together.

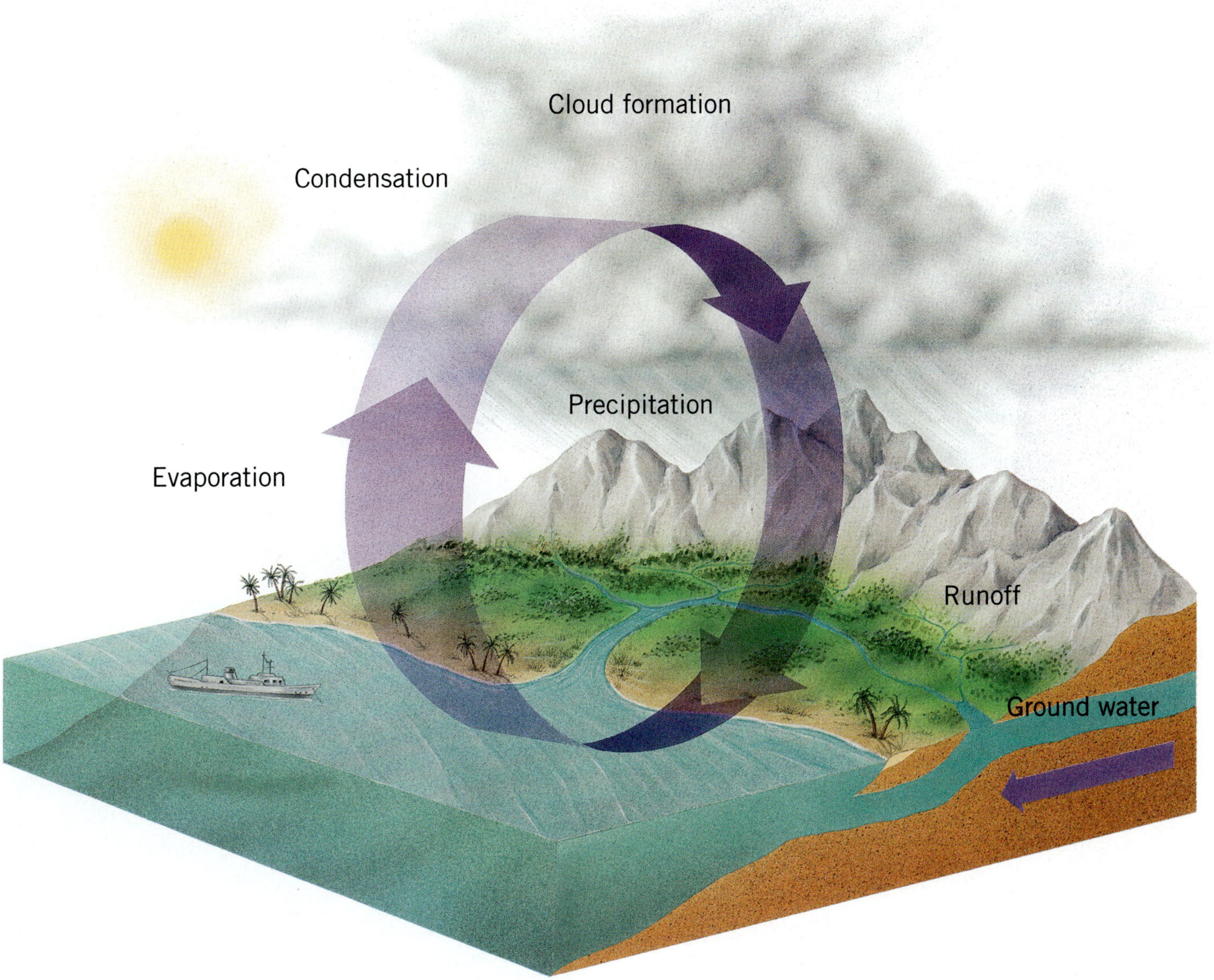

Precipitation
When the water droplets in clouds get too heavy, they fall as rain, snow, sleet, or hail.

Runoff
As precipitation falls to the earth, some of it runs into rivers and streams. Rivers and streams flow into the ocean.

Ground water
Some precipitation soaks into the earth and collects underground. This water eventually seeps into the ocean.

What are the layers of the atmosphere?

The earth's air is called the **atmosphere** (at′məs fir′). The atmosphere starts at the surface of the earth where you stand. It ends thousands of kilometers above you. Scientists divide the atmosphere into four levels that are all very different from one another.

One of the differences among the layers of the atmosphere is the density of the air particles. Density is a measurement of how crowded an area is. If an area has a high density, that means that there are a lot of objects in that area. A crowded room, for example, would have a high density of people.

The atmosphere is more dense, or has more air particles, close to the earth's surface. As you move farther away from the earth and higher into the atmosphere, there are fewer air particles. The air high in the atmosphere is less dense. Above the atmosphere, in outer space, there are no air particles.

The atmosphere is a protective shield. One layer in particular, the ozone layer, protects the earth from harmful rays of sunlight. Scientists have found a hole in the protective ozone layer. The hole may allow more of the sun's harmful rays to reach the earth. Many scientists believe the hole is caused by chemicals used in making some foam products, air conditioners, and refrigerators.

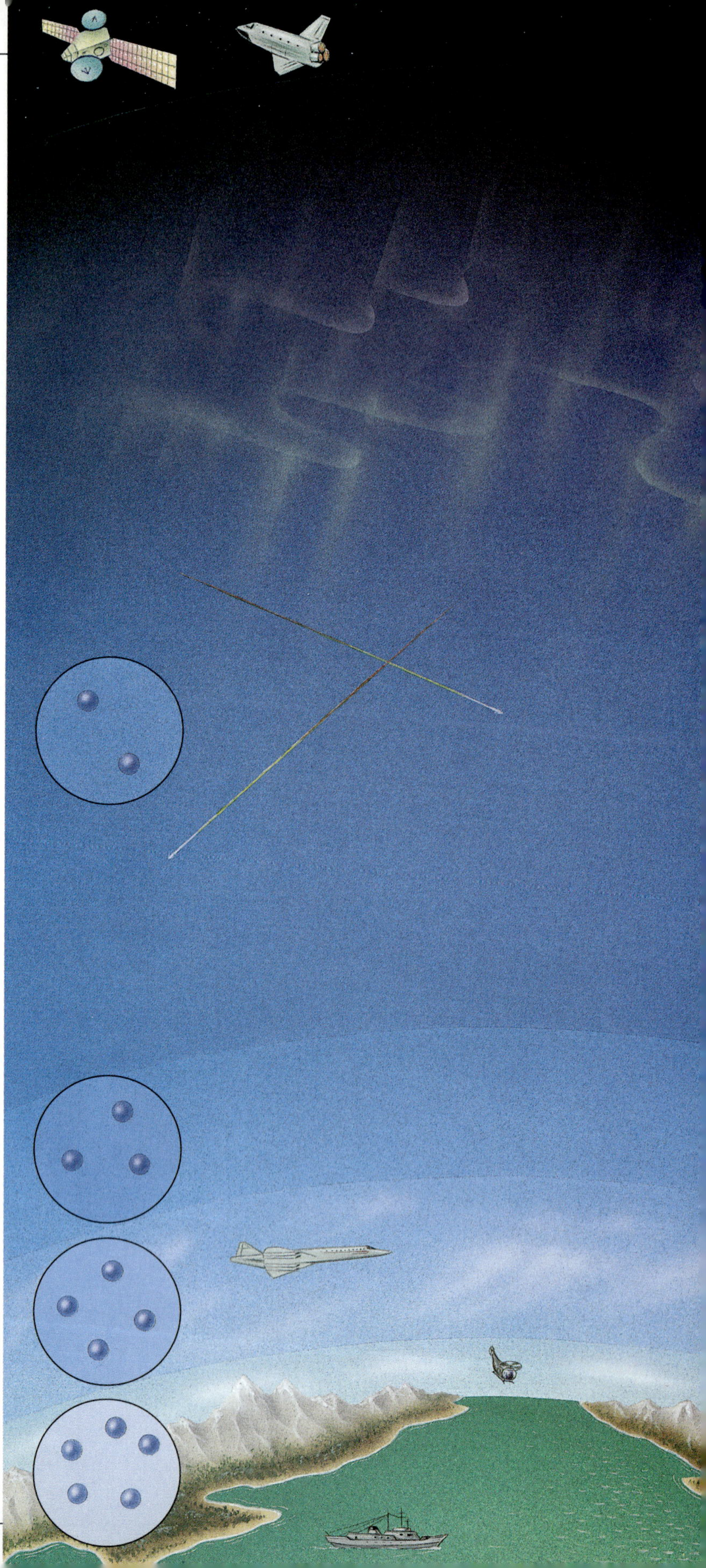

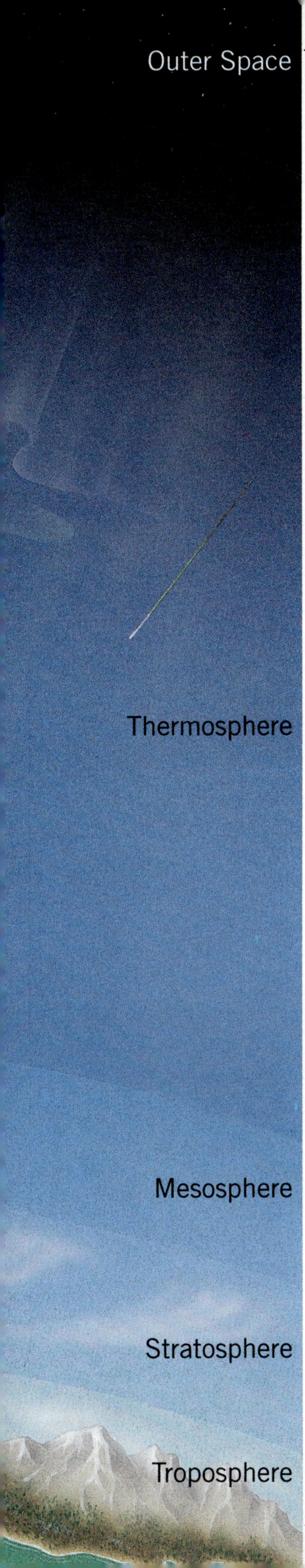

Thermosphere

This is the highest layer of air. Many satellites orbit through the thermosphere.

Mesosphere

At the top of the mesosphere, the temperature is about −100°C. This is the coldest place in the atmosphere.

Stratosphere

Where the stratosphere and troposphere meet, there is a wind called the jet stream. The jet stream blows from west to east and tends to push weather in that direction. The stratosphere is also where the ozone layer is. Ozone blocks the sun's harmful rays.

Troposphere

The clouds you see in the sky float in this layer of the atmosphere. The higher you go in the troposphere, the colder the temperature gets.

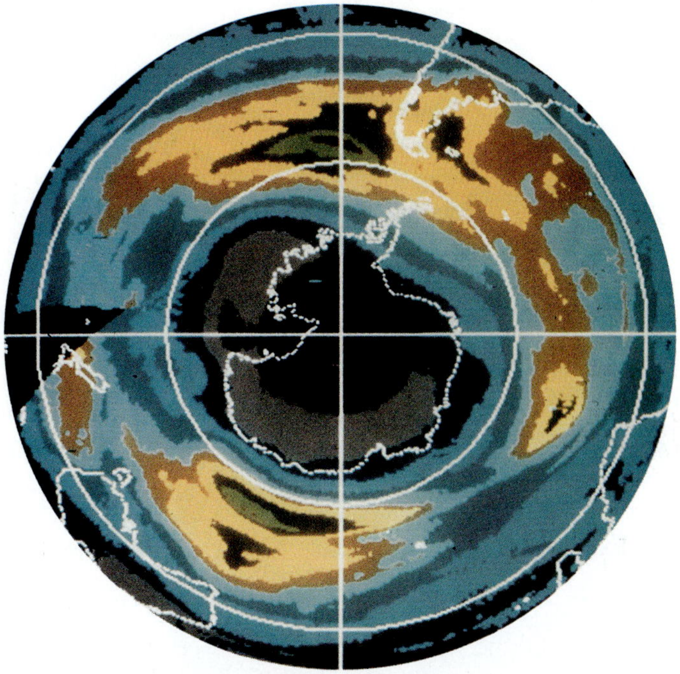

This image shows the hole in the ozone layer above the south pole. The ozone hole is shown by the gray and black areas over Antarctica.

YOU CAN HELP

Avoid using products that contain CFCs, chemicals that damage the ozone layer.

What makes the wind blow?

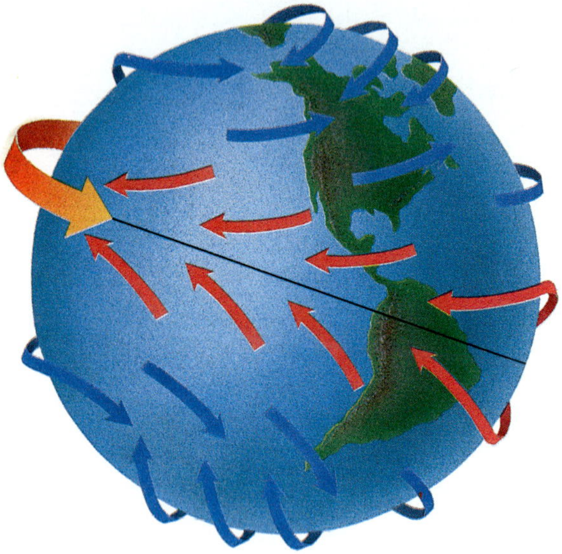

Global winds
Global winds are a result of uneven heating. The air over the equator is warmer than the air over the poles. As a result, the hot air over the equator rises, and cold air from the poles slips in under it. Global winds are curved by the earth's rotation. The direction of the earth's rotation is shown in the drawing above by the orange arrow.

During the day, the wind is blowing from the ocean to the land. At night, you notice that the wind direction has changed. Now it is blowing in the opposite direction.

Wind blows when air moves from a dense area to an area that is less dense. When air is heated, the particles spread out and become less dense, leaving more space between the particles. When air is cooled, the particles come together and air becomes more dense. In cold air there is less space between air particles. If an area of warm air is next to an area of cool air, the crowded particles in the cooler dense region flow into the more spacious warmer region. This creates a breeze.

Global winds blow over huge areas of the earth. Sea breezes and land breezes are local winds. They blow over small areas.

SCIENCE JOURNAL

Uneven heating makes air move in your home. Check your home to see where the heaters are. Also check the temperature at different heights in the rooms. Record your observations in your Science Journal.

BACK HOME

Sea breeze

When air is heated, the particles spread out. Warm air is less dense than cold air. This difference in air density accounts for wind. During the day, sunlight strikes both the Florida land and the ocean near it. But the land heats up faster than the ocean. Because the warm air over the land is less dense than the air over the ocean, the air from above the ocean spreads out toward the land. The dense, cold air pushes the less dense, warm air upward. This movement of air from the ocean toward the land forms a sea breeze.

Land breeze

At night, the land cools faster than the ocean. The warmer, less dense air over the ocean rises. Then, the cooler, denser air from over the land slides out over the ocean's surface.

How are you doing?

1. What kinds of particles make up the air?
2. Would you expect more wind on a sunny day at the beach or a cloudy day at the beach? Explain your answer.
3. **Think** If you flew to the outer edge of the atmosphere and back, what might you need on your trip to survive?

What is air pressure?

The air's density can help you predict the weather. Warm air is less dense than cold air. Clouds and rain form when air particles come closer together and squeeze out the water vapor. Wind blows when air particles move from dense areas to areas where the air is less dense.

Scientists determine how many particles are in the air by measuring how heavy the air is. Compare the weight of a full balloon with that of an empty balloon. The full balloon weighs more because it has more air particles inside. Air with more particles in it is heavier than air with fewer particles in it. The weight of the air is always pushing against you and everything on the earth. The push of the air is called **air pressure.**

Amazing!

The air pressure on the top of Mount McKinley in Alaska is less than half of what the air pressure is at sea level.

Since cold air is more dense than warm air, cold air is heavier than warm air. Air that weighs more has greater air pressure. Warm air is less dense and therefore forms low-pressure areas.

High pressure
Since there is not a lot of water vapor in high-pressure areas, they do not usually have many clouds.

A sudden change in air pressure usually means that the weather will also change. A drop in air pressure means that moist air is moving into your area. What do you think a rise in air pressure means?

Low pressure
Since air particles are spread out in low-pressure areas, there is more room for water vapor. Low-pressure areas usually contain clouds.

Be a Scientist

HANDS-ON ACTIVITY

How can you see changes in air pressure?

1. Hold two long strips of paper in front of you. They should be a few centimeters apart.
2. ACTIVITY JOURNAL Blow steadily between the strips of paper. Record your observations in your Activity Journal. How does blowing the air between the strips affect air pressure?

What are air masses?

Although you cannot see the air over your research vessel as you sail along the Florida coast, you know that it is different from the air in other parts of the country. The air around you is warm and moist, but in other areas of the country, the air is cold and dry. Any large body of air with the same temperature and humidity throughout is called an **air mass.**

The temperature and humidity of an air mass is determined by where it forms. An air mass that forms over Canada will be cold because the climate of that region is cold. In general, air masses that form over polar regions are cold. Air masses that form over deserts or tropical regions are warm.

Air masses that form over Canada are also usually dry. Since the air mass over Canada forms over land, not much water evaporates into the air. In general, air masses that form over land are dry. Air masses that form over water are humid. What do you think an air mass over the Hawaiian Islands would be like?

Global winds cause air masses to move. When air masses move, the weather changes. How the weather changes depends on the characteristics of the moving air mass, and how fast it is moving. When two air masses meet, a boundary forms.

You hear from a member of the research crew that a cold air mass from the north is moving down the coast toward your ship. What do you think the weather on your research vessel will be like when the cold and warm air masses meet?

Cold, dry air

Cold, wet air

Warm, dry air

Warm, wet air

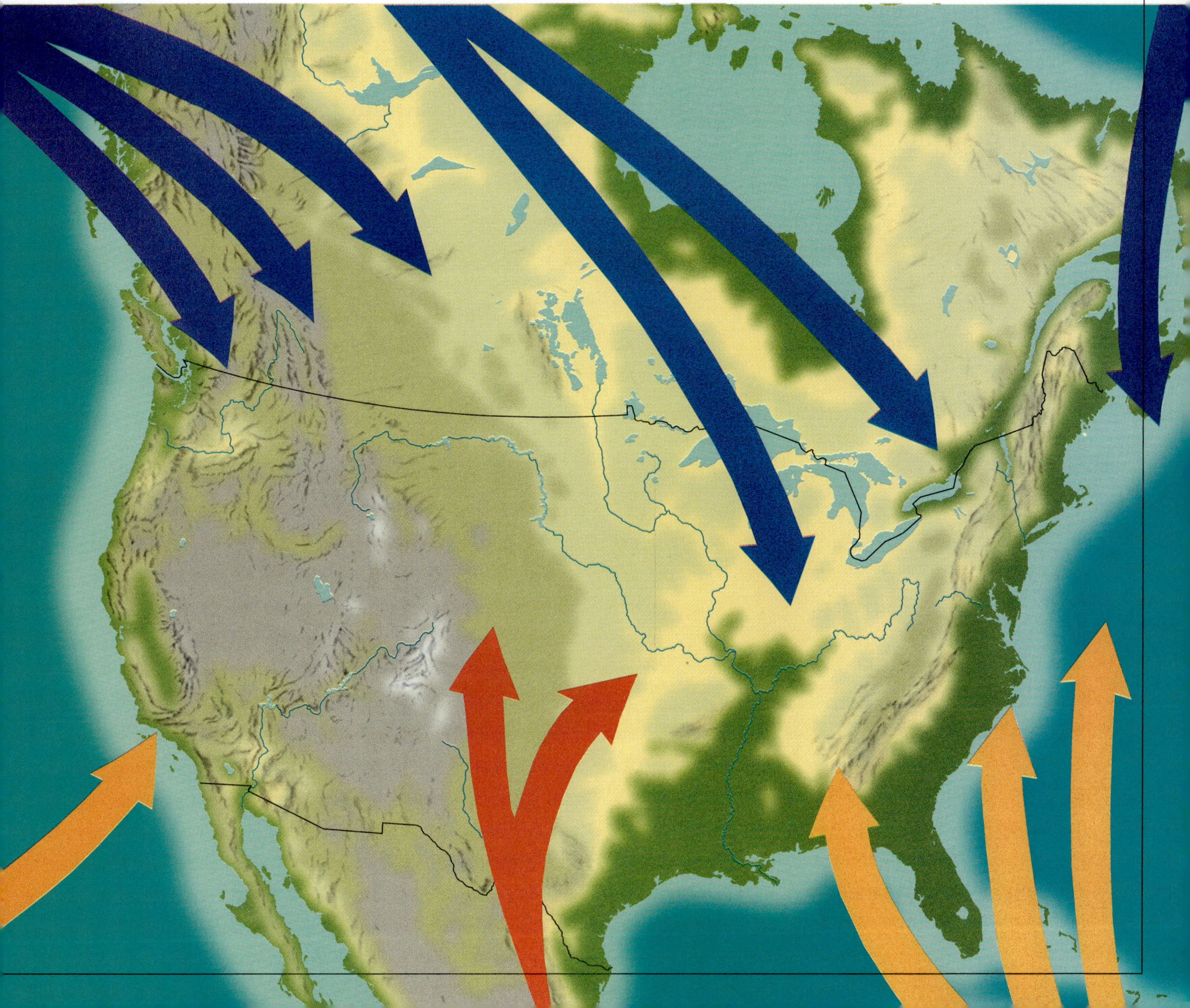

What happens when air masses meet?

The weather around your ship in the Florida Keys can be the same for several days. Then, in just a few hours, it can become very different. Moving air masses cause changes in weather. The leading edge of an air mass is called a **front.**

Fronts are named for the temperature of the advancing air mass. The greater the difference in temperature between the air masses, the greater the weather change along the front will be. In both cold and warm fronts, warm air is lifted over cold air.

Cold front

The leading edge of a cold air mass is called a **cold front.** When a cold front runs into a warm air mass, get ready for stormy weather. You may want to hunt for a sweater, because the temperature is going to drop.

Warm front

The leading edge of a warm air mass is called a **warm front.** When a warm front catches up to a cold air mass, get out your umbrella. Steady rain or snow is on the way. Temperatures will get warmer too.

This picture was taken by a satellite that collects information about weather fronts and sends it back to the earth.

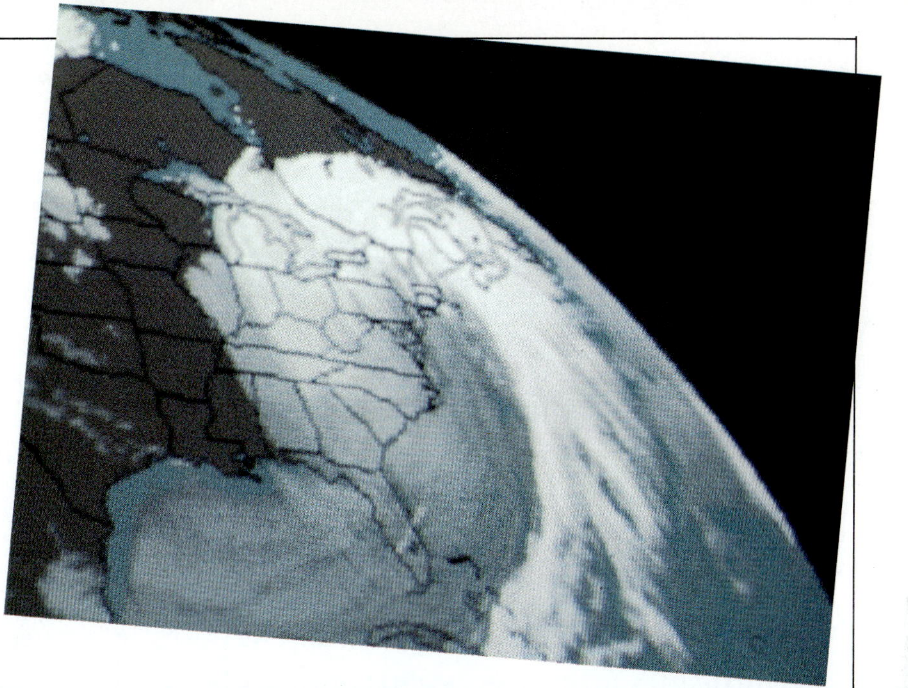

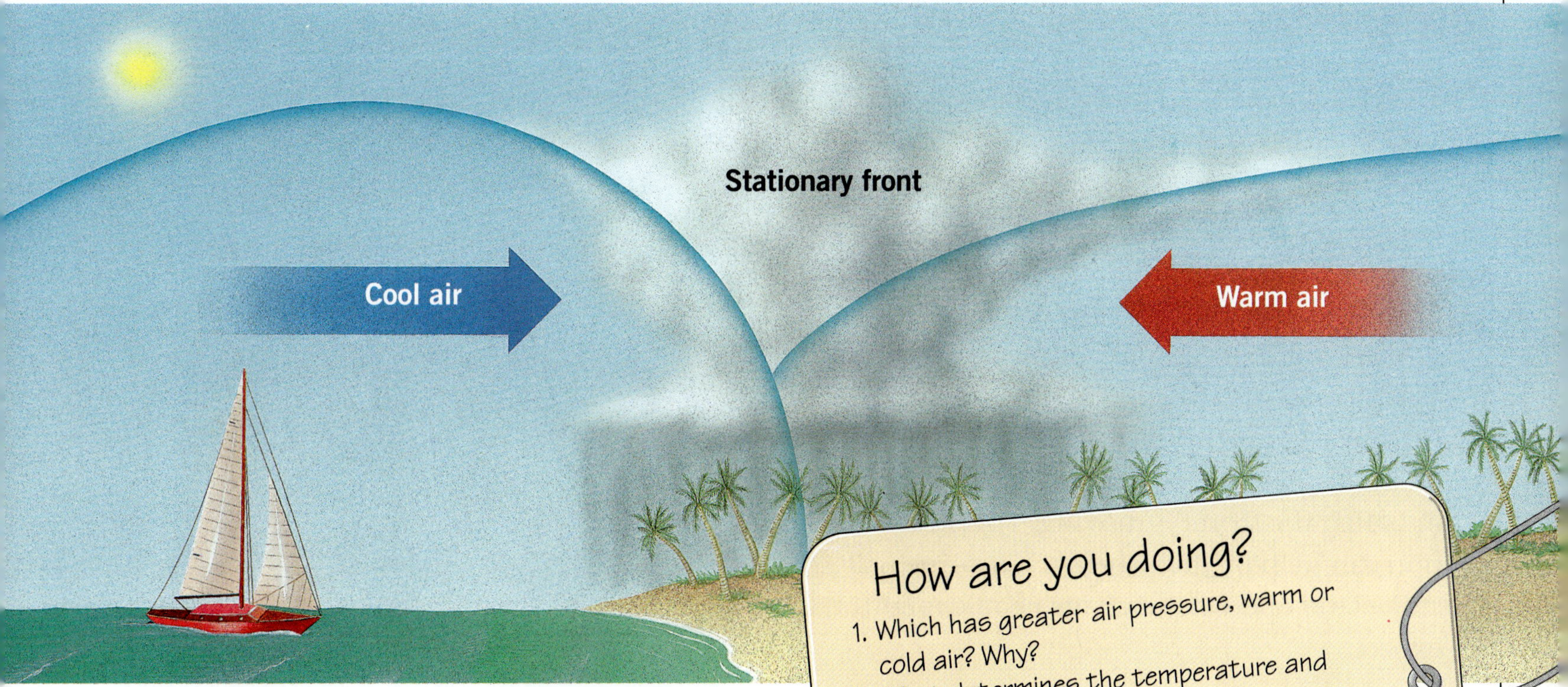

Stationary front

When two fronts lock together and stay right above your head for a few days, the result is a **stationary front.** The word *stationary* means "not moving." The weather will stay the same under a stationary front until the fronts move.

How are you doing?

1. Which has greater air pressure, warm or cold air? Why?
2. What determines the temperature and moisture of an air mass?
3. **Think** What can happen when a warm air mass cools? Describe what happens to the air particles and what weather you might expect.

Hurricane Hunter

Hurricane winds blow at speeds between 120 and 320 kilometers an hour. A hurricane gets its energy from warm air that rises from the sea. When warm air rises, cool air moves down to replace the warm air. This motion makes the air spin, and a hurricane is born. Hurricanes form over oceans or other large bodies of water. They become less severe as they move inland.

Most people head for cover when a hurricane comes. Hurricanes are powerful storms. Their storm winds can knock down trees, turn over cars, and tear roofs off houses. There are some people who actually head toward a hurricane. These weather scientists, or meteorologists, fly right at the great storms. Their planes are loaded with instruments that measure such things as the wind speed, air pressure, temperature, and the direction in which the storm is moving. This information can help predict where a hurricane will strike land and what damage people might expect.

Hurricanes like this one can cause a lot of damage.

This picture of a hurricane was taken by a weather satellite and enhanced by a computer.

MATH CONNECTION

How are air pressure and weather related?

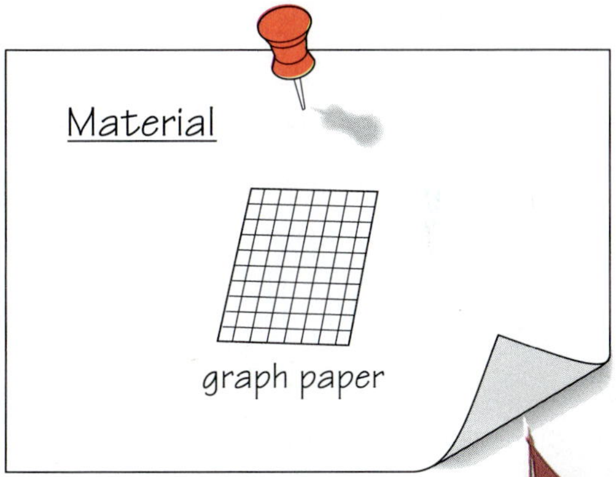

Observe and Collect Data

1. ACTIVITY JOURNAL Record air pressure and weather data from your area, or copy the chart below in your Activity Journal.

Day	Air Pressure (mm of Hg)	Weather
1	767	fair, mild temperatures
2	767	fair, mild temperatures
3	765	cloudy, mild temperatures
4	756	rain, high winds, cool temperatures
5	762	rain, cool temperatures
6	764	fair, mild temperatures
7	765	sunny, mild temperatures

2. Use your data to make a line graph of air pressure.
3. Create symbols to represent the different kinds of weather. Add the symbols to your graph.

Draw Conclusions

1. What is the relationship between air pressure and the kind of weather that occurs?
2. **Predict** the weather you would get if the air pressure readings suddenly went down.

Looking Back

MINDS-ON ASSESSMENT

Words and Concepts

Complete the following statements.

1. The particles that make up air are _____ and solids.
2. When water droplets in the air come together, they can form _____.
3. Air in the troposphere has _____ particles than the air in the thermosphere.
4. _____ is the push of air against you and other things on earth.
5. The leading edge of an air mass is called a(n) _____.
6. A(n) _____ is a body of air with the same temperature and amount of moisture throughout.

Hot air makes these balloons rise.

Applied Thinking Skills

Answer the following questions. You can use words, drawings, and diagrams in your answers.

7. What weather would you predict when a warm air mass runs into a cold air mass?
8. Explain how you think heating the air makes a hot-air balloon rise.
9. The air over a blacktop surface heats up faster than the air over grass. Draw a diagram to show which way you'd expect the wind to blow in a school yard with a blacktop surface and a grassy field.
10. **Your World** Find out what kind of air mass is over your town right now. Write a forecast for the weather you expect tomorrow.

Show What You Know

How can you forecast weather?

Weather scientists, or meteorologists, use weather maps to help forecast the weather. The maps show such things as air masses, high- and low-pressure areas, cold and warm fronts, temperatures, and precipitation.

Process Skills
Predicting, Interpreting data

Observe and Collect Data

1. Study the weather map and symbols key.
2. ACTIVITY JOURNAL **Predict** today's weather and tomorrow's weather for your area and four other areas of the country. Write your prediction in your Activity Journal. Include an explanation for each forecast.

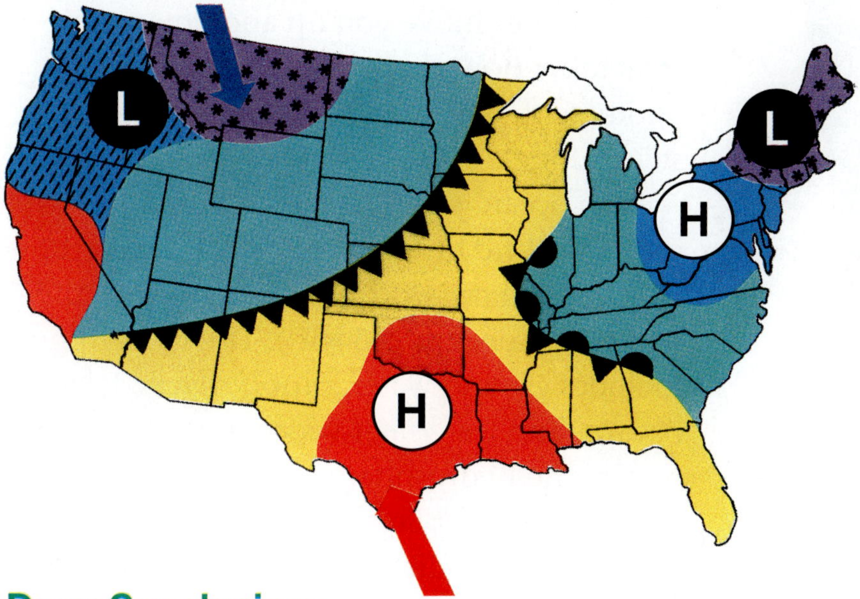

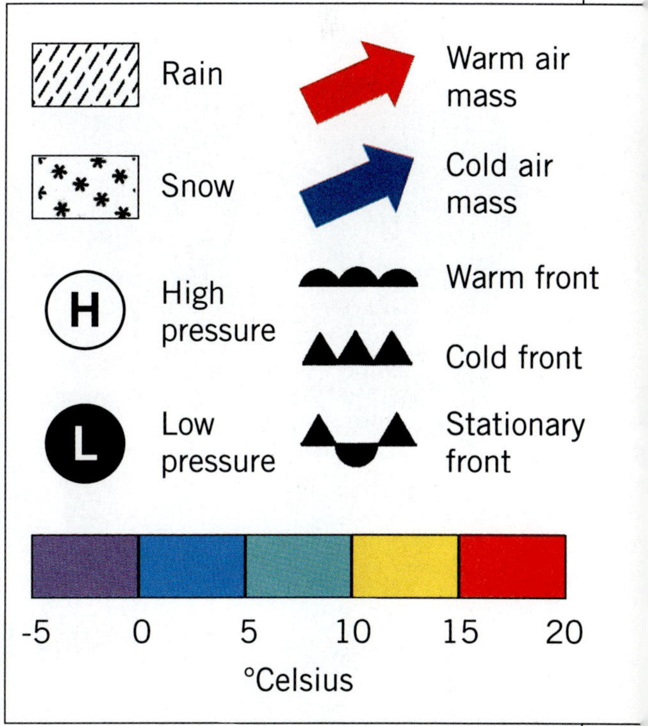

Draw Conclusions

What conditions do meteorologists take into account when making their predictions?

Chapter 2

Ocean Water

The engines of the research vessel sputter to a stop. The sun is high in the sky, and you feel hot. It's time for a swim. You pull a clear mask over your eyes. A snorkel dangles from the side of your goggles. You climb over the side of the ship and down the rope ladder after your swimming buddy.

You plunge into the ocean. Right away, the cold ocean water makes your body feel cooler. And when you lick your lips, they taste salty. You lean back, kick your feet, and float on the surface of the water.

Each wave that passes by seems to carry your floating body up and then down again. As the waves move you up and down, you remember how glad you are to have your buddy with you. You know it is not safe to swim alone.

The ocean water you're swimming in is only one kind of water found on the earth. Together, all the earth's water makes up the **hydrosphere** (hī'drō sfir'). The hydrosphere includes ground water, runoff, rivers, lakes, oceans, and ice. Water vapor in the air is also part of the hydrosphere.

SCIENCE JOURNAL In your Science Journal, describe the bodies of water you have seen or been swimming in.

FL 7054 DL

Explore Activity

Which solution has the most salt?

Process Skills
Inferring, Measuring

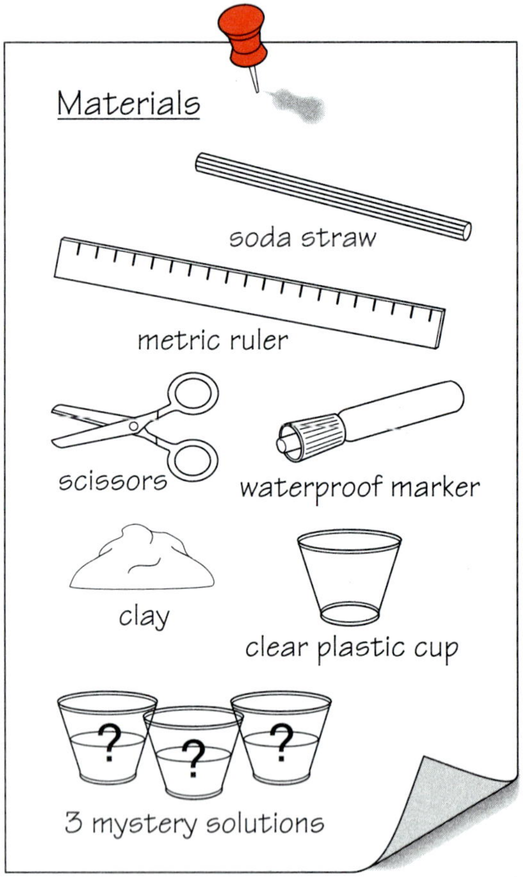

The more salt there is in a solution, the more dense the solution is. If you measure the densities of salt and water solutions, you can tell which holds the most salt.

Observe and Collect Data

1. Cut the straw so that it is 8 cm long. Starting 1 cm in from one end, use the marker and ruler to make marks on the straw 1 cm apart.

2. Use a small lump of clay to plug up the end of the straw below the first mark. Be sure the straw will not fill with water. Place the straw in a cup of water with the clay end down. The straw should float with half of the marks above the water level. Add or remove bits of clay until the straw floats this way.

3. ACTIVITY JOURNAL Gently place the straw, clay end down, into the first mystery solution. In your Activity Journal, record the number of marks that are above the solution. The more dense the solution, the higher the straw will float.

4. Repeat step 3 with the other solutions.

Share Your Results

How do the results of your group compare with those of other groups?

Draw Conclusions

1. Which solution was the most dense? Which one was the least dense?
2. **Predict** what would happen if some of the water in solution 1 evaporated.

Apply What You Know

1. If you went swimming in the ocean and in a fresh-water lake, in which would you float more easily? Explain your answer.
2. If a ship carried too much cargo, why might it be dangerous for the captain to take the ship from the ocean into a river?

What makes up ocean water?

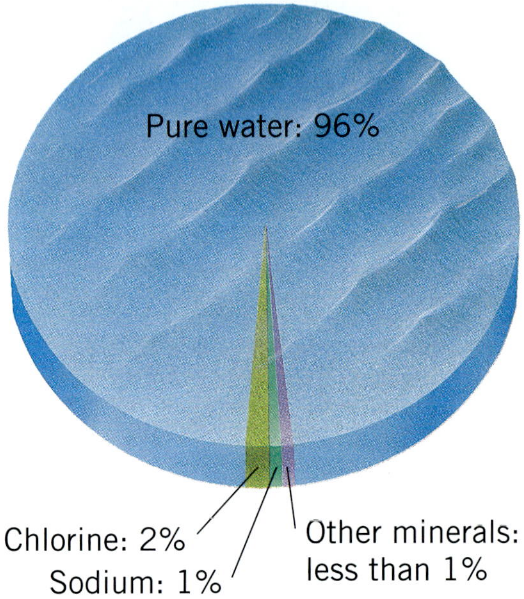

Three-quarters of the earth's surface is covered with water. Not all of the water on the earth is the same. The water in the ocean around your research vessel is salty. The water in a lake is fresh. It has little or no salt in it. Most of the water on earth is salt water. Only about 4% of the hydrosphere is fresh water.

Most of the ocean's salt comes from sodium chloride. That's the same kind of salt that people sprinkle on food. In every liter of ocean water, there are about 35 grams of salts.

Most of the salts and other minerals in the ocean come from the earth's crust. As rivers flow over land, they pick up minerals and carry them to the ocean. Minerals also enter the ocean from volcanoes and from cracks on the ocean floor.

YOU CAN HELP

Some ocean animals can be strangled by the plastic rings that hold six-packs of cans. Before throwing these rings away, cut them up.

These students are measuring the salinity of ocean water.

Things are more buoyant, or float more easily, in salt water because it is more dense than fresh water. As you've learned, density measures the number of particles in an area. Because it is more dense, salt water is heavier than fresh water.

Salinity (sə lin′ə tē) is the measure of the amount of salt in water. Salinity varies in different parts of the ocean. The lowest salinity is found where a river enters the ocean. As the water in the ocean evaporates, a more concentrated salt solution is made. Where there is more evaporation, salinity is higher. The Mediterranean Sea has a higher salinity than most other bodies of salt water.

Fresh water in the Mississippi River runs into salt water in the Gulf of Mexico. The salt water is more dense than the fresh water.

HISTORY

Gandhi's Great Salt March

People need some salt in their diet to survive. When a tax was placed on salt in India, people became angry. In 1930, the great Indian leader Mahatma Gandhi (mə hat′mə gän′dē) peacefully protested this tax.

Gandhi, with hundreds of followers, marched 320 kilometers from his home to the sea. There they evaporated sea water to get the salt that was dissolved in it. This free salt could not be taxed by the British. This event is known around the world as the Great Salt March.

What is water pressure?

As you dive deeper into the water, you feel as if something is pressing on your ears. Pressure is a force caused by something that has weight. The weight of water above you causes pressure on your ears. Your ears hurt because thin membranes inside your ears, called eardrums, are being pushed inward.

The deeper you dive, the greater the water pressure becomes. Divers who go 10 meters below the water's surface feel twice the pressure they feel at the surface. Divers must wear special equipment that makes it possible to withstand water pressure.

In the deepest part of the ocean, the water pressure is so great that the people who dive there must be inside special diving vehicles. Underwater research vessels have very strong sides. If they didn't, the water pressure would crush them. The walls of the underwater research vessel *Trieste,* for example, are 12 centimeters thick. Use a ruler to find out how thick 12 centimeters is. Compare this thickness to that of the walls in your school or home.

Your body is adapted to a certain amount of air pressure. If pressure increases, such as when you dive too far under water, you are uncomfortable. Animals in the ocean are adapted to water pressure.

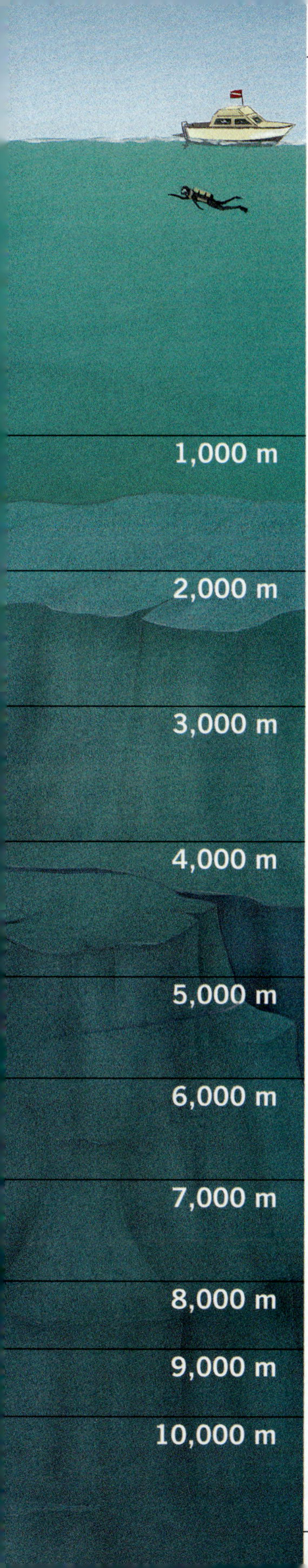

Scuba diver
An expert diver with scuba gear can go about 90 m below the ocean's surface.

Submarine
Submarines travel to depths of about 460 m or more.

Jim
The hard metal walls of a Jim suit protect the diver from the incredible pressure up to 380 m down into the ocean.

Bathysphere
This pioneer underwater research vessel was lowered more than 900 m into the ocean in 1930.

Alvin
This research vessel has gone deeper than 3,000 m to explore the ocean bottom.

Trieste
This vessel carried scientists to the deepest point in the ocean, over 10,000 m below the waves.

Be a Scientist

HANDS-ON ACTIVITY

How does depth affect pressure?

1. Use a pencil to punch holes in an empty milk carton about 4 cm apart. Cover the holes with tape.
2. ACTIVITY JOURNAL **Predict** how far water will squirt from the holes when the carton is filled with water. Record your prediction in your Activity Journal.
3. Fill the carton with water. Place it in a sink or large bucket and remove the tape. Record and explain your observations.

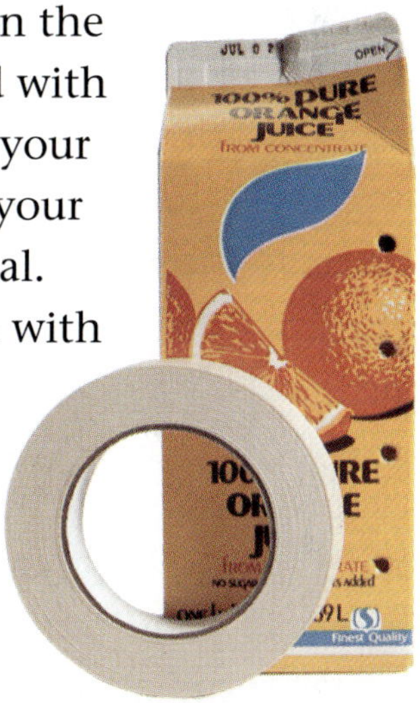

How are you doing?

1. How do salts get into the ocean?
2. How does pressure change with depth in the ocean?
3. **Think** What do you think would happen to a fish's body if it swam deeper in the ocean than it usually does?

What makes waves?

You climb out of the ocean and back onto the ship. A gentle breeze kicks up small waves. As the wind picks up speed, the waves grow larger. The speed of the wind doesn't change over the next few hours, but the waves get bigger. You radio a ship 500 kilometers away and learn that a strong wind is blowing there, too.

There are three factors that control the size of waves: the speed of wind, the length of time wind blows, and the distance over which wind blows. The largest wave ever reported was seen by the sailors on the USS *Ramapo.* It was taller than a ten-story building. What do you think the weather was like when they spotted that wave?

As you look out at the waves, it looks like the water is moving toward you. Actually, the water is only moving up and down. What you see moving toward you is wave energy. Wave energy comes from the wind.

As wind energy passes through the water, it makes the water particles move up and down, causing waves. Look at the pictures below. Notice that the wave doesn't make the ship move backward. But it does make it move up and down.

The ocean isn't the only place you can see waves. The wind makes waves move through fields of grass. People make waves in stadiums, too. Your class can do "the wave" by getting in a line and taking turns lifting your

arms up and down. When you do “the wave,” how do you move? How does the wave energy move?

As a wave moves, it may reach shallow water at a beach. If the water is very shallow, the top of the wave falls over, causing a tumbling kind of wave called a breaker.

Not all waves are caused by wind. Tsunamis (tso͞o nä′mēz), are caused by underwater earthquakes or volcanoes. The movement of the ocean floor during an earthquake or volcanic eruption causes a tidal wave to form.

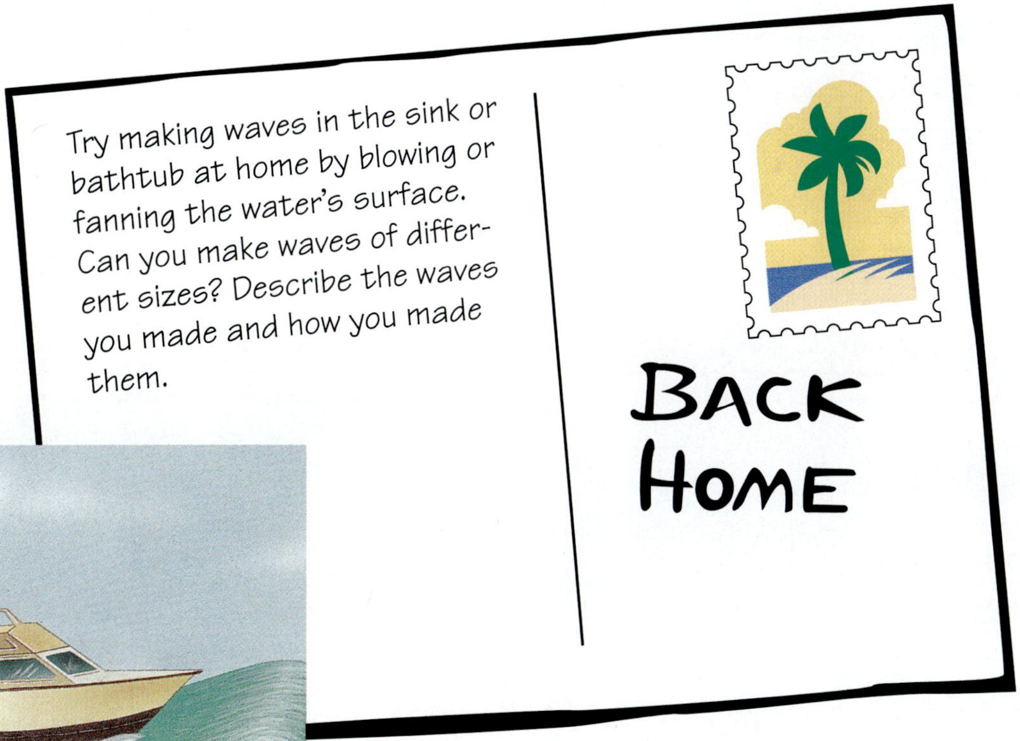

◀ Waves move objects floating on them up and down but not forward.

What causes water levels to change?

After a long day, your ship pulls into a calm area near one of the many islands south of Florida. You say good night to the crew and head to your cabin. When you go outside the next morning, you notice several rocks poking above water level. When you look for them again at noon, they're gone. The rocks didn't disappear. The ocean slowly rose. This slow change in water level is called a **tide.**

Tides are caused by the pull of the moon. All objects pull on each other. That pull is called the force of gravity. The moon's gravity pulls on the land, but the land doesn't move much because it is solid. When the moon's gravity pulls on the water, the water moves because it is liquid. Tides occur when ocean water moves toward the moon.

When the ocean water is highest, it is high tide. When you looked at the ocean at noon and saw no rocks above the water, it was high tide. When the ocean water is lowest, it is low tide. When you looked at the ocean in the early morning and saw the rocks, it was low tide. In most places tides change about every six hours.

Tides are not the same all over the world. The moon's gravity creates two large bulges of ocean water. One bulge is on the side closest to the moon. The other bulge is on the side farthest from the moon. As the earth rotates, these large bulges of water move over the oceans.

DILEMMA

Saving the Coral

Beautiful coral reefs wind around the Florida Keys. The reefs attract many colorful fish and other sea life. Coral reefs also attract millions of people every year.

Unfortunately, people are destroying the reefs. Boats pollute the water with oil and gasoline. People dump trash into the water. Swimmers break the coral by stepping on it or chipping off pieces to take home. Damaged coral dies. The animals that live around the reefs also die.

Think About It Design a poster that would make visitors aware of how they can prevent further damage to coral reefs.

What are ocean currents?

Your research vessel motors a few miles south and then the engines are turned off. Without engine power, the ship starts to drift back up north. A current causes the ship to drift.

A **current** is a river of water that moves through the ocean. Your research vessel is being pulled northward by a current called the Gulf Stream. When you take a sample of the ocean water around your ship, you notice that it is warmer than the water you sailed through before. The earth's oceans have both cold and warm currents running through them. The Gulf Stream is a warm ocean current.

There are two kinds of ocean currents: surface currents and deep ocean currents. Surface currents are kept in motion by steady winds that blow in the same direction almost all the time. In the illustration, red arrows indicate warm currents and blue arrows indicate cold currents.

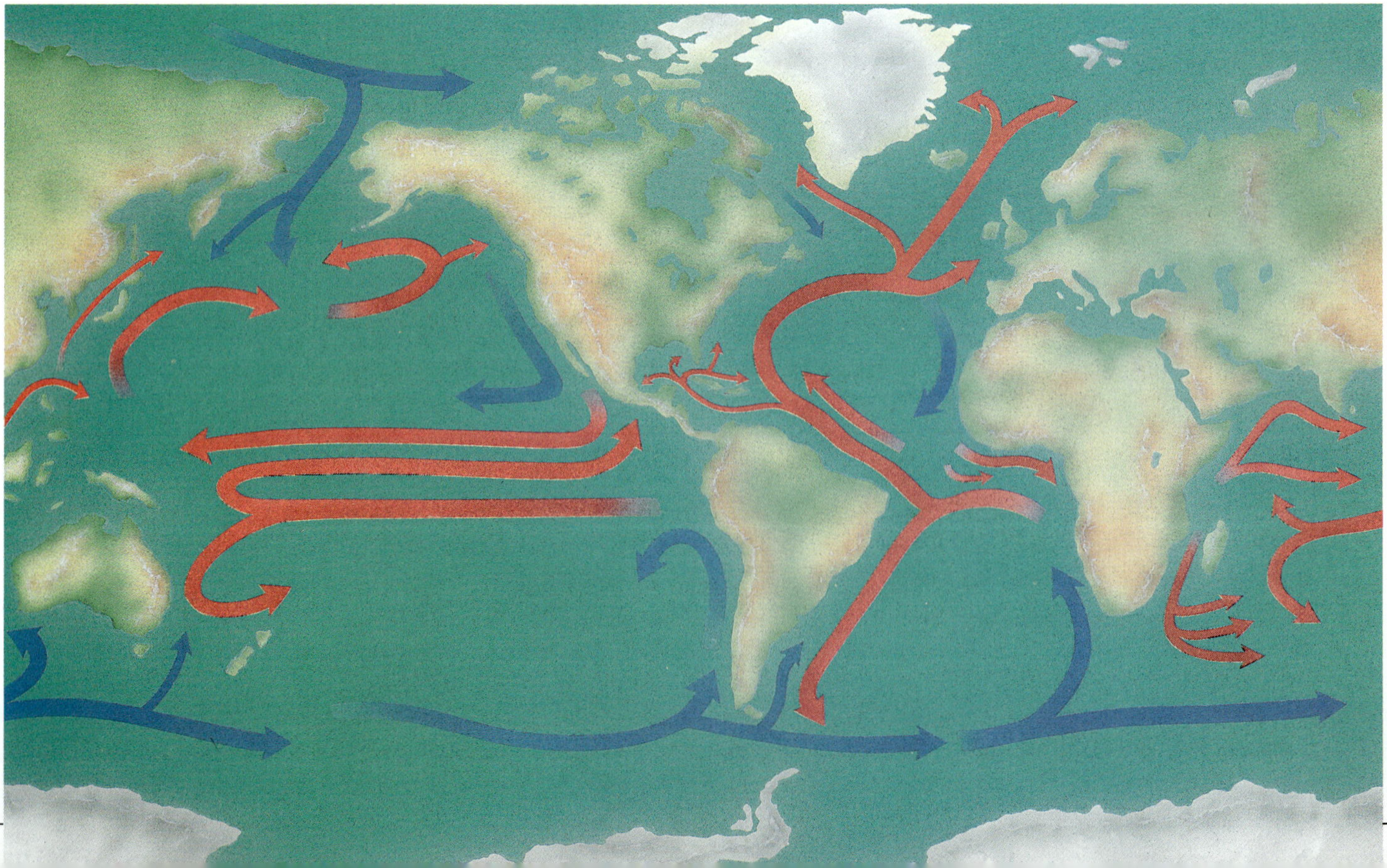

Differences in the density of cold and warm water cause deep ocean currents to form.

The way that deep ocean currents form is similar to the way that winds form. When cold and warm air meet, the heavier cold air slips under the lighter warm air. This air movement forms wind. When cold and warm water meet, dense cold water sinks under the less dense warm water. This water movement forms a deep ocean current.

Differences in the amount of salt in the water can also cause a deep ocean current. Since salty water is denser, it sinks below less salty water. The deep ocean current that runs from the Mediterranean Sea to the Atlantic Ocean is formed in this way.

How are you doing?

1. What are three factors that affect the size of a wave?
2. What force causes tides to rise and fall?
3. **Think** A research vessel off the Oregon coast turned off its engines and drifted with the current. In which direction did the vessel drift?

Science & Literature Connection

Shark Beneath the Reef

by Jean Craighead George

The following excerpt is from an adventure story about a Mexican boy who tries to catch a shark.

. . . (Tomás) ambled out to the rock reef, which was now above water. The tide was almost all the way out, exposing the rocks like the spine of a lizard. They were uncovered at about the same hour each day, for the Sea of Cortez has a twelve-hour tide, not the twice-a-day ebb and flood that exists along most of the U.S. coasts. This is due to the movement of the water as it rocks in the Sea of Cortez, and the way the gulf lies in relation to the earth's axis and the moon.

On the last stone of the reef Tomás sat himself down in a busy world. Waves of little hermit crabs that had been left high and dry by the tide scurried on their pointed toes. Carrying the heavy shells in which they lived, they ran toward the scent of water. In the tidal pool at his feet the increasing light told the sea anemones the tide was almost out. They began closing their flowerlike tendrils to survive the long hours in stale water. The *hachas,* little oysters, were already closed for the duration, while over the top of the brown seaweed danced a lively ballet troupe of Sally Lightfoot crabs. In their brilliant red armor, they all skittered backward simultaneously when Tomás lifted his hand. They swept forward like a chorus line when he sat still.

Tomás took off his clothes and . . . jumped into the water. He was quickly plunged twelve feet down to the white coral sand at the bottom of the reef. . . .

Tomás grinned as he beheld a world more fantastic than anything he could conjure up in his imagination. Blue, green, black, yellow, orange and purple fish floated dreamlike from the top of the reef to the bottom. On the rocks clung animals that looked like flowers, fans, strings, rubber tires, spaceships and Aztec gods. And they were all real. . . .

Once more his lungs hurt. Determined to increase their capacity, he held on to the rock and sat resolutely on the bottom. Just in front of him lay an overhang. The sea currents that rushed along the reef here had eroded it, leaving the deep, dark overhang. Tomás swam a short distance under it, looking for his friend the jewfish, which lived in the cave at the bottom of the sea. The fish had large, black eyes that had evolved for night hunting, the time when the jewfish fed. When it did not appear, Tomás forced himself to hold his breath yet longer and swam farther under the overhang.

And then he saw something else. Far to his right loomed the tail of a huge shark. He could not see the head, for the beast was moving in and out of focus in the darkness of the cavern. But what he saw was big.

Think About Your Reading

1. How do you think Tomás feels about the sea and its creatures? What details told you this?
2. Name two effects the changing tide has on animals in this excerpt.

Predicting Choose an animal Tomás sees in the ocean. Make a sketch of what you think the animal might look like. Predict two behaviors the animal might have. Then look up the animal at the library. How close were your predictions?

Where to Read More

Pearl S. Buck, *The Big Wave,* (Thomas Y. Crowell, 1948)
Jiya's whole fishing village is lost in a tidal wave. Will he learn to live with his fear?

Looking Back

Words and Concepts

Read each statement. If a statement is true, write *true* as your answer. If a statement is false, change the underlined word or phrase to a word or phrase that will make the statement true.

1. The deeper you go in the ocean, the <u>greater</u> the pressure becomes.
2. Three factors that control the size of the waves are the <u>temperature</u> of wind, the length of time wind blows, and the distance over which wind blows.
3. A tide is the change in water level caused by the <u>moon's</u> gravity.
4. When cold and warm waters meet, the cold water <u>sinks under</u> the warm water.
5. Steady winds set the <u>deep-ocean currents</u> in motion.
6. If you put an object in samples of ocean water and fresh water, it would sink deeper in the <u>ocean</u> water.

Applied Thinking Skills

Answer the following questions. You can use words, drawings, or diagrams in your answers.

7. If you could push a balloon down to the bottom of the ocean, how would you expect the balloon to change?
8. If you wanted to go surfing, what weather information could you gather to predict the size of the waves?
9. You want to send a message in a bottle across the ocean. Choose a coast from which to launch your bottle. Describe which current would carry it. **Predict** where your message would end up.
10. **Your World** What parts of the hydrosphere are near your home? Would you expect the water to be fresh or salty?

Show What You Know

How can you model currents?

Observe and Collect Data

1. Fill the jar halfway with warm water. Add several drops of red food coloring to the water and stir.
2. ACTIVITY JOURNAL Gently drop a colored ice cube into the warm water. Watch what happens in the water for the next 5 minutes. In your Activity Journal, describe or draw what you see.
3. After 30 minutes, observe the water again and record your observations.

Draw Conclusions

1. What kind of ocean current did you model, a surface current or a deep ocean current?
2. How is the ocean current you modeled similar to an air current?

Process Skills
Observing, Inferring, Making models

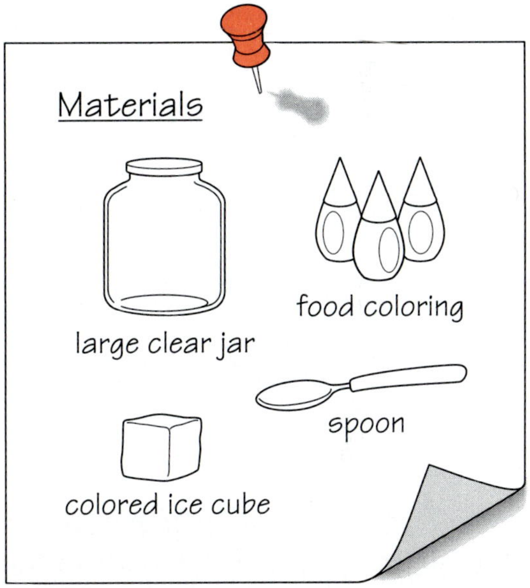

Chapter 3

Ocean Features

You put on your scuba diving equipment and jump into the water. Although the water on the surface is choppy, all is calm just a few meters down. Using your fins, you head down to deep water. You breathe easily, thanks to your tank full of air. Your mask keeps the stinging salt water out of your eyes, so you have a clear view ahead of you.

Looking down, you see sand and a few scattered rocks. Moving more like a graceful bird than a fish, a black manta ray almost twice your size glides by. You swim on. Ahead, a living forest seems to spring out of the sand. This is a coral reef. Small fish of all shapes and colors dart among the branches of the coral.

The ocean bottom gently slopes deeper. Then, suddenly, the shelf seems to vanish into darkness. The edge of a cliff drops off below you. You and the other divers float above the cliff. You can't follow it down. The water pressure that deep would be too much for you. What does the rest of the ocean floor look like? How can we find out?

In your Science Journal, draw a picture of what you think the bottom of the ocean looks like.

Divers must wear special suits to withstand the pressure of the deep ocean.

Explore Activity

How can you map what you can't see?

Process Skills
Measuring, Collecting data, Interpreting data

Observe and Collect Data

1. Use the clay to make a model in the shoe box of what you think the ocean bottom looks like.
2. Cut a narrow slot from one end of the box top to the other with the scissors. Make marks along the slot one centimeter apart. Tape the top on the box and exchange your box with another student.
3. ACTIVITY JOURNAL Tie the washer to the end of the string. Lower the string into the slot until the washer hits bottom. Using your fingers, mark the string where it touches the box top. Pull the string out and measure the length from your fingers to the bottom of the washer. Record the length in your Activity Journal.
4. Move the string and weight to the next mark and measure and record the distance from the box top to the base of the washer. Repeat this step at each centimeter mark along the slot.
5. Use the measurements to draw a cross section of the model in the shoe box.

Share Your Results

Open the box and compare your drawing to the shape of the clay. Whose map of the ocean floor is more like the clay model? Did others use special techniques?

Draw Conclusions

1. How accurate was your map?
2. Why might the method you used be difficult to use to map the ocean floor?

Apply What You Know

What other methods could be used to map the ocean floor? Describe another method. Compare your method with the one you used during this activity.

How can you find what you cannot see?

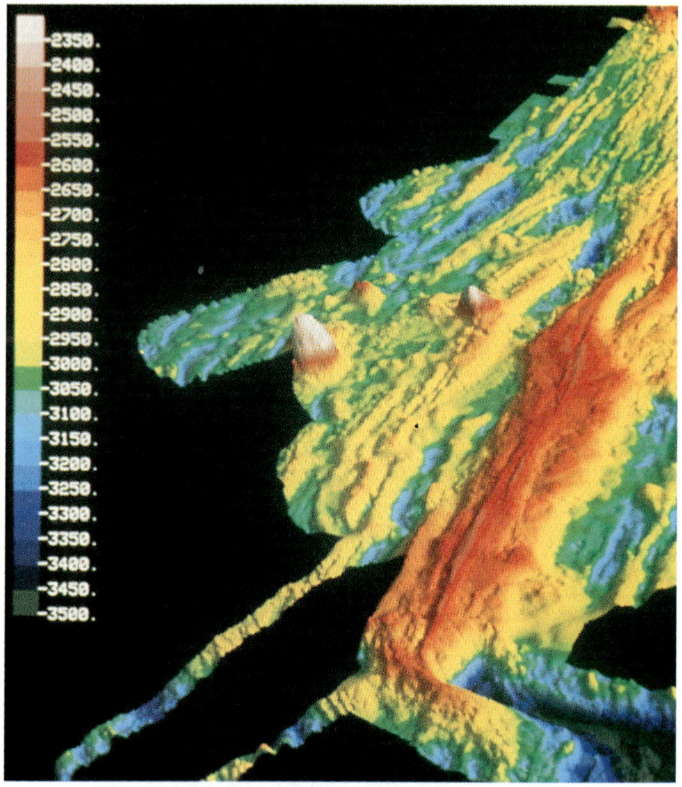

A computer created this map of the ocean floor using sonar signals. The colors on this map show different depths in the ocean.

Scientists didn't lower a rope into the ocean to map its depths; they used sound to determine the depth of the ocean. Boats sent sound waves through the water. After the sound waves hit the ocean bottom, they bounced back upward as a ball might bounce off the ground. The method of using sound to measure depth or to find objects in the water is called **sonar** (sō′när).

The scientists measured the time it took the sound to make the round trip from their ship to the ocean bottom and back again. They divided this number by two to figure out how long it took the sound to travel one way to the ocean bottom. By multiplying the time it took the sound to travel one way by the speed of sound, scientists calculated the distance from the ship to the ocean floor. Today, research ships use electric sound signals to map the ocean floor. The signals go to a computer, which makes a map on its screen.

Scientists aren't the only ones who use sound to find objects that are under water. Whales and porpoises use sound too. From sound, these animals sense things such as the direction to a seamount and the distance to another animal.

Be a Scientist

HANDS-ON ACTIVITY

How can you use sound to judge distance?

1. ACTIVITY JOURNAL Divide into groups. Practice dropping and catching a tennis ball at different distances from the floor. While you do this, have a partner time how long it takes the ball to hit the ground and bounce back up. Other group members should measure the distance from your hand to the ground each time. Record the times and distances. Compare the time it takes the ball to travel up and down and the distance the ball travels.
2. Have other group members close their eyes. Drop the ball from various heights. Say "start" as you drop the ball and "stop" as you catch it. Based on what they hear and on their observations in step 1, have them predict the distance the ball traveled. Record the predictions and the actual distance in your Activity Journal.
3. Switch roles and repeat step 2 so that every group member gets to drop and listen.

What does the ocean floor look like?

If you looked at a sonar map of the ocean floor, the world beneath your research vessel might surprise you. The longest mountain chain on the earth lies hidden beneath the waves. Deep valleys and canyons, wide plains, and steep cliffs also lie at the bottom of the ocean. The deepest trench in the ocean is seven times deeper than the Grand Canyon.

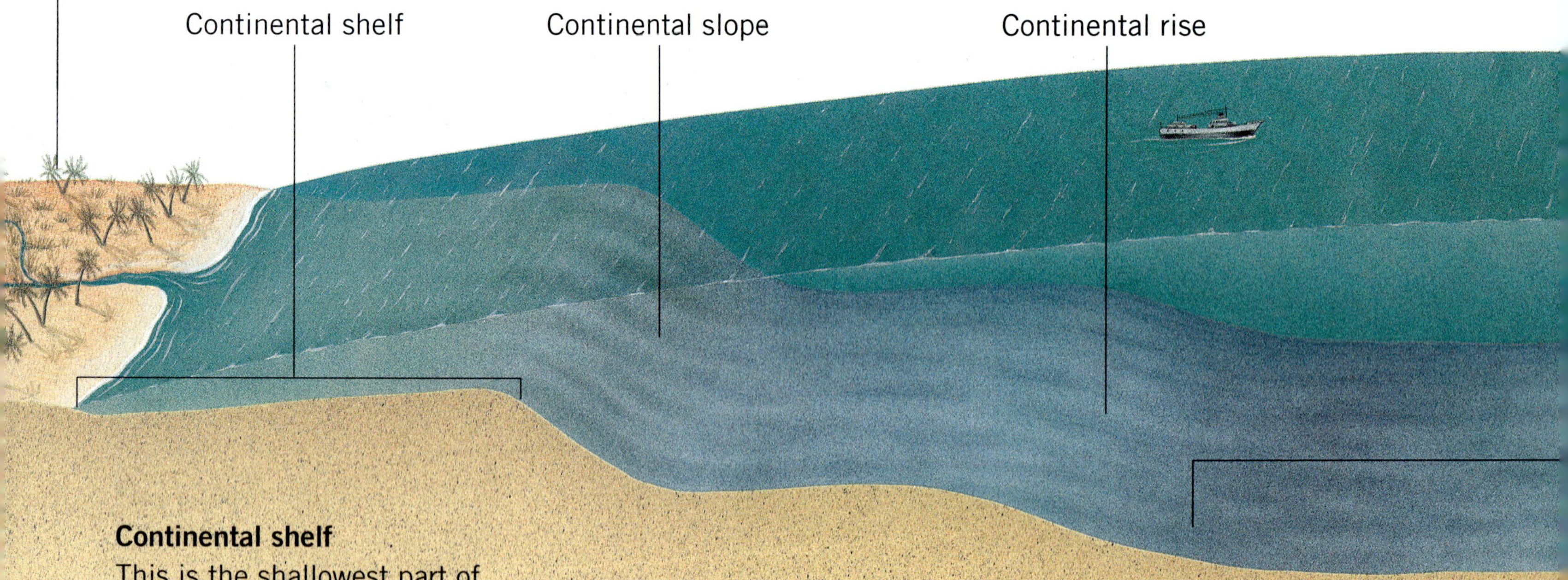

Continental shelf
This is the shallowest part of the ocean. Near the Florida Keys, the shelf extends 90 km out from the shoreline. In other areas, it is hundreds of kilometers wide.

Continental slope
Here the ocean depth increases to several thousand meters over just a few kilometers' distance.

Continental rise
This more gradual slope is made of sediment that rolled down the continental slope.

SIDE TRIP

The Ring of Fire

There is a circle of volcanoes in the Pacific Ocean called the Ring of Fire. Volcanoes can erupt out of the ocean floor just as they do on land. After a volcano releases lava into the sea, the lava hardens and forms a mountain in the sea. Sometimes these mountains rise above the ocean, forming islands. Scientists believe that many islands were formed this way.

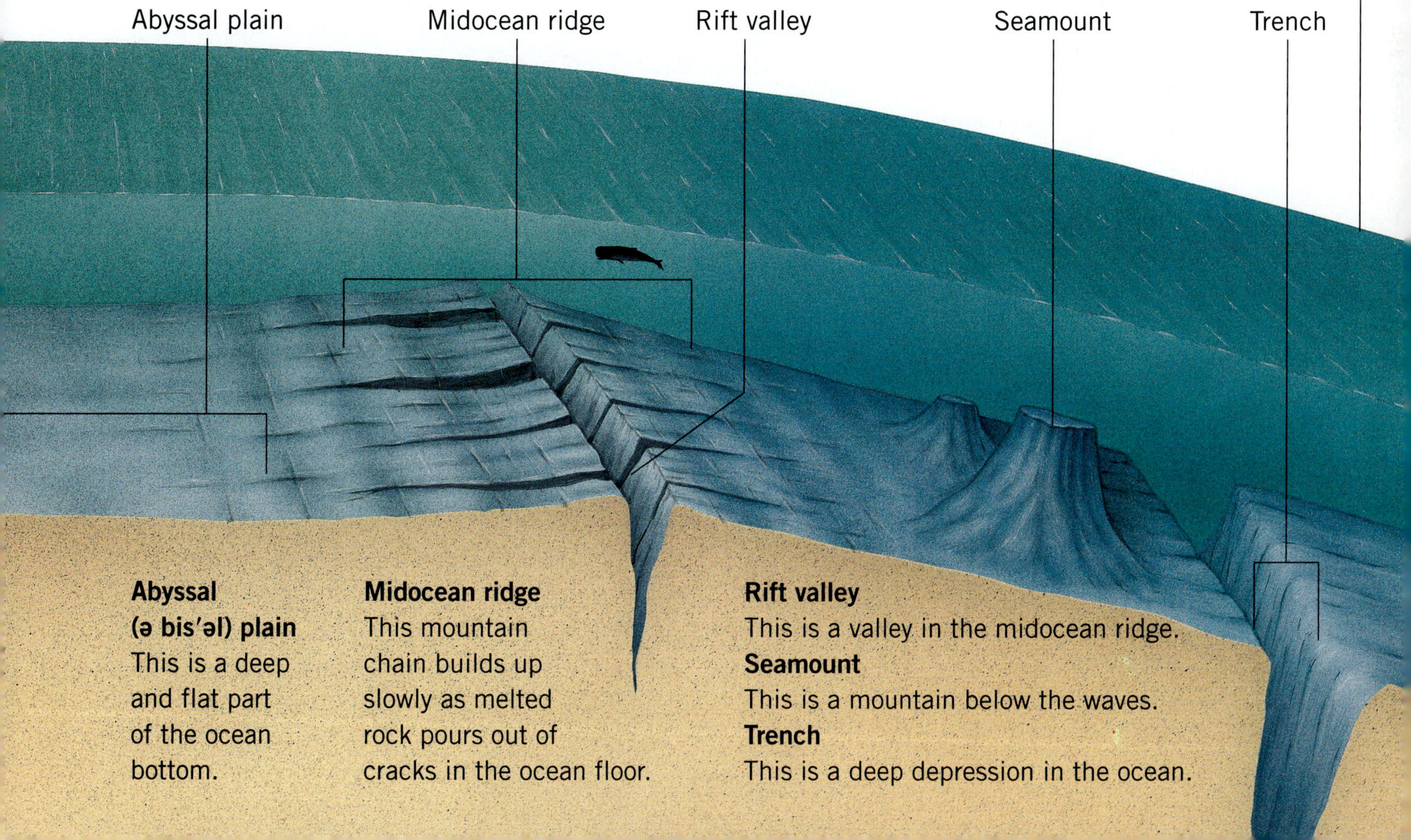

Abyssal (ə bis′əl) plain
This is a deep and flat part of the ocean bottom.

Midocean ridge
This mountain chain builds up slowly as melted rock pours out of cracks in the ocean floor.

Rift valley
This is a valley in the midocean ridge.

Seamount
This is a mountain below the waves.

Trench
This is a deep depression in the ocean.

What are hot spots on the ocean floor?

Some thermal vents have hot, smoky chimneys spewing iron sulfide. Other vents leak minerals into the ocean water much less dramatically.

New species from this strange ecosystem at the bottom of the ocean are still being discovered.

If you wanted to see the ocean floor with your eyes instead of your ears, you would have to climb into an underwater vessel. Scientists would gently lower the vessel into the ocean. Soon you would be skimming just a few meters above the ocean floor.

Because sunlight does not reach the ocean floor, underwater vessels use spotlights to light the ocean bottom. As you peer out of the thick glass portholes, you might see fountains of water spurting out of cracks in the floor. These fountains of hot water are called **thermal vents.**

The heat from thermal vents comes from inside the earth. The inside of the earth holds melted, red-hot rock. It's this rock that flows out of volcanoes as lava. Somewhere on the ocean floor, water seeps through cracks until it reaches these hot rocks. Then the water becomes heated and rises back through thermal vents.

The water around these vents is so hot that it can melt metal. Just a few meters above some thermal vents, the water turns into a smoky black plume. The plume turns black because the water shooting up from inside the earth contains an element called sulphur that combines with ocean water to make a black mineral called iron sulfide.

Career Corner

Oceanographer

Imagine cruising the world's oceans to track the habits of whales or explore the nature of the deep sea. That's what I do. My name is Sylvia Earle and I am an oceanographer. Oceanographers study many things having to do with the ocean's rocks, water, plants, and animals. Oceanographers map the ocean floor, analyze sea water, and study ocean life. I may spend months at sea or on land collecting and analyzing data. And I use special equipment, such as underwater cameras and diving gear. To become an oceanographer, you must study math and science at a college or university.

There are many vents on the bottom of the Atlantic and Pacific Oceans. If you saw a thermal vent, you would also see many living things. Animals that live near thermal vents use the heat and chemicals that spew from the thermal vents to stay alive. You might see tube worms as tall as your teacher or giant white clams that are bigger than your head. You might also see huge crabs crawling across the ocean floor and long brown mussels clinging to rocks.

How are you doing?

1. Which gets deeper faster: the water above the continental shelf or the water above the continental slope?
2. Describe thermal vents.
3. **Think** The sonar readings become shorter as your ship crosses part of the ocean. What can you conclude about the ocean floor below you?

What natural treasures are in the ocean?

Huge oil rigs get oil by drilling deep into the ocean floor.

Many minerals that are found on land are also found in the ocean. Some minerals, such as copper, nickel, and manganese, are found in potato-sized rocks, called nodules, on the ocean floor. Other minerals, such as gold and silver, are dissolved in the water.

Minerals and other resources also lie below the ocean floor. Many areas of the continental shelf contain deposits of oil and natural gas. Your ship's engines, and many other machines, depend on oil which may have been taken from the ocean floor.

YOU CAN HELP

The more oil we conserve, or save, the fewer oil rigs will have to be built. If there are fewer oil rigs, fewer accidents are likely to occur. Encourage adults to recycle motor oil.

Salt is one of a few minerals that can be separated from ocean water. Not only do people use the separated salt to season food, but people also use the water it is separated from as drinking water.

Be a Scientist

HANDS-ON ACTIVITY

How can you clean up an oil spill?

1. Fill a large pan with water and add a small amount of oil.
2. Invent a way to clean up the oil spill. You might try using paper towels, soap, detergents, sawdust, or other materials.
3. ACTIVITY JOURNAL In your Activity Journal, describe your cleaning method, how much time it took, and how well it worked. Compare your method with methods other students used. Could your method be applied to oil spills in the ocean? How would your method affect the environment?

One problem with offshore drilling is the effect of accidents. Oil spills can send thousands of tons of oil into the ocean. Spilled oil travels on ocean currents and spreads to many areas. Many plants and animals are killed by oil spills.

What are the ocean's living treasures?

An oyster can create a pearl around a single grain of sand.

There are many living things in the earth's oceans. All of them are important and should be treasured. Some living things are particularly valuable to us, because they provide food or other useful materials.

Each year, 70 to 75 million tons of fish are caught. Most of this catch is used to feed people and other animals. Shellfish are also a valuable source of food. To increase the supply, many people raise fish and shellfish in underwater farms.

Sushi, a popular Japanese dish, can include fish, shellfish, and seaweed.

SCIENCE JOURNAL

In your Science Journal, write a list of the things in your home that come from the ocean. Include minerals, oil, and living resources.

BACK HOME

The supply of the ocean's living and nonliving treasures is limited. Some kinds of whales, for example, have almost died out because humans hunt them for food and oil. Many fish are taken from the sea faster than they can reproduce. Water pollution has also damaged many ocean ecosystems.

To prevent ocean life from becoming endangered, many nations are trying to stop over-fishing by setting up fishing limits and restrictions.

Today, most people use sponges that are made in factories. For centuries, however, people used natural sponges. Natural sponges, like those shown here, are the soft skeletons of animals that live in the ocean. The living cells are removed before the sponge is sold.

Seaweed toothpaste? Seaweed contains agar, which is used to thicken toothpaste, ice cream, yogurt, and gelatin.

How are you doing?

1. Name three nonliving resources that are found in the ocean.
2. Name three resources that come from living things in the ocean.
3. **Think** Plan a menu that uses products from the ocean. Explain how the items in your menu came from the ocean.

Looking Back

Words and Concepts

Match the description in Column A with the ocean feature in Column B.

Column A

1. Hot underwater fountains that release iron sulfide
2. Steep surface above which ocean depth increases to several thousand meters over a short distance
3. A form in which some minerals, such as copper and manganese, are found on the ocean floor
4. Ocean volcano that does not rise above the water
5. Mountain chain on the ocean floor

Column B

a. Continental slope
b. Seamount
c. Midocean ridge
d. Thermal vents
e. Nodule

Looking back on the ocean

Applied Thinking Skills

Answer the following questions. You can use words, drawings, or diagrams in your answers.

6. Why do you think it might be important to have maps of the bottoms of rivers, lakes, and shallow ocean waters?
7. Describe how sonar signals would change as your ship traveled over an abyssal plain and a trench.
8. Would you expect to find plants growing near thermal vents? Why or why not?
9. Describe environmental and technical problems people might have mining minerals from the ocean.
10. **Your World** List any kinds of food you have eaten that came from the ocean.

Show What You Know

MINDS-ON ASSESSMENT

How does sonar show the ocean floor?

Observe and Collect Data

1. Use the data in the table to make a profile of part of the ocean floor. Graph the sonar position versus the depth. Begin with 0 meters (sea level) and graph downward.
2. Make another graph of time versus depth.

Sonar Position	Time (in seconds)	Depth (in meters)
1	1	762
2	3	2,301
3	4	3,608
4	6	4,602
5	9	6,903
6	10	7,660
7	6	4,602
8	5	3,935
9	1	762

Process Skills

Making a graph, Interpreting data

Material

graph paper

Draw Conclusions

1. What kind of feature does your profile show?
2. How is this mapping technique similar to the one used in the Explore Activity? How is it different?
3. Look at your graph of depth versus time. Describe the relationship between the time it takes a sonar signal to travel and the depth of the ocean floor.

Air and Water

Show what you know about the earth's air and water. Work by yourself, with a partner, or in a group. Choose one activity.

Science-Fiction Writer Write a story about the crew of a research ship that finds the Loch Ness Monster. Include a description of the monster and the instruments used to find it.

Poet Write a song or poem about the air or ocean. Include information about the characteristics of air and water and the motion of air and water.

Environmentalist Make a poster that tells people about the properties of the earth's air or water, how they are being polluted, and what people can do to stop the pollution.

Treasure Hunter Pretend you are going to look for a sunken ship that holds a great treasure. Create a plan for locating the ship and removing the treasure. Present your plan to the class in a song or as a play.

Meteorologist Write a fictional radio weather report for your area. Be sure to include a description of weather conditions and air masses. Give today's weather and predict tomorrow's weather, explaining what you based your prediction on.

Castaway You are the only survivor of a shipwreck. You find yourself on an island in the Pacific Ocean. Luckily, several things from your ship and from the ocean have washed up on the beach. What could you use to survive and send for help? How would knowing about the air and ocean help you?

Glossary

air mass (er mas) Any body of air with the same temperature and amount of moisture throughout. (page E18)

air pressure (er presh′ər) The push caused by the weight of the air. (page E16)

atmosphere (at′məs fir′) The layers of air that surround the earth. (page E12)

cold front (kōld frunt) The leading edge of a cold air mass. (page E20)

current (kər′ənt) A river of water that moves through the ocean. (page E38)

front (frunt) The leading edge on an air mass. (page E20)

humidity (hyo͞o mid′ə tē) The amount of water vapor in the air. (page E10)

hydrosphere (hi′drō sfir′) All of the earth's water. (page E26)

salinity (səl in′ə tē) The measure of the amount of salt in water. (page E31)

sonar (sō′när′) A method using sound to measure distances or find objects in the water. (page E48)

stationary front (stā′shə ner′ē frunt) A weather front that is not moving; this occurs when a cold front meets a warm front. (page E21)

thermal vents (thər′məl vents) Fountains on the sea bottom through which hot, mineral-rich water flows. (page E52)

tide (tīd) The rise and fall of the ocean's surface level caused by the moon's gravity. (page E36)

warm front (wôrm frunt) The leading edge of a warm air mass. (page E20)

Unit E Index

Boldface numerals denote glossary terms. Italic numerals denote illustrations.

Credits

Photographs

1 GHP Studio*; 2–3 Tim Davis*; 4BR Tim Davis*; 4L D. C. Lowe/AllStock; 4TR Larry Lipsky/Tom Stack & Associates; 5B Brian Parker/Tom Stack & Associates; 5T Ken Karp*; 6–7 Bert Sagara/AllStock; 7 E. R. Degginger/Earth Scenes; 9 Elliott Smith*; 10 GHP Studio*; 13B Ken Karp*; 13T NASA; 16 Massimo Borchi/Bruce Coleman Inc.; 17 Willie L. Hill, Jr./Stock, Boston; 17 Ken Karp*; 18B Randy Wells/AllStock; 18BC David L. Brown/The Stock Market; 18T Breck P. Kent/Earth Scenes; 18TC Stephen J. Krasemann/DRK Photo; 21 Anne Dowie*; 22B NASA; 22C W. Faidley/Weatherstock; 22T Ken Karp*; 23 Ken Lax*; 24 Spencer Swanger/Tom Stack & Associates; 26B Ken Lax*; 26T Dan Harding/Adventure Photo; 27 Stephen Frink/The WaterHouse; 28 GHP Studio*; 29 Elliott Smith*; 30L Ken Karp*; 30R Tim Davis*; 31L NASA; 31R The Bettmann Archive; 33 GHP Studio*; 36 Stephen Frink/The WaterHouse; 37R Stephen Frink/The WaterHouse; 42B Stephen Frink/The WaterHouse; 42T Paul Humann/Jeff Rotman Photography; 43 Tim Davis*; 44 Paul Steel/The Stock Market; 44–45 Al Giddings/Images Unlimited, Inc.; 45 Al Giddings/Images Unlimited, Inc.; 47 Elliott Smith*; 48 Dr. Ken C. MacDonald/Department of Geological Science, University of California; 51 Harvey Lloyd/The Stock Market; 52B WHOI, D. Foster/Visuals Unlimited; 52T Reter Ryan/Scrupps/SPL/Photo Researchers; 53 Deep Ocean Exploration and Research; 54L Stacy Pick/Stock, Boston; 54R Ken Karp*; 55B Paul Fusco/Magnum; 55T Nikolay Zurek*; 56L Breck P. Kent/Animals, Animals; 56R GHP Studio*; 57 Ken Lax*; 57R GHP Studio*; 58 Stephen Frink/The WaterHouse; 59 GHP Studio*

Special thanks to Marine Science Institute, Redwood City, California; Malcolm X Elementary School, Berkeley, California; Franklin Year-Round School, Oakland, California; Carl B. Munck Elementary School, Oakland, California; Hintil Ku Ka Child Care Center, Oakland, California.

*Photographed expressly for Addison-Wesley Publishing Company, Inc.

Illustrations

Molly Babich 40
Nea Bisek 8T, 23, 28, 43, 46, 59
Carlyn Iverson 10, 11, 12–13, 14, 15, 16T, 17, 18, 19, 20, 21, 25, 30, 32–33, 34, 35, 36, 37, 38, 39, 49, 50, 51
Maryland CartoGraphics 19
Jane McCreary 8B, 16B, 29, 47
Randy Vergoustraete 60–61

Text

40–41 From Jean Craighead George, *Shark Beneath the Reef* (New York: Harper & Row, 1989). Copyright ©1989 by Jean Craighead George. Reprinted with permission of HarperCollins Publishers.

You're in the final seconds of the game. Your heart is pounding. Your team gets the rebound and the ball is passed to you. Sweat drips down your chin as you turn and dribble the ball down the court.

Now you are only a few feet from the basket. You feel a sudden surge of energy. You leap and shoot the ball. It bounces off the backboard and falls cleanly through the basket. All those weeks of practice to get ready for the game have paid off. You've scored!

Recreation Center

Are you ready to have some fun? Do you like being active? Do you want to exercise and enjoy yourself at the same time? Then come to the recreation center!

Look around. There's a lot going on. Join a game of basketball or volleyball, or take a swim in the pool. There is also a track where you can run. Whatever you choose to do, you can get a good workout.

When you exercise, you breathe harder and your heart beats faster than when you are at rest. These changes occur because your body is working harder. When you are working harder, your body needs nutrients and oxygen to keep going.

Your lungs and your heart are part of body systems that transport raw materials to your body cells. Because their main function is moving nutrients and oxygen, these systems are called transport systems. Your cells use the nutrients and oxygen to produce the energy you need.

- How does exercise make your heart feel?
- How does exercise affect your breathing?
- What habits will help you stay healthy?

Unit F

TRANSPORT SYSTEMS

Activities

Features

Chapter 1

Circulation

You continue a fast-paced game of basketball. A player on the other team shoots and misses. You leap up, get the rebound, and dribble the ball quickly down the court. Your breathing is fast, and your heart is pounding. You fake a pass to a teammate and shoot. The ball spins on the rim and goes in—two points! No time to rest. You head back up the court, heart still pounding, ready to stop the other team from scoring.

Basketball certainly is good exercise. After the game, it takes several minutes for your heart to slow down and beat at its normal rate. What connection is there between exercise and the increase in heart rate that you experience? What other situations sometimes cause your heart rate to change?

SCIENCE JOURNAL In your Science Journal, list some things that cause your heart rate to speed up. Make another list of times your heart rate is slow.

Explore Activity

How does your pulse rate vary?

Process Skills
Measuring, Collecting data

Material

clock or watch
to measure seconds

Observe and Collect Data

1. In your Activity Journal, make a copy of the data table below. Place your fingers on the side of your neck under your jaw, as shown in the picture. Move your fingers around until you feel a beat. This beat is your pulse.

Activity	Pulse Beats in 15 Seconds	Pulse Beats in 1 Minute
Rest		
10 jumping jacks		
20 jumping jacks		

2. Sit quietly for several minutes, and then find your pulse. Use the clock or watch to count how many pulse beats occur in 15 seconds. Multiply your count by four and record this number as beats in one minute.
3. Do ten jumping jacks. Again, take your pulse for 15 seconds and multiply by four. Record your results.
4. Do twenty jumping jacks. Then take your pulse again for 15 seconds and multiply by four. Record your results.

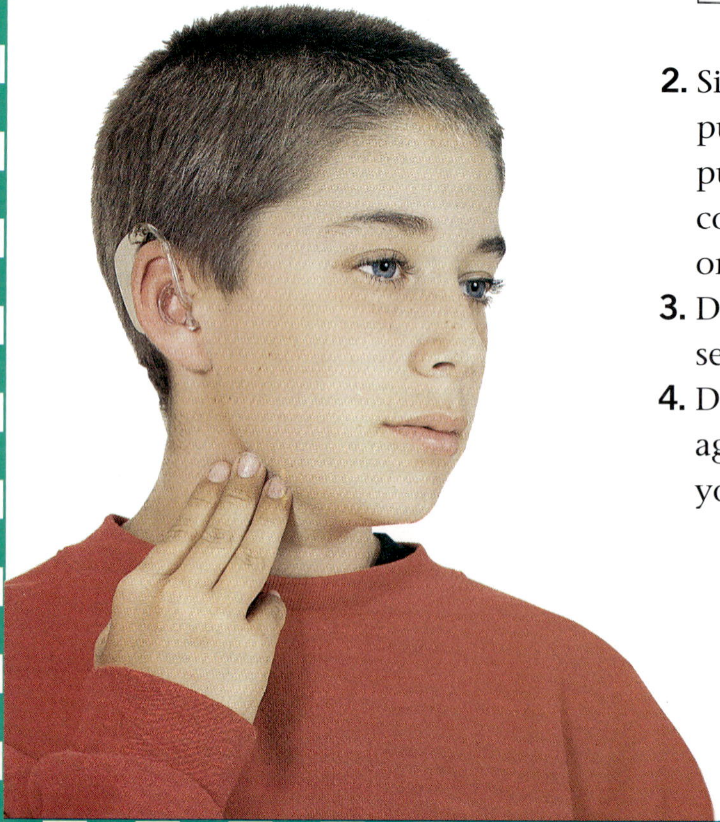

Share Your Results

Compare the pulse rates you recorded with those of two other students. How do your data compare?

Draw Conclusions

1. How does your pulse rate change when you exercise?
2. Why do you think your pulse changes?

Apply What You Know

1. **Predict** what your pulse rate would be after doing fifty jumping jacks.
2. Do you think that your pulse rate would keep rising as long as you exercised? Explain your reasoning.

What does your circulatory system do?

As you play basketball, your body is working harder than when you are at rest. Your legs need energy to run up and down the court. Your arms need energy to dribble and shoot. Your cells get this energy using the food you eat and the air you breathe.

Nutrients and oxygen, the ingredients your cells need to get energy, must be transported to every cell in your body. The system that transports these materials is called the

SCIENCE JOURNAL

Ask the adults in your home about sports and other physical activities they have enjoyed doing. In your Science Journal, make a list of these activities. Which ones do you think would make someone's heart beat fastest?

BACK HOME

circulatory (ser′kyo͞o lə tôr′ē) **system.** Your circulatory system includes your blood, your blood vessels, and your heart.

Your blood is a mixture. Part of your blood carries oxygen, which enters your body when you breathe in. Another part of your blood carries nutrients from digested food. There are also parts of your blood that fight infections. Different parts of your blood work together to form clots that stop cuts from bleeding.

Blood flows through tubes called vessels. Blood vessels are like hoses. If you bend a hose, the stream of water slows down. If you straighten it out, the water flows again. The same thing happens with blood vessels. Have you ever felt a tingling feeling in your hand or foot after sleeping on it or twisting it the wrong way? That tingling feeling is a message to your brain that your cells aren't getting enough oxygen.

Your heart is a muscle that pumps your blood. Your heart is like an engine that keeps your circulatory system running. It beats about sixty to eighty times per minute, day and night. It pumps faster when you play basketball or other sports in order to deliver more oxygen to your cells.

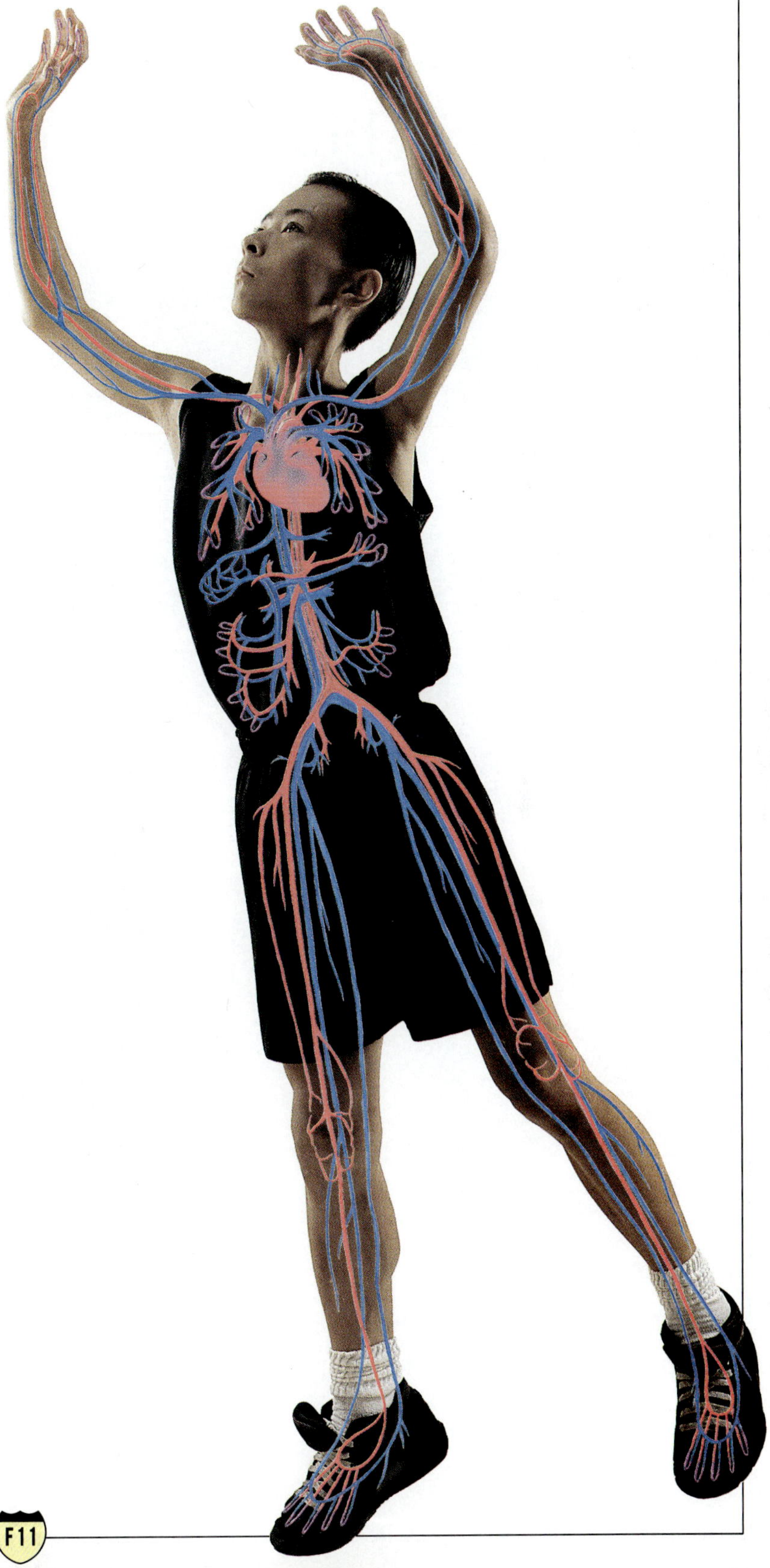

What is in blood?

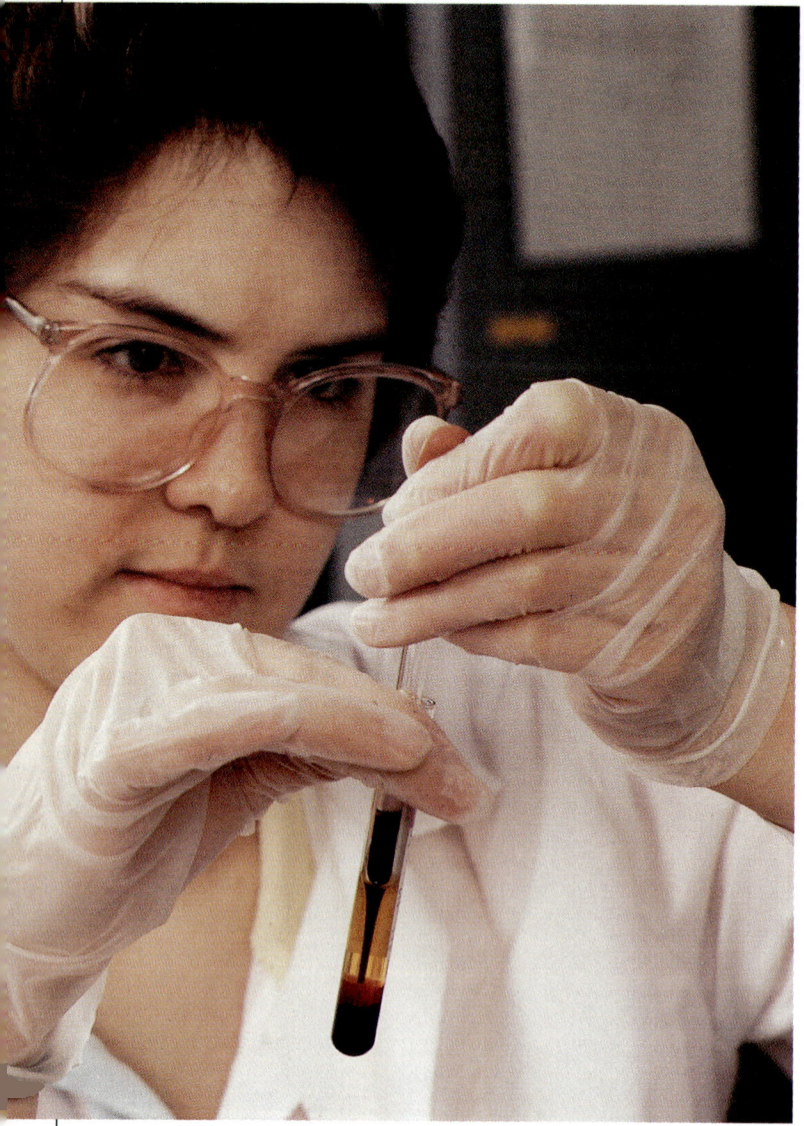

If blood is spun rapidly, the solid parts settle toward the bottom. Plasma is found at the top.

Blood transports oxygen, nutrients, carbon dioxide, and other materials through your body. Blood is a mixture of a liquid and several kinds of solids. An average adult carries three to five liters of blood in his or her body. The body replaces blood if some is lost. It is safe for healthy adults to donate blood several times a year. Encourage adults you know to donate blood.

The liquid part of blood is called **plasma** (plaz′mə). It makes up more than half of the volume of blood. Many people think that this part of the blood is red, but plasma is actually yellowish in color. The solid parts of your blood are what give it a red color.

Plasma consists mainly of water. In fact, it is more than 90 percent water. Plasma also contains sugar, salts, and some proteins. These substances are dissolved in the water making up plasma. One of the proteins in plasma, fibrinogen (fī brin′ə jən), is needed for blood to form a clot.

The solid parts of blood are made up of three kinds of cells: red blood cells, white blood cells, and platelets (plāt′lits). Your plasma is like a stream that carries the solid parts of your blood to and from your body cells.

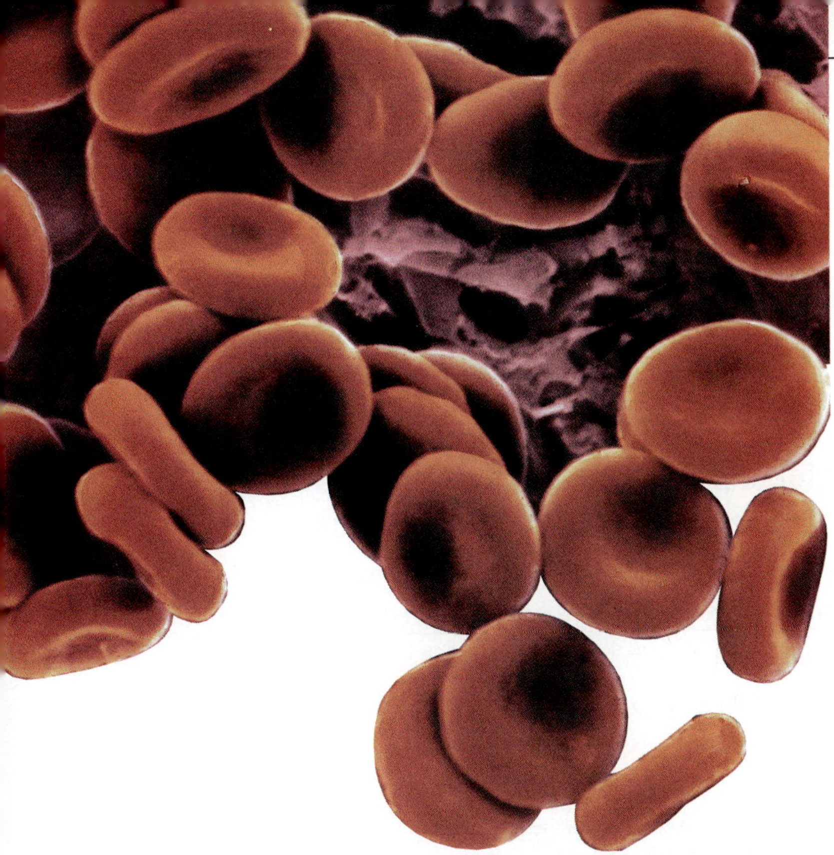

There are millions of red blood cells in each drop of blood.

Blood delivers oxygen to your body cells. **Red blood cells** are disk-shaped cells that carry oxygen. These cells contain a protein, called hemoglobin, that binds to oxygen. Red blood cells pick up oxygen as they pass through the lungs. When carrying oxygen, the cells turn bright red. After they pick up the oxygen, the red blood cells are pumped to the heart and then to the rest of the body. As they flow through the body, they release oxygen to the cells and pick up carbon dioxide from the cells.

When you play basketball or any other sport, your cells need more oxygen. So when you exercise, your heart beats faster, pumping more red blood cells to your muscles.

PEOPLE

Charles Drew

Charles Drew was a surgeon who developed a new way to store and preserve blood. This made it possible to save it for a longer period of time for blood transfusions. It saved the lives of thousands of wounded soldiers in World War II and continues to save lives today.

During World War II, Drew was the medical director of the Red Cross blood bank program. After the war, he taught surgery at Howard University and was chief of surgery at Freedman's Hospital.

What happens when you cut yourself?

You were diving for the ball, and you ended up skidding across the gym floor on your knee. The skin on your knee has broken and you are bleeding. Time out! Somebody get the first aid kit!

How can you stop a cut from bleeding? First, put a clean cloth or bandage over the cut. Then apply some pressure on top of the bandage. This should help the blood form a clot and the bleeding to stop.

Platelets are a part of blood that helps blood to clot. Platelets stick to one another at the wound. A tangle of protein fibers also forms at the break in the blood vessel. These fibers and platelets work together to form a clot. The clot seals the cut.

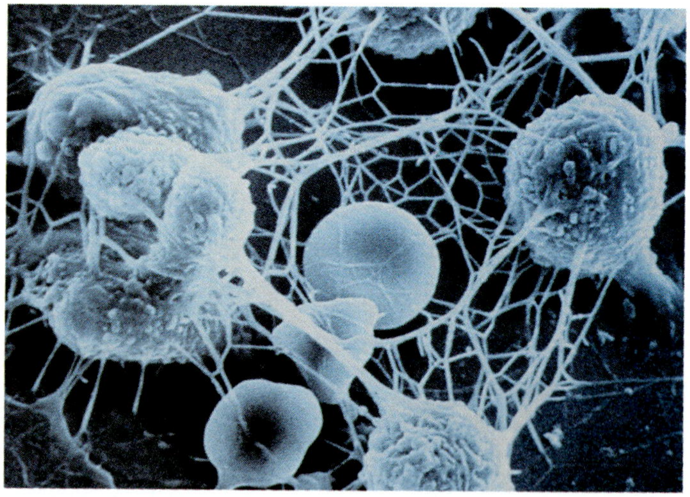

Platelets and protein fibers together form a clot. The clot stops the bleeding from a broken blood vessel.

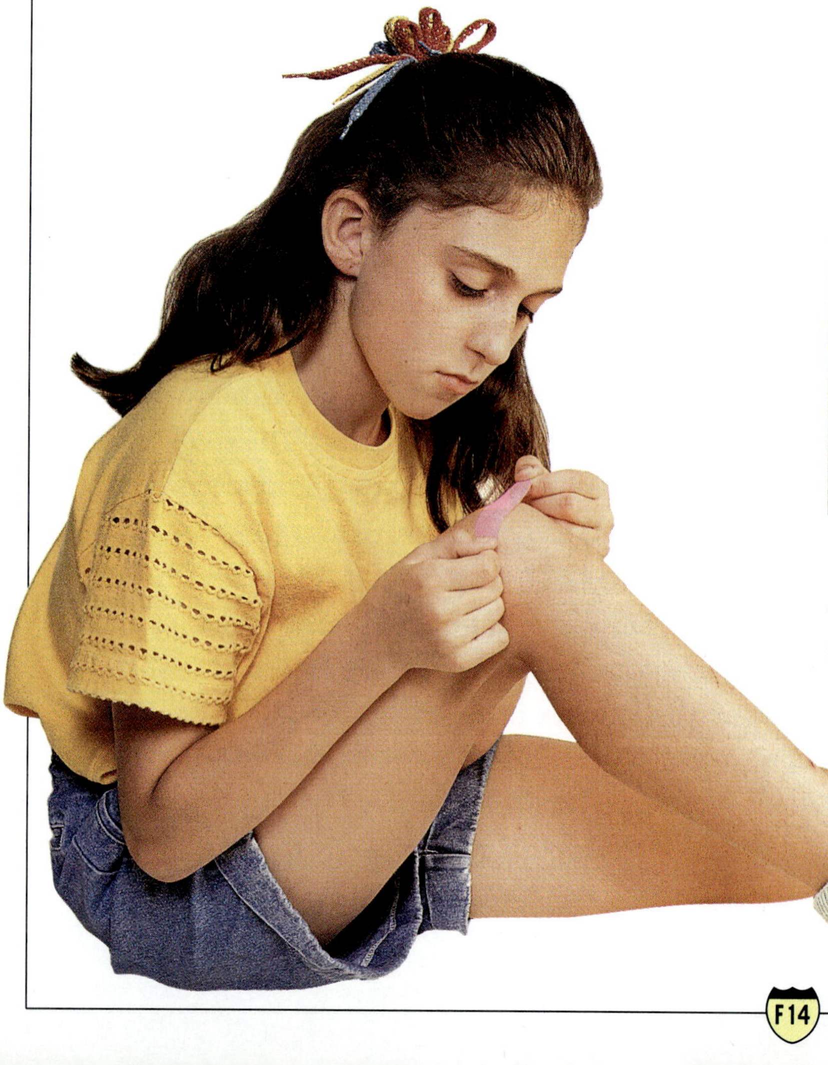

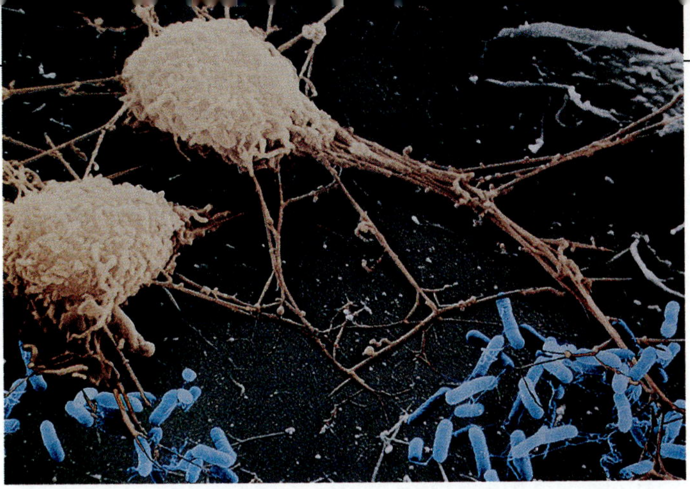

Some white blood cells surround bacteria and destroy them. In this photo the white blood cells are light and the bacteria are blue.

Before going back to the game, you ask the nurse to check the cut. He cleans your scraped knee and puts some antiseptic (an′tə sep′tik) on it. The antiseptic kills some bacteria that could cause infection.

A healthy body can also defend itself against invading bacteria. Blood cells that fight infection are called **white blood cells.** These cells kill bacteria that enter your body. White blood cells can also kill some of the bacteria that might make you sick.

A cut that is left dirty is more likely to become infected than one that is cleaned. If bacteria get into a cut, the white blood cells may not be able to kill all of the bacteria. In fact, some white blood cells might die. The pus in an infected wound is formed, in part, from dead white blood cells. A cut can heal more quickly if it does not become infected.

Be a Scientist

HANDS-ON ACTIVITY

What are the parts of blood?

1. Place a prepared slide of blood on the stage of a microscope.
2. Look at the slide through the microscope.
3. ACTIVITY JOURNAL In your Activity Journal, draw and label what you see.

How are you doing?

1. What is the function of the circulatory system?
2. What are the parts of blood and what do they do?
3. **Think** The virus that causes AIDS destroys some white blood cells. Why do people with AIDS have to watch out for infections?

What kinds of blood vessels do you have?

Your body has three kinds of blood vessels—arteries (ärt′ər ēs), veins (vāns), and capillaries (kap′ə ler′ēs). These vessels carry blood to and from every cell in your body. If all the blood vessels in your body were placed in a straight line, they would circle the earth four times.

Arteries carry blood away from the heart. As the heart pumps, it pushes blood into the arteries. This stretches the thick artery walls. When the heart relaxes, the artery walls spring back. This pushes blood along. The stretching out and relaxing of the artery walls is called the pulse. You can feel your pulse when you put your fingers against an artery in your neck. Can you find your pulse anywhere else?

From the arteries blood passes into tiny **capillaries.** As red blood cells flow through capillaries, oxygen and nutrients pass through the thin walls of the capillaries and into nearby cells. Capillaries also pick up waste products from the cells.

Artery
As the heart beats, blood is forced into two large arteries. These large arteries branch into smaller arteries. Arteries take oxygen to all parts of the body.

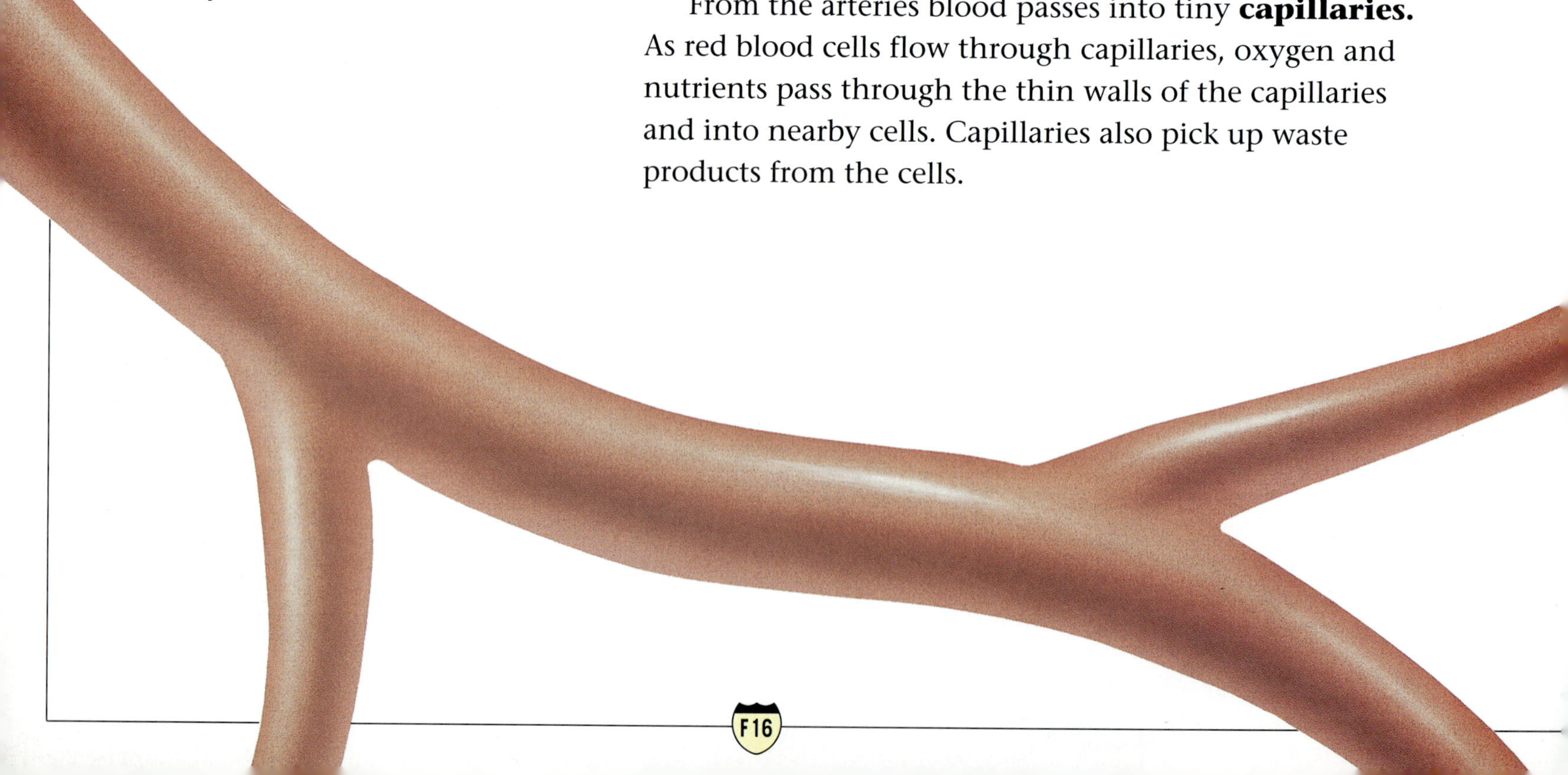

Veins carry blood to the heart. Muscles in your body help push blood through your veins toward your heart. Your veins contain one-way valves that keep the blood from flowing backwards, away from the heart. Some veins are close to your skin. If you look at the inside of your wrist, you might see some of your veins.

Vein

Blood that leaves the capillaries enters small veins. Small veins join together to form larger veins. Veins carry waste products away from body cells and back to the heart.

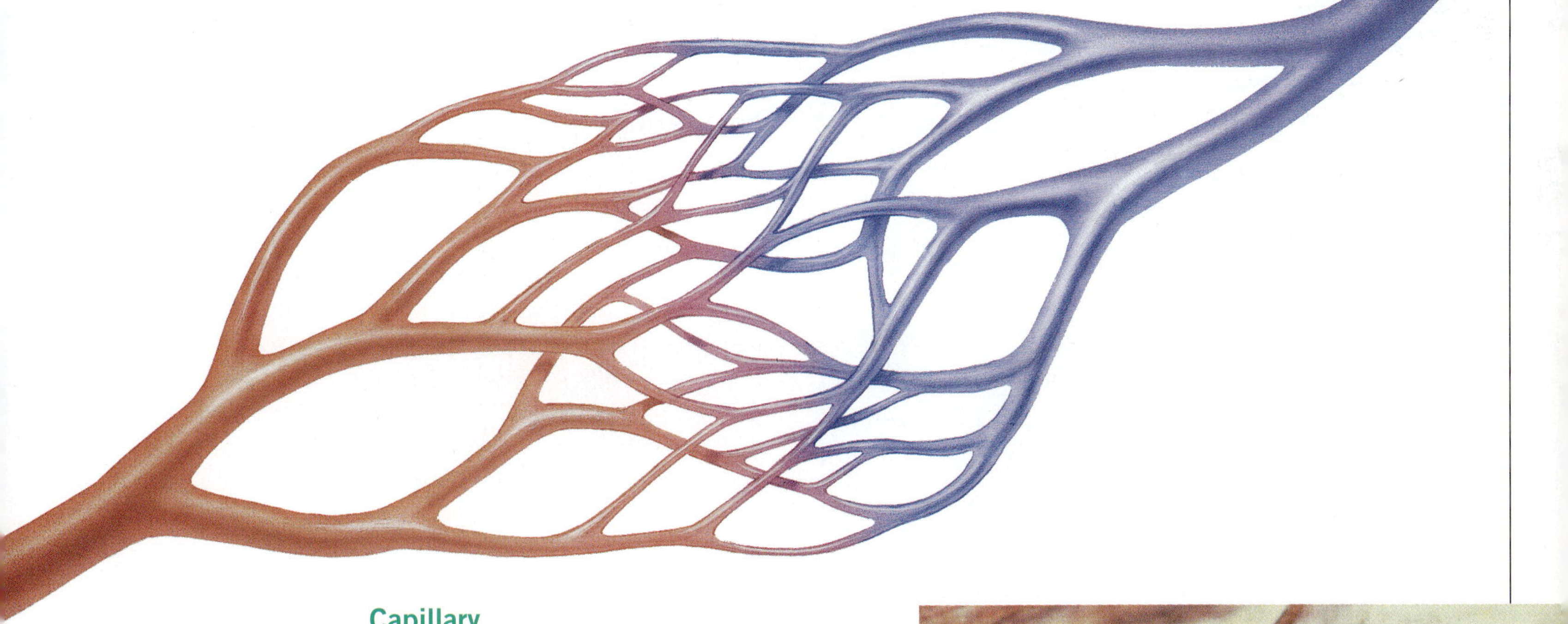

Capillary

Capillaries connect small arteries with small veins. Capillaries pass through all tissues of the body. They are so small that red blood cells must move through them in single file.

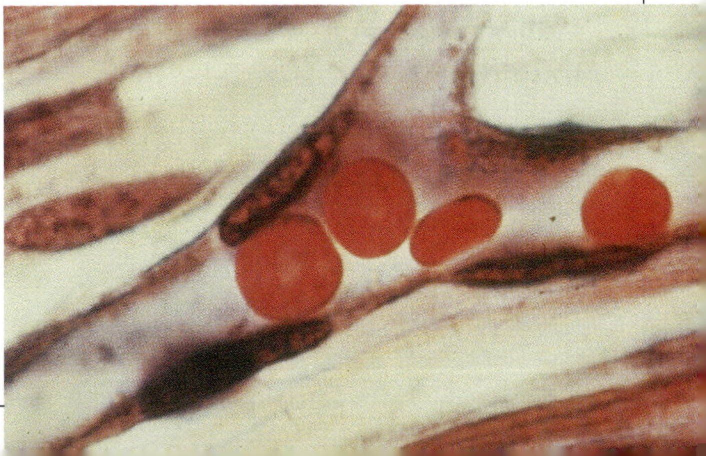

What are the parts of your heart?

Your leg muscles are working hard as you run up and down the court and jump at the net. The muscles in your arms are moving as you dribble, pass, and shoot. Which muscle in your body do you think is working the hardest? No matter what you're doing, the answer is: your heart.

Your heart is about the size of your fist. Place your fist slightly to the left of the center of your chest. Make sure your fist is level with your armpit. This is about the location of your heart within your body.

Inside your heart there are chambers. The chambers are called atria (ā'trē ə) (singular: atrium) and ventricles (ven'tri kəlz). The **atria** are chambers that receive blood coming into the heart. The atria pump blood into the ventricles. The **ventricles** are chambers that pump blood out of the heart.

Each heartbeat is actually two sounds. The sounds are often described as "lub-dub." The closing of the valves creates the sounds. Valves prevent blood from flowing back toward the heart. The "lub" sound is produced as the valves between the atria and ventricles close. The "dub" sound is caused by the closing of valves in the two large arteries that lead from the heart.

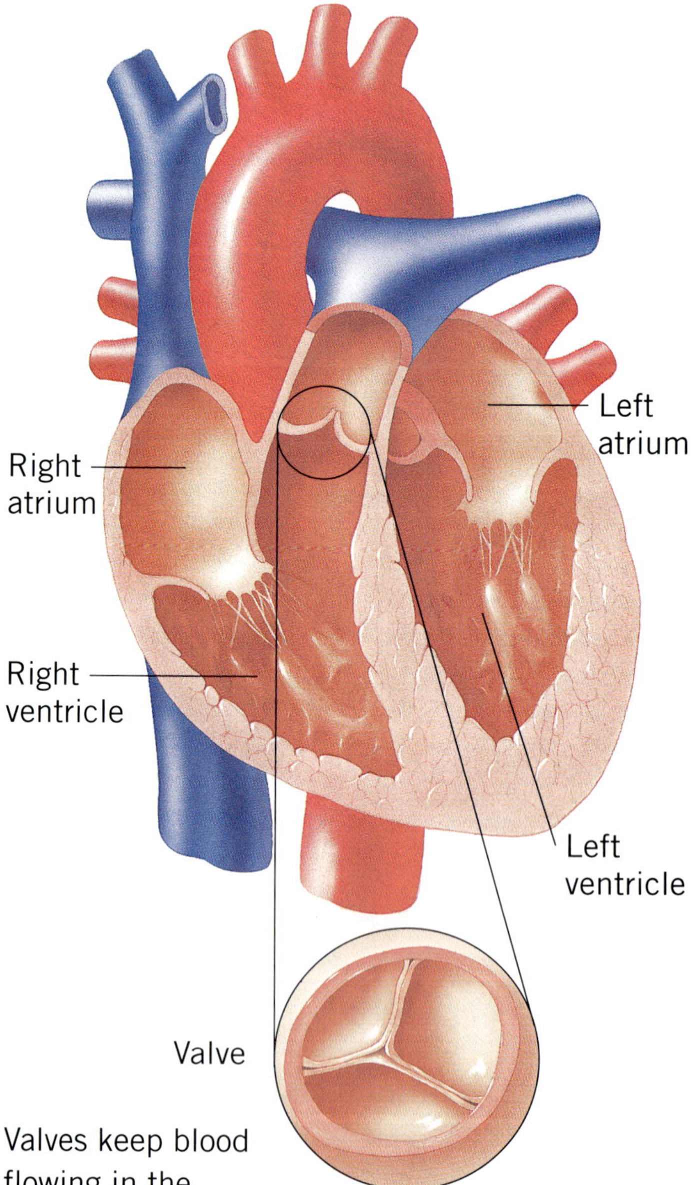

Valves keep blood flowing in the proper direction.

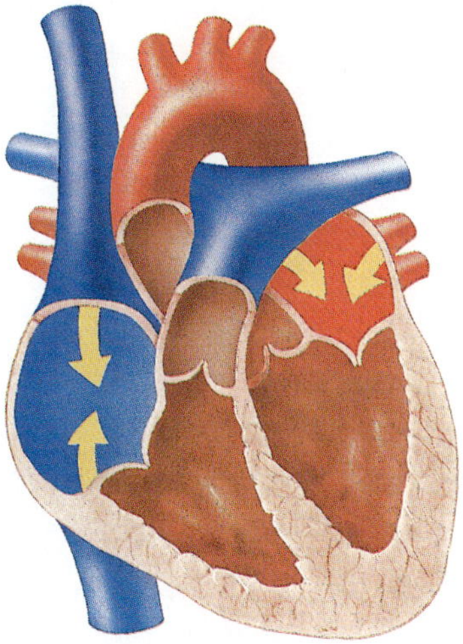

The atria receive blood from the body.

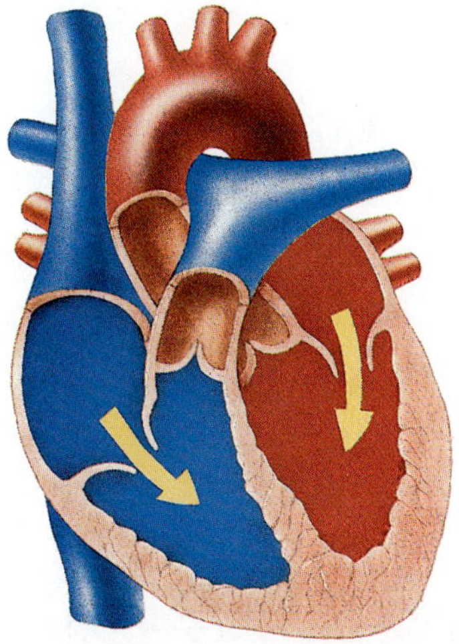

The atria pump blood into the ventricles.

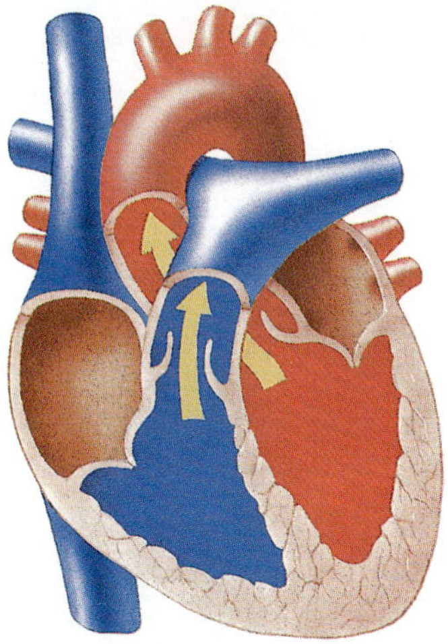

The ventricles pump blood to the body.

Be a Scientist

HANDS-ON ACTIVITY

How do heart valves work?

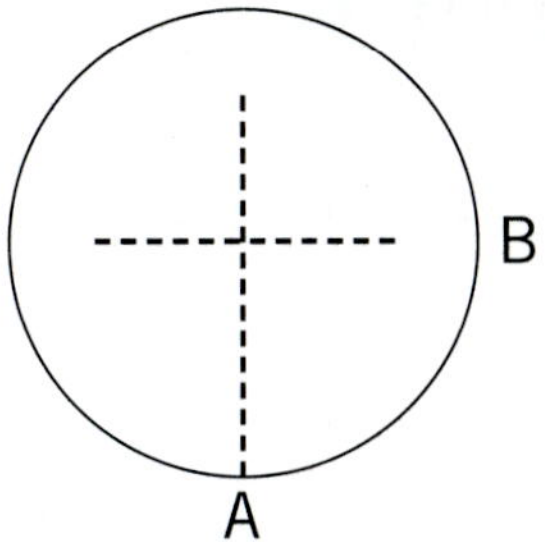

1. Cut a piece of paper into a circle. Cut slits into the circle as shown.

2. Form a cone by bringing point A to point B and taping them together.

3. ACTIVITY JOURNAL Try to push a pencil through the slit from the outside of the cone. Try again from the inside. Record your observations in your Activity Journal. How is your model like the valves in the heart?

Amazing!

It only takes about one minute for a blood cell to travel through your whole circulatory system.

What is blood's path around the body?

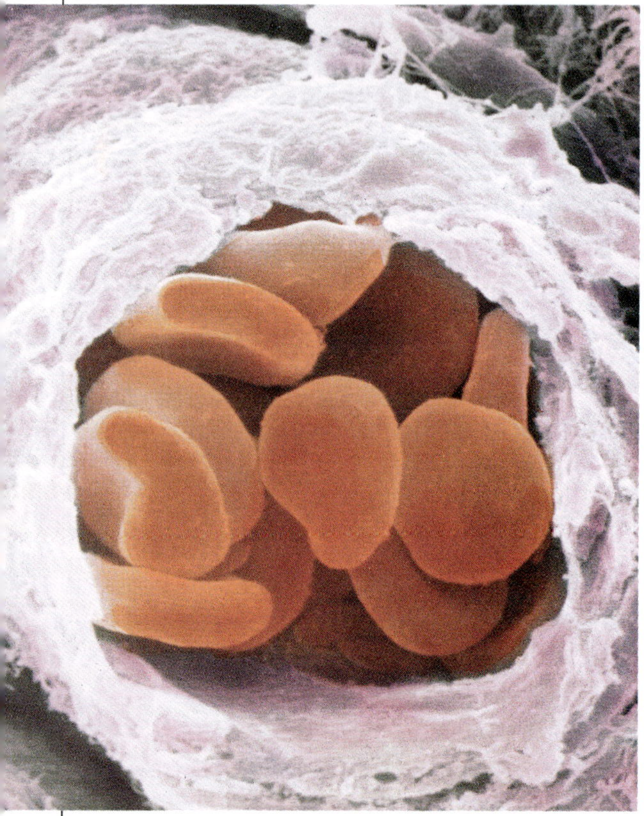

Oxygen-rich blood travels through arteries such as this one.

You've had a good workout at the recreation center. It's time for a shower and then some rest. Even as you relax, your heart will stay active, sending blood throughout your body.

The heart is really a double pump. The right side of the heart pumps blood to the lungs. The left side pumps blood to the rest of the body.

Two large veins receive blood from throughout the body and carry the blood to the right atrium. This blood contains carbon dioxide, one of the waste products blood picks up from the cells. The right atrium fills and then contracts, forcing blood into the right ventricle. The right ventricle contracts, forcing blood into an artery and then into smaller capillaries going to the lungs.

In the lungs, blood picks up oxygen and gets rid of carbon dioxide. Blood returns to the heart from the lungs through veins and fills the left atrium. The left atrium contracts, forcing blood into the left ventricle. The left ventricle contracts, forcing blood into a large artery called the aorta (ā ôr'tə).

The aorta branches into smaller arteries, like the trunk of a tree divides into smaller branches. The arteries carry blood to all the parts of your body. Small arteries branch into tiny capillaries. The capillaries then flow together to form small veins. The small veins continue to merge to form large veins. These large veins return blood to the right atrium where it starts the trip again.

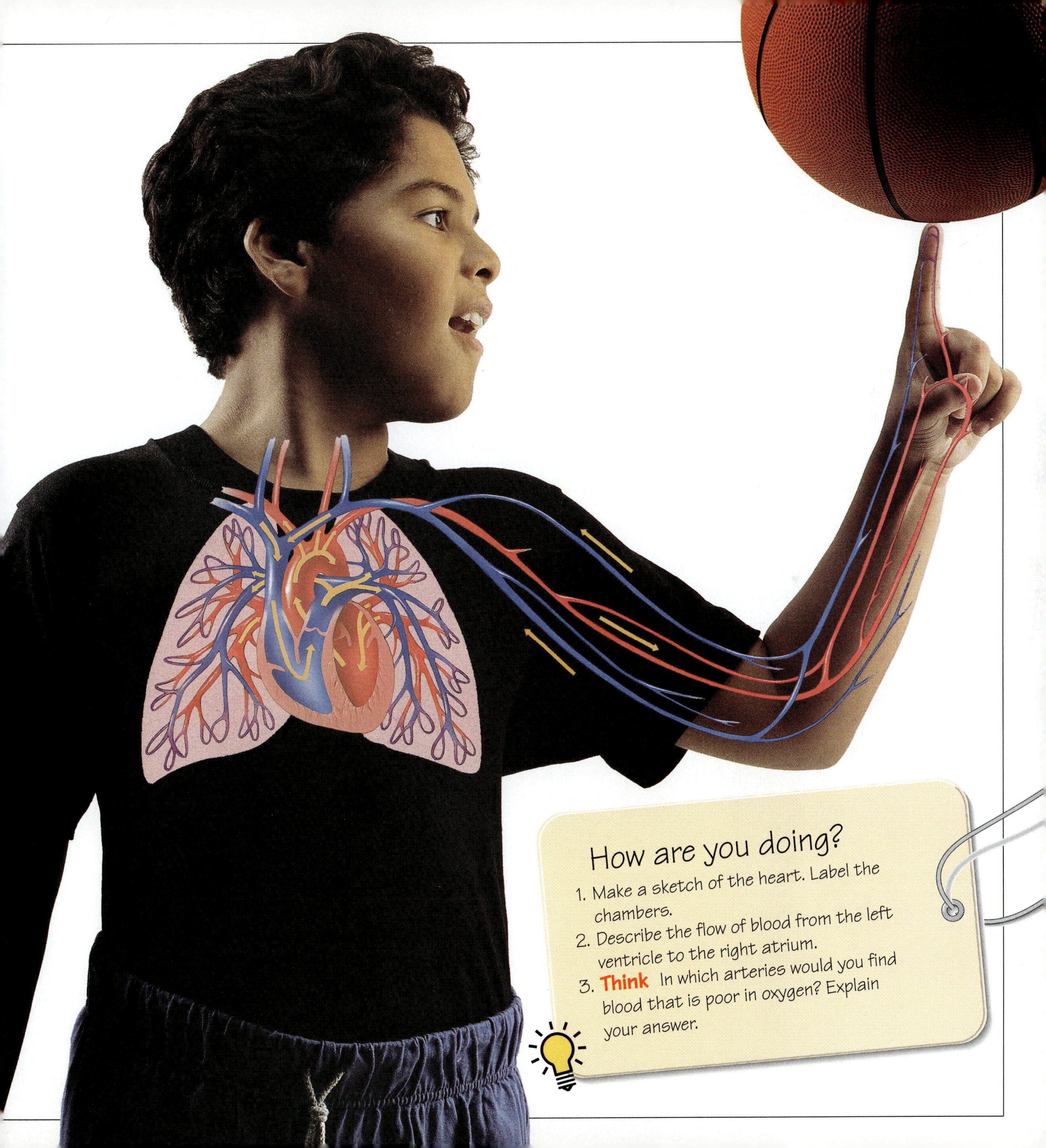

How are you doing?

1. Make a sketch of the heart. Label the chambers.
2. Describe the flow of blood from the left ventricle to the right atrium.
3. **Think** In which arteries would you find blood that is poor in oxygen? Explain your answer.

Science & Literature Connection

Racing the Sun

by Paul Pitts

The following excerpt is from a novel about a Navaho family.

"Brandon," Grandfather whispered, and his rough hand shook my shoulder.

"What?" I said almost in panic.

"It's time."

"Time?"

"To run."

I sat up. "You mean run as in 'to walk real fast, to jog'?"

"If you get up early each morning and run to greet the sun, you'll always be healthy and quick." . . .

I felt the bed wiggle as Grandpa lay back down on his bunk. My heart was racing. Maybe getting scared to death gave my circulatory system just as good a workout as running would. My heart slowed down, but my eyes stayed open. All right, I'll humor him, I thought. He's only going to be here for a few days. . . .

I started off at an easy lope. "Race the sun!" I heard him call softly before I reached the corner.

I ran for another block, then stopped to look at the sky. The old sun was in no hurry to rise. I walked for another block, then sat down on a bench at the bus stop to rest for a few minutes.

The sun finally peeked above the trees, so I started back. I set a pretty good pace so I was sweaty and winded by the time I reached my grandfather.

"What a great idea for Sunday morning," I puffed.

"That's good for the first time." Grandpa smiled. "Tomorrow you'll do better."

"Tomorrow! You want me to do this again?"

"The right way is to do it every day." He grinned at the stricken look on my face. "And tomorrow you must run the whole way so that you can greet the sun with pride."

Think About Your Reading

1. Which really gave Brandon's circulatory system a better workout: getting scared or running? How did you draw that conclusion?
2. List the main events in this excerpt in the order in which they occur.

Hypothesizing What changes would you feel in your body if you ran at least a half mile every day for two weeks? Write a hypothesis. If you can, try it. Record how far you run each day and how you feel.

Where to Read More

The Visual Dictionary of the Human Body, (Dorling Kindersley, 1991) See and read about your insides, from your nerve cells to your heart.

Looking Back

Words and Concepts

Match the statement with the letter that corresponds to the part of the circulatory system shown in the two diagrams on this page.

1. Vessels that carry oxygen-rich blood away from the heart to the body cells
2. Where blood from the lungs enters the heart
3. The organ that pumps blood
4. Vessels that take blood to the heart
5. The chamber of the heart that pumps blood throughout the body

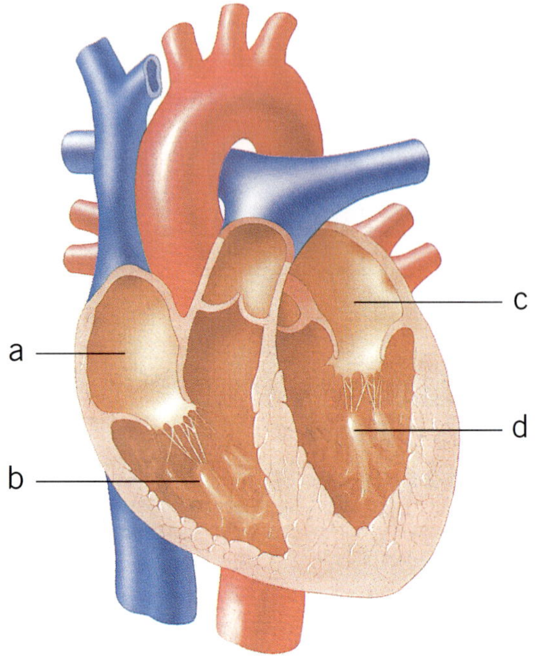

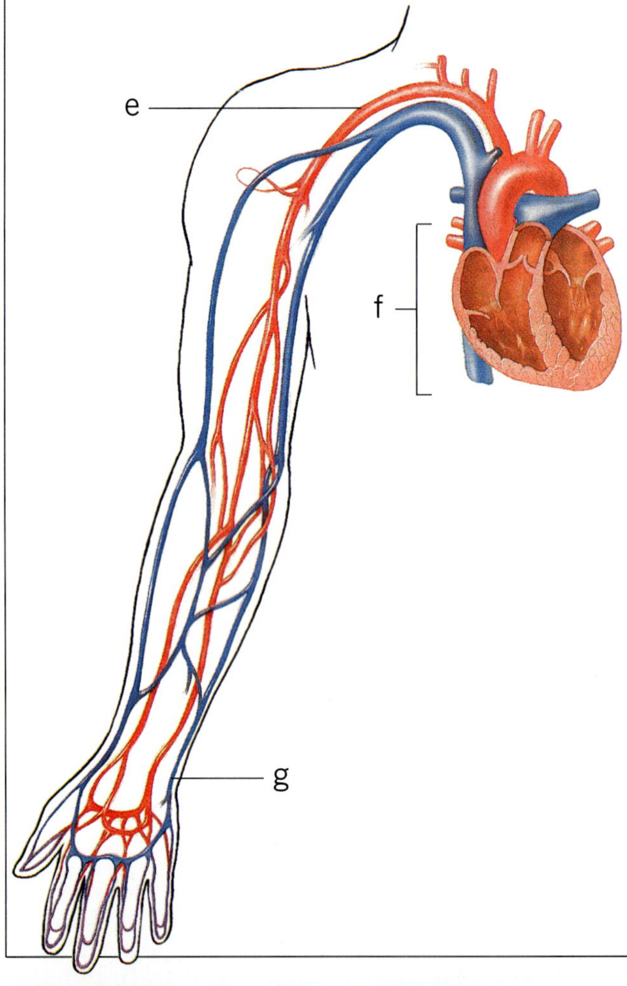

Applied Thinking Skills

Answer the following questions. You can use words, drawings, and diagrams in your answers.

6. Red blood cells are destroyed in victims of a disease called malaria. Why do you think victims of malaria might feel weak?
7. How are arteries, veins, and capillaries like a system of highways and local roads?
8. Do you think the number of white blood cells increases or decreases when you are sick? Why?
9. Compare the right atrium with the left atrium. Also compare the left ventricle with the right ventricle.
10. **Your World** Imagine that in the course of a day you took a walk, ate lunch, sat in class, and played basketball. At which point do you think your pulse was fastest? Explain your answer.

Show What You Know

What does your circulatory system look like?

Observe and Collect Data

1. Spread a large piece of butcher paper on the floor. Have your partner trace the outline of your body on the butcher paper.
2. Draw a heart in the outline. Divide the heart into four chambers. Label each chamber.
3. With the red yarn representing arteries and the blue yarn representing veins, tape yarn onto the paper to show the path of blood throughout the body.
4. Draw the lungs in the outline. Use the yarn to show the path that blood takes from the heart to the lungs and back.

Process Skill
Making models

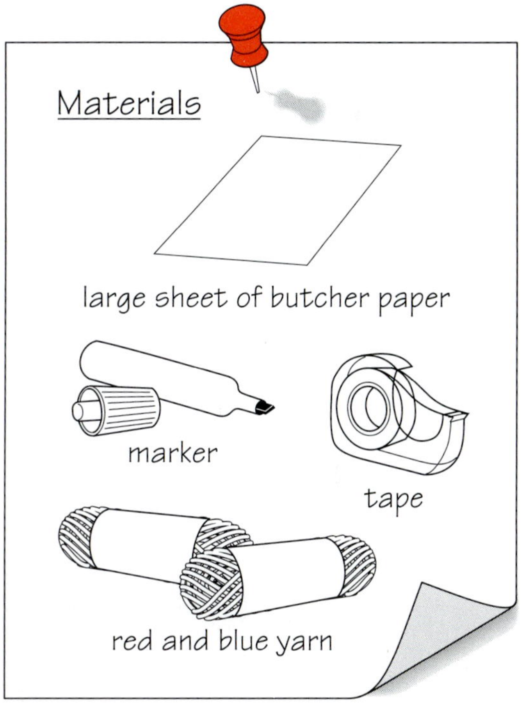

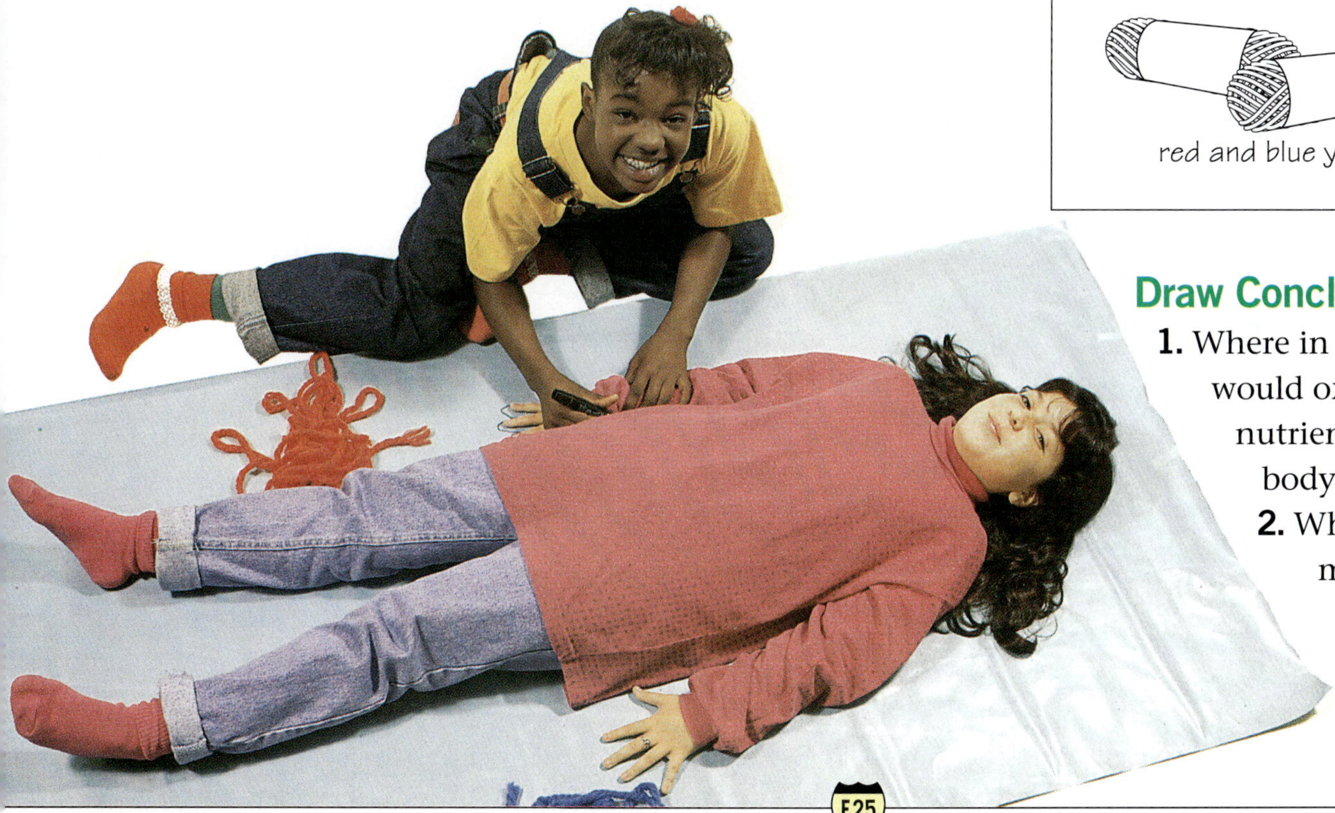

Draw Conclusions

1. Where in your model would oxygen and nutrients move into body cells?
2. Where in your model would carbon dioxide leave blood?

Chapter 2

Respiration

You feel strong as you dive into the pool. You cut through the water, legs kicking and arms swinging. At first you breathe after every two strokes, but after a few laps you breathe on every stroke. You are also breathing more deeply, taking in more air with each breath.

As you exercise, both your heart rate and your breathing rate are fast. The air that you breathe in contains oxygen. Your body needs a constant supply of oxygen. Red blood cells in your circulatory system transport oxygen from your lungs, through your heart, and then to the cells of your body. Red blood cells also transport carbon dioxide to your lungs so your body can get rid of it.

Oxygen and carbon dioxide are exchanged when you breathe. Breathing involves bringing air into the body. It also involves forcing air out of the body. How do you think the air that you breathe in is different from the air that you breathe out?

SCIENCE JOURNAL In your Science Journal, write what you think happens to air that enters your body. Also write how you think air you breathe in differs from air you breathe out.

LA
arena
SAN RAMON

Explore Activity

What is your lung capacity?

Process Skills

Measuring, Collecting data, Estimating

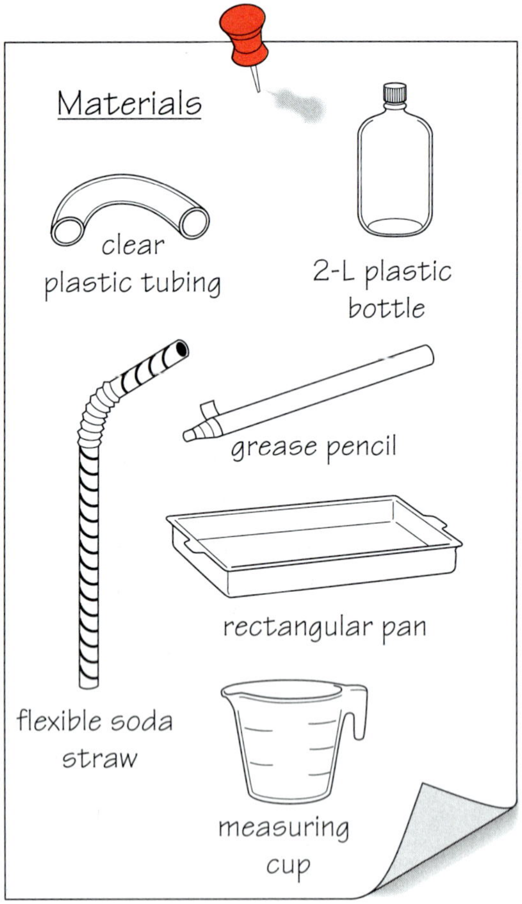

Observe and Collect Data

1. Use the measuring cup to add 250 mL of water to the bottle. Use the grease pencil to mark the water level and label it "250 mL." Repeat this procedure adding labels at measurements such as 500 mL, 750 mL, 1,000 mL, and so on until the bottle is full.
2. Add water to the pan to fill it halfway to the rim. Place your palm over the mouth of the bottle. While holding your palm against the mouth of the bottle, turn it upside down. Lower the bottle into the pan of water so that the mouth of the bottle is near the bottom of the pan. Carefully remove your hand and have your partner hold the bottle steady.
3. ACTIVITY JOURNAL Place one end of the plastic tube into the mouth of the bottle. Attach a flexible straw to the plastic tube. Using the marks you made, record the water level in the bottle in your Activity Journal. You may have to estimate if the water level is between markings.
4. Take a deep breath. Hold your nose and blow into the straw until you cannot force any more air out of your lungs. Note that water has been forced out of the bottle. Determine how much air is in the bottle by using the milliliter lines that you drew.
5. Throw the straw you used away and replace it with a new straw. Switch positions with your partner and repeat the activity.

Share Your Results

Compare your lung capacity with the lung capacity of several other students. What differences do you observe?

Draw Conclusions

1. How much air did you exhale?
2. What is your approximate lung capacity?

Apply What You Know

Do you inhale and exhale as much air during normal breathing as in this activity? Use your data to support your answer.

What does your respiratory system do?

The air is filled with oxygen, carbon dioxide, and other gases. To survive, you must exchange the air inside your body with the air outside your body. The system that transports air into and out of your body is called the **respiratory** (res′pər ə tôr′ē) **system.**

You breathe because your cells need oxygen to unlock the energy in food. Without oxygen, some cells would die in three to five minutes. When your body needs more energy, your cells need more oxygen. You breathe harder when you exercise in order to get more oxygen to your cells.

YOU CAN HELP

Burning charcoal pollutes the air. Lighter fluid and charcoal that contains lighter fluid are even worse for the air. Protect the air you breathe. If your family barbecues, encourage them to avoid using lighter fluid.

During one day a person breathes in and out as much as 12,000 liters of air. The air you breathe in is about one-fifth oxygen and contains almost no carbon dioxide. After your blood cells release carbon dioxide and absorb oxygen, the air in your respiratory system changes. The air you breathe out still has oxygen in it, but it contains more carbon dioxide than the air you breathed in.

While you're swimming, you must think about each breath as you decide when to lift your head above the water. Take a deep breath. Take a number of short, shallow breaths. You can control your breathing if you think about it. But you don't always control your respiratory system. When you sleep or when you're not thinking about it, your respiratory system keeps going, exchanging oxygen and carbon dioxide.

Breathing is controlled by a part of your brain called the respiratory center. This part of your brain is very sensitive to carbon dioxide. When the amount of carbon dioxide in your blood reaches a certain level, the respiratory center in your brain signals your body to breathe faster. This helps your body get rid of excess carbon dioxide and bring in more oxygen.

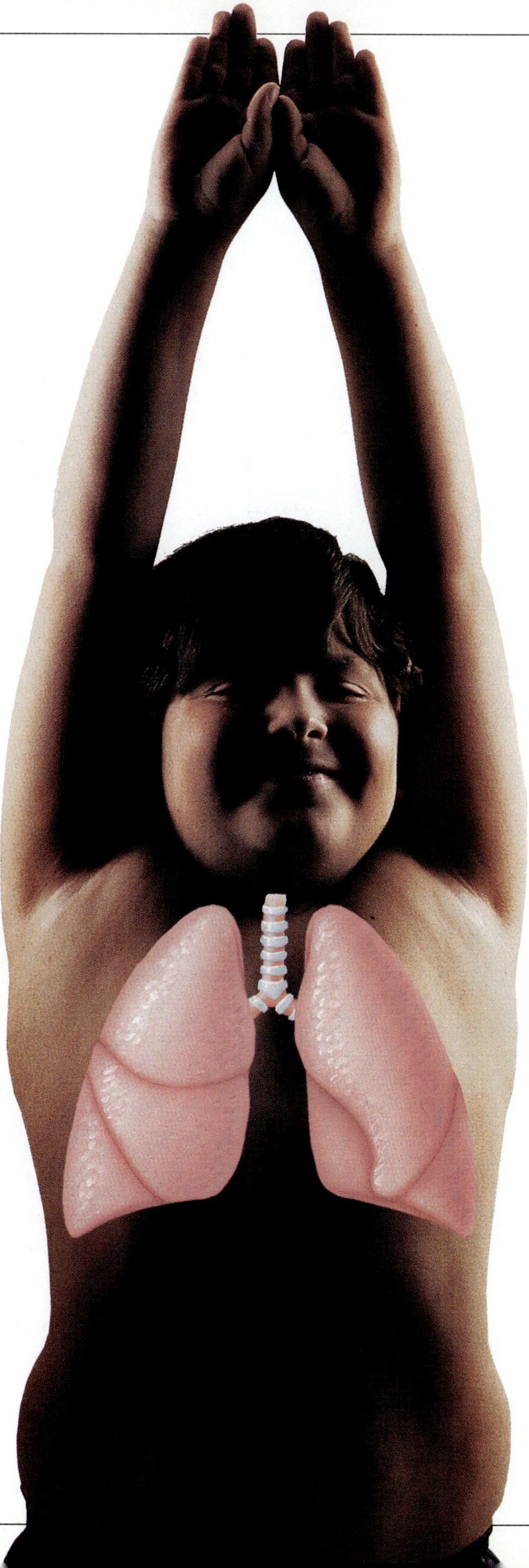

Be a Scientist

HANDS-ON ACTIVITY

How does exercise affect your breath?

Carbon dioxide causes bromthymol (brōm thī′môl) blue to change color from blue to yellow.

1. ⚠ Add 10 mL of bromthymol blue to a cup. Do not drink the bromthymol blue. It could make you sick.
2. Use a straw to blow into the cup. Note how long it takes for the bromthymol blue to turn completely yellow.
3. Add 10 mL of bromthymol blue to a second cup. Jog in place for two minutes. Use a straw to blow into the cup. Note how long it takes for the color to change this time. Does exercise affect the amount of carbon dioxide in the air you breathe out? Explain your answer.

How do you breathe?

When you swim, you breathe each time you lift your face out of the water. When you breathe in, you **inhale** (in hāl′). When you breathe out, you **exhale** (eks hāl′).

Your lungs do not have any breathing muscles. Your respiratory system uses the muscles surrounding the lungs to help you breathe. The muscles surrounding your lungs are called respiratory muscles. Respiratory muscles include your chest muscles and a muscle called the **diaphragm** (dī′ə fram′) that is below your lungs.

When you inhale, your respiratory muscles get tense, or contract. Your chest muscles pull your rib cage upward and outward when they contract. Your diaphragm flattens and moves downward when it contracts. When this happens, your chest cavity gets larger. Your lungs expand to fill this space and air is sucked in.

When you exhale, your respiratory muscles relax, making your chest cavity smaller. This forces air out. Your lungs are never empty. They keep about one breath's worth of air as a reserve. Place your hands on both sides of your ribs. Take a couple of deep breaths. What do you feel?

When you inhale, the respiratory muscles contract. As space inside the chest increases, air rushes into the lungs.

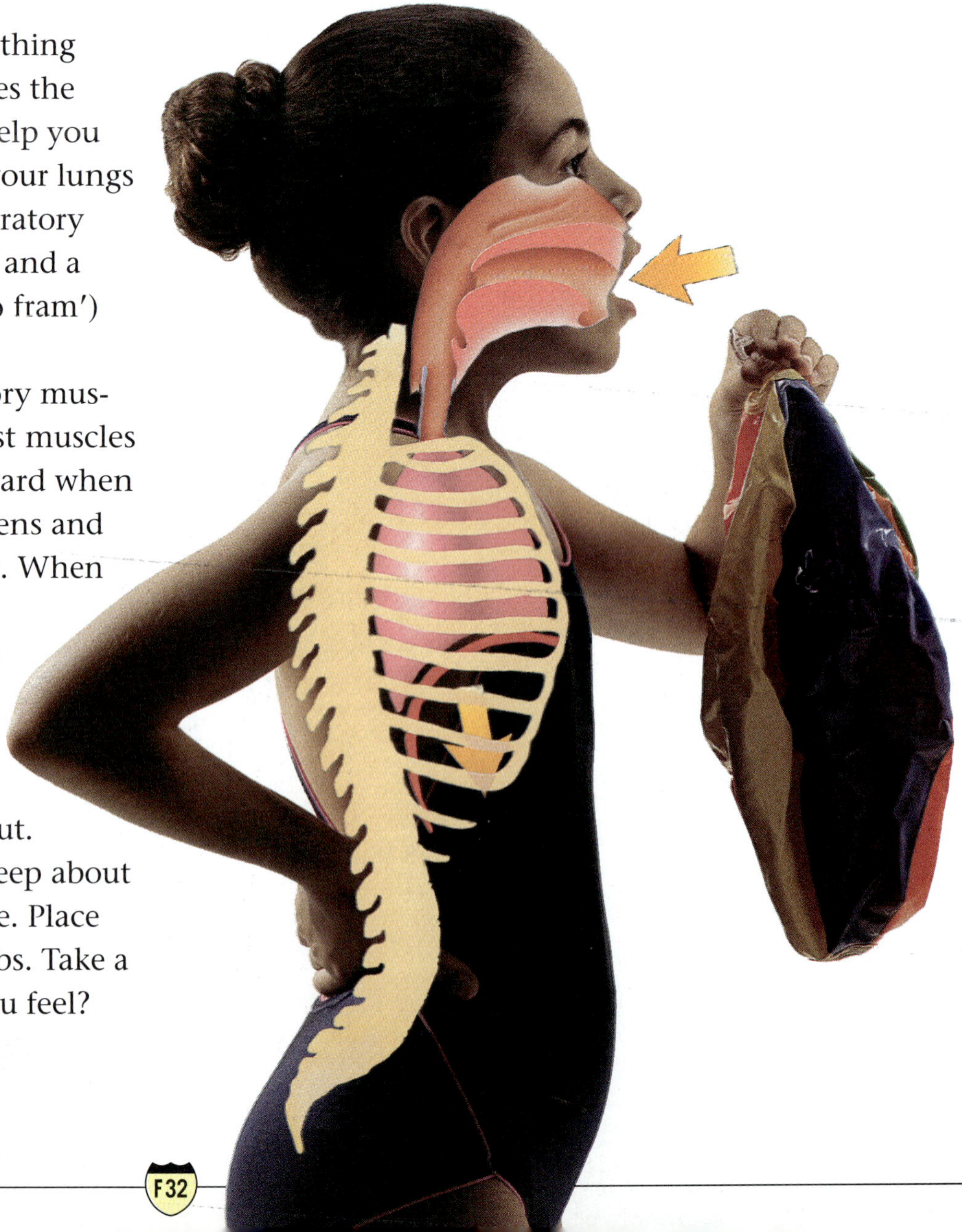

When you exhale, the respiratory muscles relax. As the chest cavity shrinks, air is pushed out of the lungs.

SCIENCE JOURNAL Take home some balloons and ask each member of your family to see how full he or she can make a balloon with one breath. Who has the greatest lung capacity? Record your observations in your Science Journal.

BACK HOME

How are you doing?

1. What two gases are exchanged by the respiratory system?
2. Describe what happens when you inhale and exhale.
3. **Think** How does the movement of the diaphragm change during exercise? How does this let more air into the lungs?

What is the path of air in and out of the lungs?

You are breathing heavily as you climb out of the pool. After resting for a few minutes, your breathing rate returns to normal. But whether you are breathing normally or rapidly, the path that the air takes in and out of your body is the same.

You can breathe in and out through either your nose or your mouth. Your nose is designed not only to smell what is in the air, but also to change the air that enters your body. Air is warmed up as it travels through your nasal passages. The mucus in your nose moistens the air. Tiny hairs inside your nose also help filter dust, smoke, and other solids from the air.

Sometimes you breathe through your mouth. The air that enters your respiratory system this way might not get as warm or well-filtered as air that enters through your nose. Breathing through your mouth has its advantages, however. You are able to take in more air at a faster rate through your mouth than you can through your nose. When do you breathe through your mouth? When do you breathe through your nose?

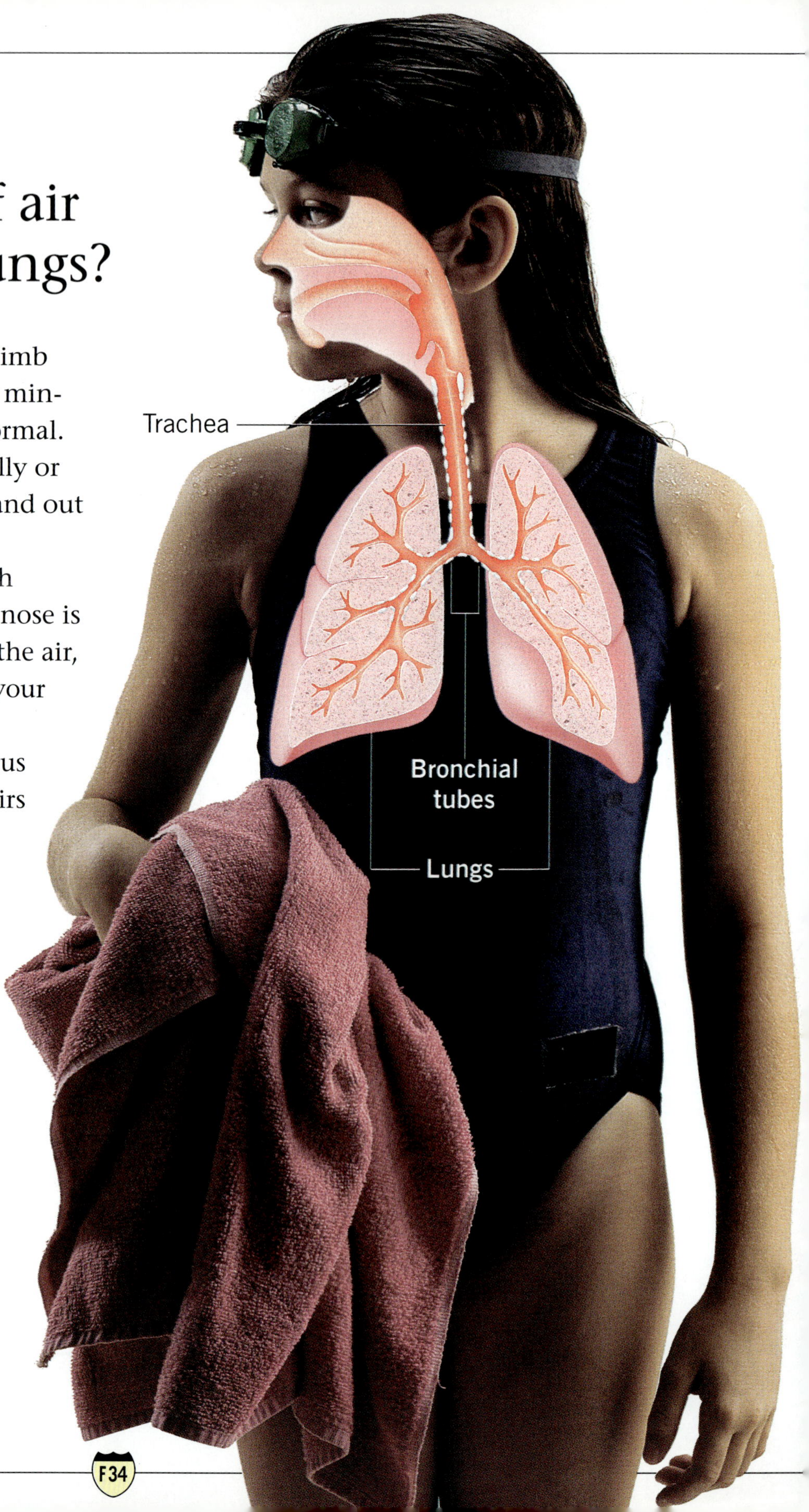

After air comes into your mouth or nose, it is funneled into the throat. Your throat, like your nose, is lined with mucus and tiny hairs that filter the air. Your throat connects your nose and your voice box. Your voice box contains your vocal cords. The sound you make when you talk is caused by the vibrations of your vocal cords.

From the throat, air passes through the **trachea** (trā′kē ə), or windpipe. The trachea has rings around the outside. These rings are made of strong, flexible tissue. You can feel them when you touch your neck. These rings help keep the trachea open as you turn your head or bend your neck.

In the chest, the trachea divides into two tubes called **bronchial** (brän′kē əl) **tubes.** One bronchial tube enters each lung. The bronchial tubes branch off into hundreds of smaller tubes. Some of these tiny bronchial tubes are thinner than the period at the end of this sentence.

The **lungs** are spongelike organs. They inflate with air when you breathe in. They deflate as you breathe out. Each lung is about the size of a football.

SIDE TRIP

The Snack Shop

Choking usually occurs when food becomes stuck in the trachea. Coughing is your body's way of trying to get the stuck food out of your throat. If coughing doesn't get the food out, the best way to remove an object that is stuck in the trachea is the Heimlich maneuver.

Some restaurants post a chart showing how to perform the Heimlich maneuver. Does your school cafeteria or nearby snack shop display such a chart?

Where are oxygen and carbon dioxide exchanged?

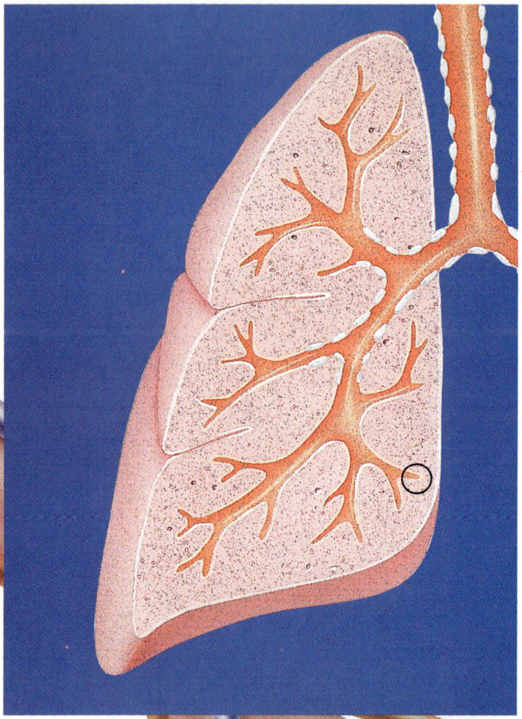

After you rest, you dive back into the water. As you swim across the pool, an exchange of gases is going on between your lungs and the outside environment. When you swim underwater, you hold your breath. But deep inside your lungs an exchange of gases is taking place that never stops.

You've learned that the bronchial tubes branch off into smaller tubes. These tubes in the lungs end in clusters of tiny spheres called **air sacs.** There are about 300 million air sacs in a pair of lungs.

Groups of air sacs look like small bunches of grapes.

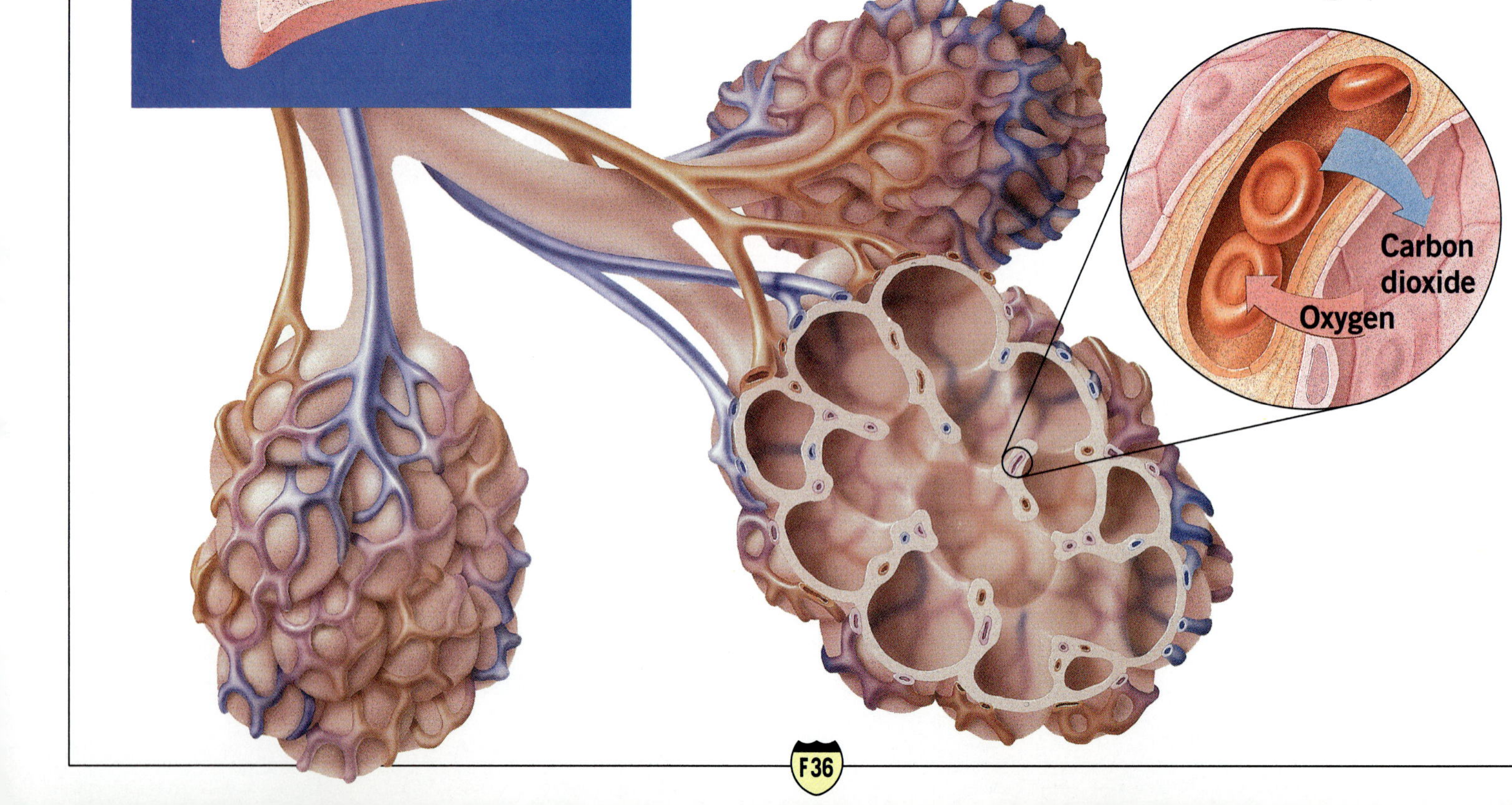

The walls of air sacs and the walls of capillaries are both very thin. Air sacs are so thin that if 500 air sacs were flattened and stacked on top of each other, they would only be as thick as this page. Because the walls of air sacs and capillaries are so thin, oxygen and carbon dioxide can pass through them.

The gas exchange occurs through a process called diffusion (di fyo͞o′zhən). In diffusion, matter tends to move from areas of higher concentration to areas of lower concentration. After you inhale, the air sacs have a high concentration of oxygen. Blood in the capillaries, on the other hand, has a low concentration of oxygen. Oxygen therefore moves by diffusion from an air sac into the capillary that surrounds it. When it enters the lungs, blood has a higher concentration of carbon dioxide than the air sacs. Carbon dioxide therefore moves from a capillary to the air sac.

This exchange of gases between a capillary and an air sac takes less than a second. After gases are exchanged, carbon dioxide that has been released into the air sac leaves the lung by the same path the oxygen-rich air entered the lung.

Be a Scientist

HANDS-ON ACTIVITY

How does oxygen get into blood?

1. Add three drops of green food coloring to a small cup of water.
2. Fold a paper towel several times. Put several drops of the green water on top of the paper towel.
3. ACTIVITY JOURNAL After a minute, observe the bottom surface of the towel. Record your observations in your Activity Journal. How is this similar to what happens in the air sacs?

How are you doing?

1. Describe the path that air takes into and out of the lungs.
2. Make a diagram that shows what happens to air that enters the air sacs.
3. **Think** How might your breathing rate be affected if you were in a room where the amount of oxygen in the air was slightly less than normal? Why?

VIEWPOINT

The Effects of Emotions

Does your heart beat or breathing rate ever increase when you're not exercising? Emotions can affect your circulatory and respiratory systems. Think about how you feel when you watch an athletic event or a scary movie. Compare your heart beat and breathing rate when you watch an exciting athletic event to your heart beat and breathing rate when you are exercising.

SCIENCE JOURNAL

In your Science Journal, write about a time you felt strong emotions. Did these feelings affect your heart beat or breathing rate? Do you always react the same way to similar situations? Check your pulse and breathing rate next time you get tense or excited, and see how your circulatory and respiratory systems are affected by emotions.

Data Collection and Analysis

MATH CONNECTION

How many Calories are used in different activities?

Oxygen is needed to release energy from food. But some activities use more energy—and therefore, more oxygen—than others. The following table compares the oxygen used in different activities.

Activity	Oxygen Used per Hour (L)	Calories Released
Basketball	90	450
Bicycling	55	
Dancing	100	
Jogging	120	
Sitting	25	
Swimming	120	
Walking	60	

Observe and Collect Data

1. ACTIVITY JOURNAL The energy released from food is measured in Calories. About five Calories of energy are released for each liter of oxygen used. In your Activity Journal, copy the table above.
2. Calculate the Calories released by multiplying the amount of oxygen used in an activity by five. Use your results to fill in the Calories released column in the table in your Activity Journal.
3. Make a bar graph that shows the number of Calories used per hour for the activities listed in the table.

Draw Conclusions

1. How much energy is required to dance for an hour, compared with sitting for an hour?
2. How much energy is used to play basketball for two hours?
3. Which activities would you recommend to someone who wants to burn many Calories? Explain your reasoning.

Looking Back

MINDS-ON ASSESSMENT

Words and Concepts

Match the letters on the diagram of the respiratory system with the descriptions below.

1. Small spheres at the end of the bronchial tubes
2. Chambers with thin walls where carbon dioxide leaves the blood and oxygen enters the blood
3. The tube in your throat through which air enters and leaves the chest area
4. Two branched tubes that carry air into each lung
5. Two large lobes where oxygen and carbon dioxide are exchanged

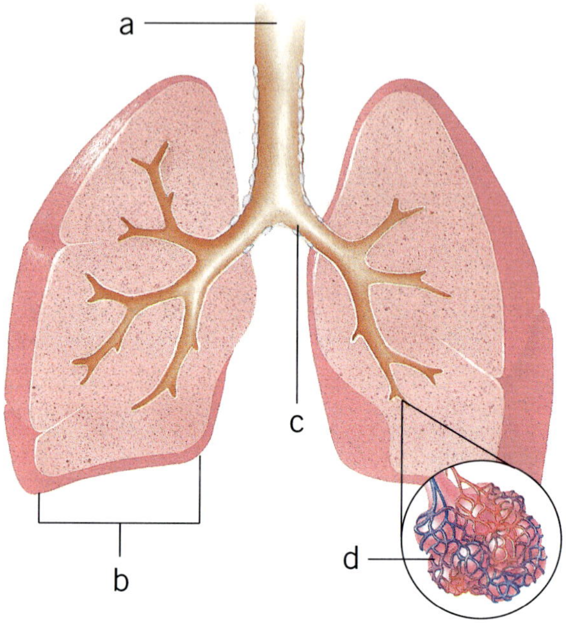

Applied Thinking Skills

Answer the following questions. You can use words, drawings, and diagrams in your answers.

6. Describe what happens to your lungs and respiratory muscles when you inhale and when you exhale.
7. What is the main function of the respiratory system? How do the circulatory and respiratory systems interact?
8. Describe how oxygen and carbon dioxide are exchanged in the respiratory system.
9. How is the air you inhale different from the air you exhale? Why is it different?
10. **Your World** Breathing exercises can help bring more air into your lungs with each breath. How might this help you in athletic competition?

Show What You Know

How does the diaphragm work?

Observe and Collect Data

1. Attach the small balloon to one end of the straw with the rubber band.
2. Slip the other end of the straw through a hole in the bottom of the cup so that the small balloon dangles inside the cup. Seal the hole around the straw with a bit of clay.
3. Cut the neck off the large balloon. Stretch the large balloon tightly over the open end of the cup.
4. Pull down slowly on the large balloon and observe what happens to the small balloon.

Draw Conclusions

Use your model to explain how the diaphragm causes breathing to occur.

Process Skills
Making models,
Defining operationally

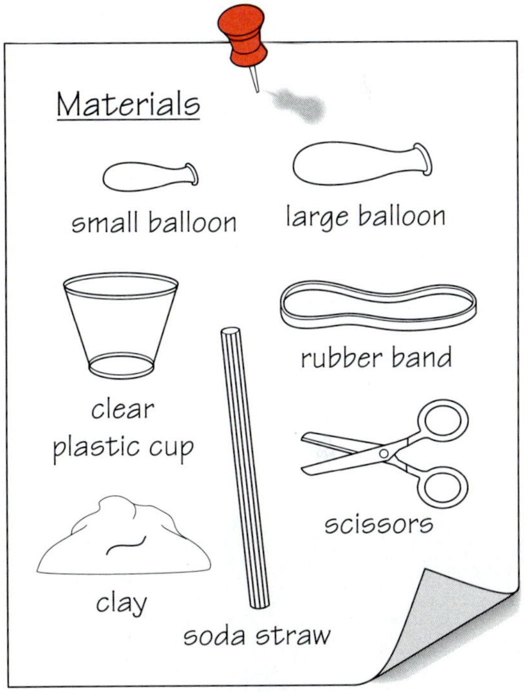

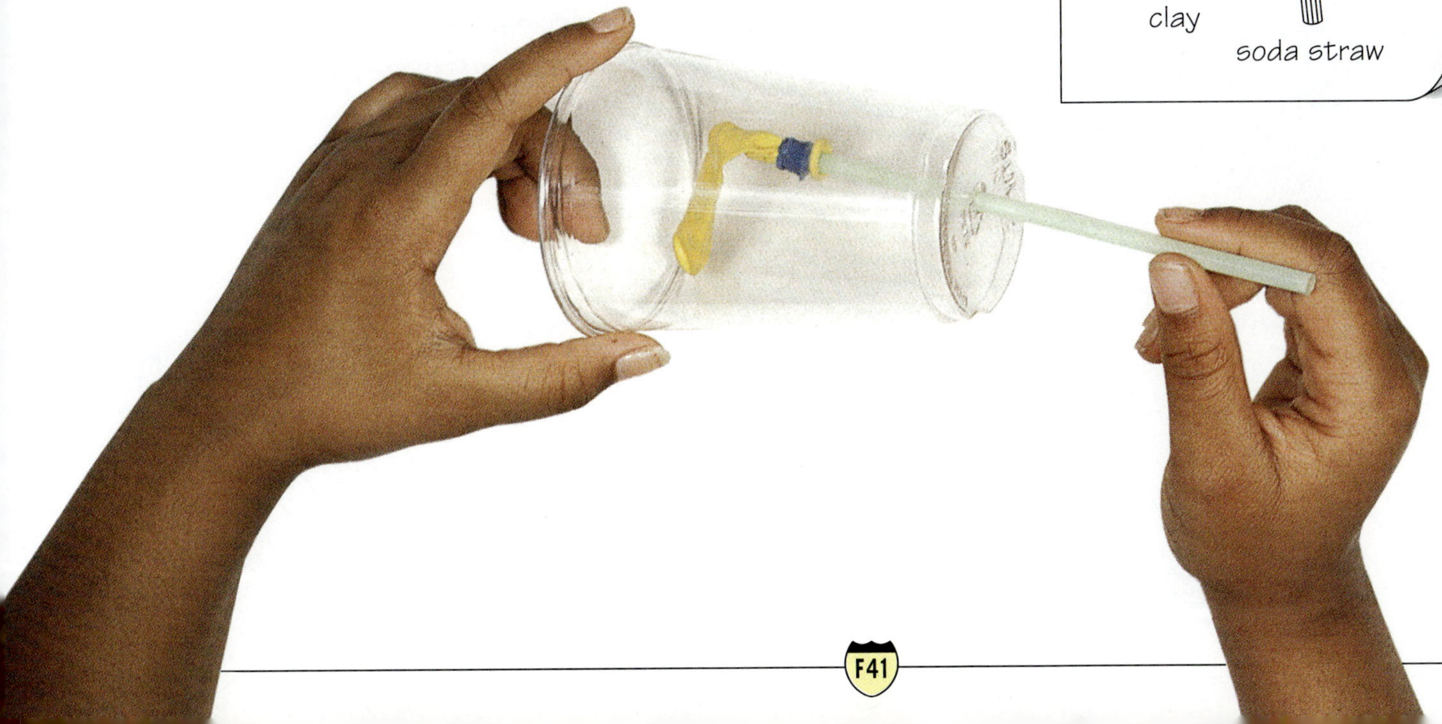

Staying Healthy

Are you going to the recreation center tomorrow? If you are, you may be choosing fun and good health at the same time. Healthful habits begun at an early age can mean better health when you are older.

You spend a couple of hours at the recreation center several days a week. Your muscles get a good workout playing ball or swimming. It's great fun. But did you know that it's also good for your circulatory system and respiratory system? Exercise keeps these systems in shape, which in turn helps keep you healthy.

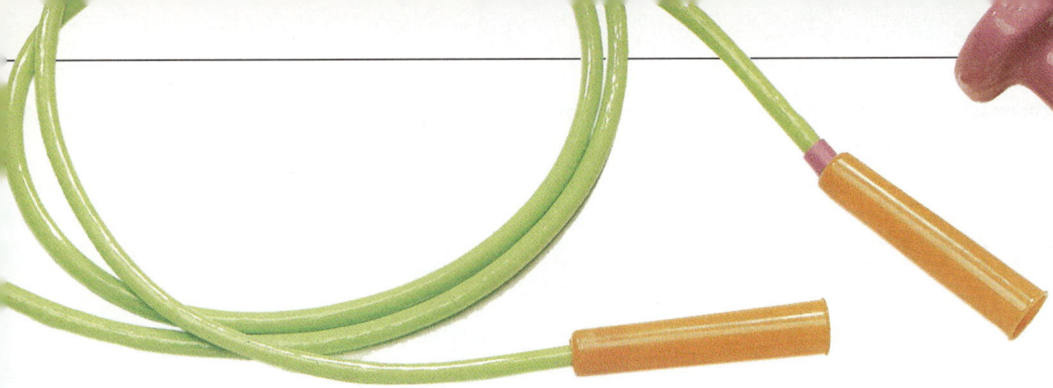

Good habits can help you maintain or improve the health of your transport systems. Having efficient circulatory and respiratory systems will not only help you excel at the recreation center, but it will also give you more energy at home and at school. Good health habits will also help prevent problems with your transport systems. Good health habits include eating healthful foods, exercising regularly, protecting yourself from harmful bacteria, and not smoking.

You are influenced by messages, such as those in ads and commercials, to make certain choices. Watch for messages about the health of the circulatory system and respiratory system. Also watch for messages in ads for products that might hurt these systems.

In your Science Journal, record the kinds of messages that you see and hear. Which kinds of messages are most common?

Explore Activity

How can you prevent bacteria from being spread?

Process Skills
Observing, Inferring, Predicting

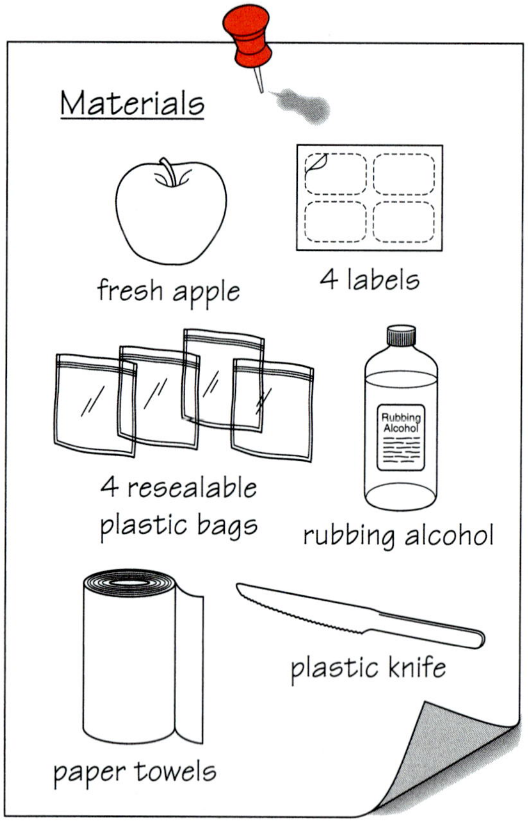

Observe and Collect Data

1. Use the labels to number the plastic bags.
2. Cut the apple into four sections using the plastic knife. Breathe on one section. Place this section in bag 1. Rub your hands on a second section. Place this in bag 2. Wash a third section in water and dry it off. Do not touch this section after it has been washed. Handling it with a paper towel, place this section in bag 3. Use a paper towel to clean the last section with alcohol. Place this section in bag 4 without touching it.
3. ACTIVITY JOURNAL **Predict** what the apple sections will look like in one week. Record your prediction in your Activity Journal.
4. Store the bags in a dark place for one week.
5. After a week, compare the apple sections. Record your observations in your Activity Journal.

Share Your Results

Compare your results with those of other students. Did all the apple sections change in the same way? If not, how did they differ?

Draw Conclusions

1. What do you think caused the changes that you saw in the apple sections?
2. How might some germs be spread?

Apply What You Know

What are some steps you could take to help to stop the spread of germs?

How does exercise affect your circulation?

All of the running and playing you do at the recreation center exercises your muscles. But you don't have to go to the recreation center to exercise. You can go for a walk, ride a bike, dance, and do other physical activities. Exercise strengthens your muscles, and your heart is your hardest-working muscle. Exercising several times a week helps keep your heart healthy and strong.

Your heart is a powerful pump. As blood rushes into the arteries when the heart contracts, the arteries expand from the force of blood. The force of blood against the walls of the arteries is called blood pressure.

Blood pressure goes up when you exercise. This rise in pressure is normal. Some people, however, have higher than normal blood pressure almost all the time. Such high blood pressure is a disease called hypertension (hī′pər ten′shən). Over many years, hypertension weakens arteries. Blood pressure can be checked easily, so everyone should have it checked regularly.

There are ways you can reduce your chances of having hypertension. Both smoking and eating too much salt can cause your blood pressure to rise. Don't smoke, and limit the amount of salt in your diet. Regular exercise will also help to keep your blood pressure normal.

Your pulse rate increases when you exercise. It returns to normal some minutes after you stop exercising. Regular exercise can result in a slower resting pulse. A slower pulse usually means that the heart does not have to work as hard.

Exercise makes your heart stronger. A strong heart can pump more blood with each beat. This means the heart can rest longer between beats. Exercise also stimulates the growth of more blood vessels in the heart.

Career Corner

Emergency Medical Technician

Have you ever seen an ambulance crew in action? The people who staff the ambulance are emergency medical technicians, or EMTs. My name is Jane Smith and I started my career as an EMT. Today I teach high-school graduates the skills they need to become EMTs.

EMTs give first aid to people who are sick or injured and help get them ready to be moved to a hospital. We have radios in the ambulance so we can discuss with doctors the best ways to treat our patients.

How does diet affect your circulation?

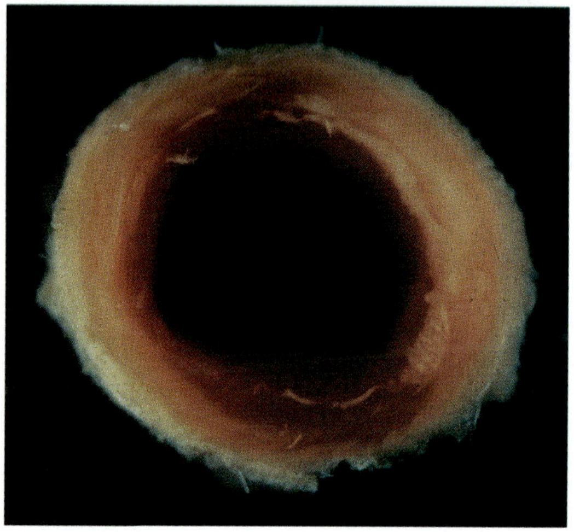

Normal artery

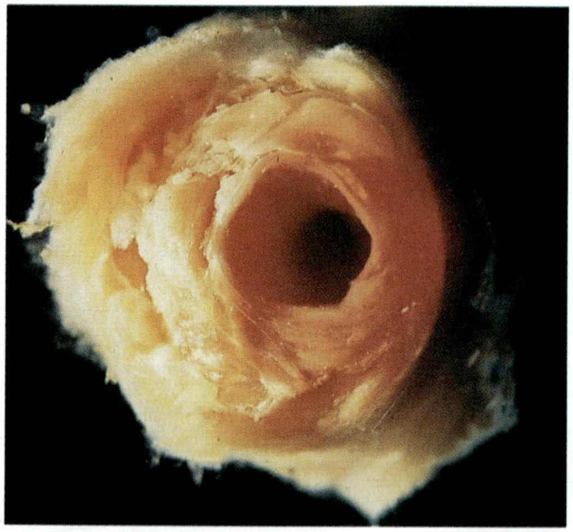

Clogged artery

The physical activities that you do at the recreation center and elsewhere help to keep your circulatory system in good shape. What kinds of food do you eat after you exercise? Your choice of food also affects the health of your circulatory system.

Over many years, eating too many foods that are high in fat can damage your circulatory system. After food is digested, fats can float around your bloodstream. Sometimes fats will attach to the inside of artery walls. If fats build up, the passage through the artery will get narrow. If the passage becomes totally blocked, the flow of blood will be stopped.

If an artery carrying blood to the heart muscle becomes blocked, the heart muscle may die. Your heart muscle, like the rest of your body, needs oxygen to function. The heart cannot do its job if a large area of heart muscle dies. When this happens, it is called a heart attack. If blood flow is not restored to the heart muscle, the heart attack victim may die.

Foods high in fats usually come from animals. Foods from plants, such as fruits and vegetables, are lower in fat and better for your circulatory system.

To have a healthy heart and circulatory system as an adult, you need to make the right choices now. Exercise and a sensible diet are two of the most important things you can do to keep your circulatory system healthy today and in the future.

Instead of this:	Eat this:
Doughnut	Toast and jam
Fried chicken	Baked chicken
Ice cream	Frozen fruit bar
French fries	Baked potato
Whole milk	Skim milk
Sour cream	Yogurt
Peanuts	Popcorn
Waffle	Oatmeal
Potato chips	Pretzels

Be a Scientist

MINDS-ON ACTIVITY

What is your plan for staying healthy?

ACTIVITY JOURNAL

Design an activity program that will help keep your heart and circulatory system healthy. The program should involve exercise. You can vary the activities from day to day. Be sure that the activities exercise the heart muscle. Encourage your classmates to join you in your program. Record your activity program in your Activity Journal.

What kinds of activities are best for exercising the heart? After using your program for a week, decide if you need to improve it.

How are you doing?

1. How does exercise help make the circulatory system healthy?
2. What is hypertension and how can it be avoided?
3. **Think** What would you tell a friend who says the amount of fat you eat is important only if you already have heart disease?

How can you help your respiratory system?

Like the heart, the diaphragm is a muscle. Exercise strengthens the diaphragm. Exercise also increases the lungs' capacity, meaning the lungs can take in more air. This makes the respiratory system more efficient because more air sacs can be used.

Exercising helps the fitness and health of your respiratory system in other ways too. A stronger diaphragm can work longer and harder. This means that you can do hard physical activity for a longer time without tiring. For example, you can swim or run faster and farther. When you sing, you can hold a note longer. A stronger diaphragm helps supply more oxygen to your body even when you are resting.

Have you ever had a "stitch," or a pain in your stomach, during exercise? Sometimes this pain is the result of a cramp in your diaphragm muscle. The best way to get rid of this cramp is to lift your hands over your head. This stretches out your diaphragm muscle. The stronger your diaphragm muscle, the less likely it is to get a cramp.

For the next minute, count the number of breaths that you take. You know that your breathing rate goes up when you exercise. An athlete in top condition may have a low resting breathing rate. But during physical activity, an athlete's breathing rate may triple. This increase is a sign of the fitness and health of the respiratory system. A healthy respiratory system supplies a lot of oxygen to the body with little effort.

Hiccups seem to be caused by a series of brief muscle spasms of the diaphragm. How does your family cure hiccups? Compare your family's cures with those of your classmates' families.

BACK HOME

Aerobic activity, such as running, is one of the best ways to keep your respiratory system in shape.

What's in the air you breathe?

Bacteria, dust, pollen, and other particles that float in the air are brought into your body with every breath. Your body has defenses against these particles.

Your nose contains hairs that filter these particles from the air. The tubes of the respiratory system are also lined with tiny hairs, called cilia (sil′ē ə), and a layer of mucus. The mucus traps particles that you breathe in and the cilia push them out of the system.

When there are too many particles in the air, your body will produce extra mucus. Your body will also try to get rid of irritating particles by coughing or sneezing.

Be a Scientist

HANDS-ON ACTIVITY

What are your air filters?

1. Fill a cup with water and add several pinches of dirt. Cover the bottom of a baking pan with petroleum jelly.
2. Tilt the end of the pan. Slowly pour the dirty water through a wad of cotton into the pan.
3. ACTIVITY JOURNAL Examine and describe the cotton and the petroleum jelly. In your Activity Journal, describe how your nose and its mucus filter the air.

Keep your germs to yourself. Always cover your mouth and nose when you sneeze and wash your hands to stop the spread of viruses and bacteria that cause respiratory infections.

The most common respiratory problem is the common cold. There are more than one hundred different kinds of viruses that cause the common cold. Viruses and bacteria can cause other illnesses such as tuberculosis, pneumonia, and strep throat.

Plants usually release pollen into the air in the spring and in the fall. Some people are allergic to pollen. This allergy causes some of the same symptoms you have when you have a cold.

Air pollution can also irritate your respiratory system. Cars and factories are a major source of air pollution.

YOU CAN HELP

To reduce the amount of air pollution, ride your bike, take public transportation, or walk instead of having someone drive you someplace.

How are you doing?

1. Identify some ways exercise increases the health of the respiratory system.
2. How does the respiratory system clean the air that enters the body?
3. **Think** What might happen to your health if you didn't have hair and mucus to filter the air?

How does smoking affect circulation?

As you are leaving the recreation center for home, you notice a sign that you've seen before. You read the words *No Smoking* and look at the symbol above the words. Of course, the sign means that smoking is not permitted. Smoking is dangerous for the person who smokes. It also is dangerous for nonsmokers who are near people smoking.

Cigarette smoke contains more than 4,000 different chemicals. Not all of the effects of these chemicals are known, but many are poisonous. Three of these poisonous chemicals in cigarette smoke are nicotine, carbon monoxide, and tar.

SCIENCE JOURNAL

Find out if anyone you know was a smoker who gave up the habit. Ask the person if it was difficult to quit smoking. Ask the person how he or she feels about having given up cigarettes. Record his or her responses in your Science Journal.

BACK HOME

In America, 390,000 people die each year from smoking-related diseases.

When a body needs a substance, it is called addiction. Nicotine is the chemical in cigarettes that causes people to become addicted to cigarettes. Nicotine reaches the brain a few seconds after a person inhales cigarette smoke. This temporarily satisfies the cigarette smoker. But the nicotine eventually breaks down. The tissues of the brain begin sending the signal to send more nicotine.

Nicotine causes arteries to become narrower and blood pressure to rise. It also speeds up the heart rate by ten or more beats per minute, so the heart is working harder but the body's cells are getting less blood.

Smoking also damages the blood vessels and increases the chances of having a stroke. People who smoke a pack of cigarettes a day are twice as likely to have a heart attack or stroke as are nonsmokers.

Carbon monoxide is inhaled in cigarette smoke. Carbon monoxide attaches to red blood cells, just as oxygen does. However, carbon monoxide's ability to attach to red blood cells is 250 times stronger than oxygen's ability, and carbon monoxide displaces the oxygen. So the heart is pumping blood around the body but the blood holds less oxygen! This is why many smokers become "out of breath" more quickly than nonsmokers when exercising.

Cigarette smoking can also lead to blocked arteries because it increases the amount of fats that can be deposited on artery walls. Smoking increases the chance that platelets will form clots in your blood vessels. Although it's good for clots to form on a cut to stop bleeding, clots that form inside your body can be harmful. The clots the platelets form in arteries can block the flow of blood and lead to a heart attack or stroke.

How does smoking affect respiration?

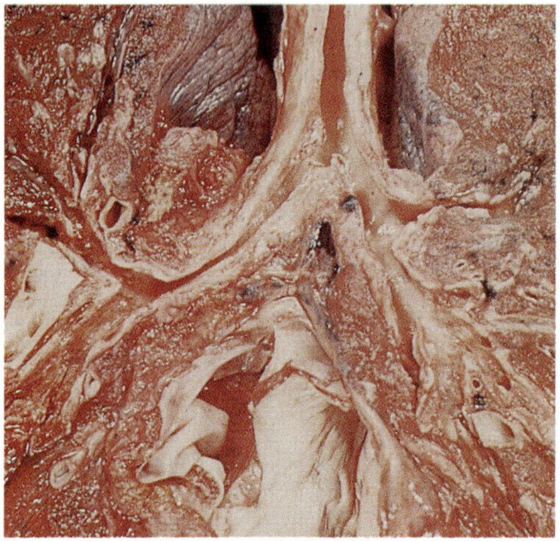

Cross-section of nonsmoker's lung

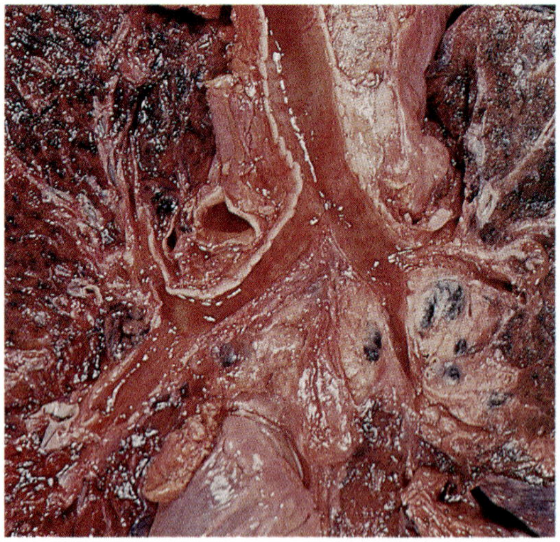

Cross-section of smoker's lung

Cigarette smoke damages the respiratory system even more than it damages the circulatory system. The tars in the smoke cling to the inside of the lungs. Smoking also damages air passages by paralyzing the tiny hairs that line the trachea and bronchial tubes. These tiny hairs, called cilia, sweep dirt or germs out of the respiratory system. Without cilia, a smoker must cough to clear dirt and germs from the trachea.

People who smoke often develop chronic bronchitis (brāŋ kīt'is), or "smoker's cough." People who have chronic bronchitis can't stop coughing. The longer a person smokes, the more tar builds up inside the lungs, and the harder it is to clear them. If it is not taken care of, chronic bronchitis can lead to heart failure.

Over a period of time, the tars and nicotine begin to damage the air sacs in the lungs. When the air sacs break apart, there are fewer areas where oxygen and carbon dioxide can be exchanged. As more and more sacs become damaged, breathing becomes more difficult.

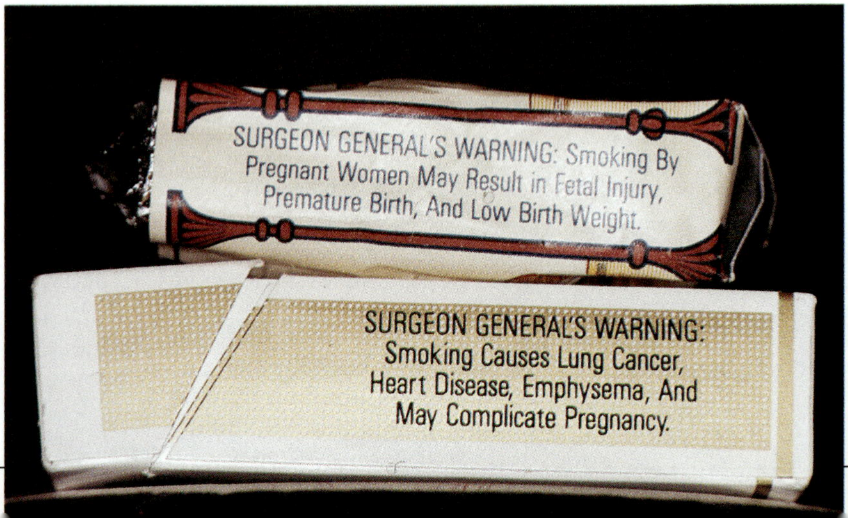

Air sacs do not grow back by themselves. Once they are destroyed by the chemicals in cigarettes, they are gone for good. A disease, called emphysema, is caused by damaged air sacs. People with emphysema (em′fə sē′mə) have a hard time breathing. This disease restricts their activities so much that many people with emphysema cannot even walk across a room without getting out of breath. There is no cure for emphysema.

Tars and other chemicals in cigarette smoke can also cause lung cancer. Cancer involves the growth of abnormal cells. These cells crowd out normal cells, but do not do the work of normal cells. The lungs of people with lung cancer become unable to do their job of bringing oxygen into the body. Lung cancer is usually fatal. About 90 percent of lung cancer deaths are related to smoking.

DILEMMA

Secondhand Smoke

Current research shows that smoking not only damages the smoker's respiratory and circulatory systems, but also those of the people around the smoker. Despite the health hazards to themselves and those around them, people have a right to smoke.

Think About It Should smoking be banned or restricted in public places? Why or why not? What else can be done to protect the health of nonsmokers?

How are you doing?

1. How does smoking cigarettes damage the circulatory system?
2. How does smoking cigarettes damage the respiratory system?
3. **Think** How do you think being in a room with a smoker affects the respiratory system of a nonsmoker?

Looking Back

MINDS-ON ASSESSMENT

Words and Concepts

Mark each statement true or false. If the statement is false, change the underlined word or words to make the statement true.

1. The force of blood against the walls of the arteries is called blood pressure.
2. Hypertension is blood pressure that is higher than normal almost all the time.
3. Too much fat in the diet can cause the air sacs to become clogged with fatty deposits.
4. Regular exercise helps to strengthen the diaphragm.
5. Cilia and mucus help to trap tiny particles that enter the respiratory system with inhaled air.
6. Nicotine is an addictive chemical in cigarettes.

Applied Thinking Skills

Answer the following questions. You can use words, drawings, and diagrams in your answers.

7. List some benefits from regular exercise to the circulatory system.
8. Create a meal plan that includes healthful foods. Create another meal plan with foods that are not good for your circulatory system. Describe how each meal plan, over many years, might affect your circulatory system.
9. How is coughing one way that the respiratory system cleans itself?
10. **Your World** Explain how you play an important role in determining your future respiratory and circulatory health.

Show What You Know

What are the dangers of smoking?

Observe and Collect Data

1. Look through old magazines and find five different advertisements for cigarettes. Cut out the advertisements and tape each one to a sheet of paper.

2. ACTIVITY JOURNAL In your Activity Journal, make a chart listing adjectives the ads use to describe cigarettes. List adjectives that you would use to describe cigarettes. Compare your lists with the warning labels in the advertisements.

3. Design your own advertisement for why people shouldn't smoke.

Process Skills
Observing, Classifying

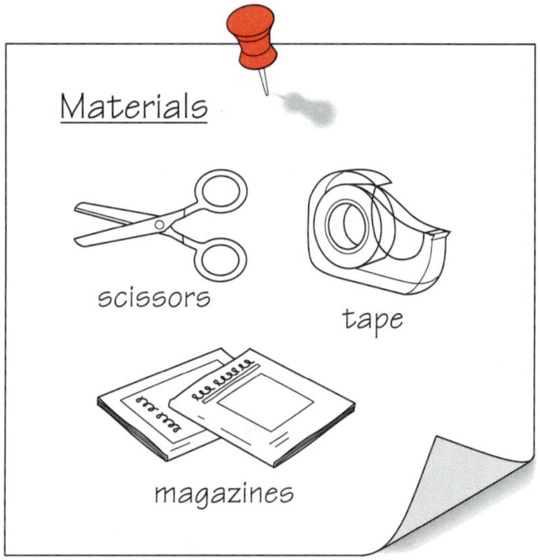

Draw Conclusions

Do any of the advertisements seem to be aimed at particular groups of people, such as women or young people? What observations support your conclusions?

Transport Systems

Work by yourself, with a partner, or in a group to show what you know about transport systems. Select one activity.

Songwriter Write a song about how you use your respiratory or circulatory system when singing or playing a musical instrument. Include changes that take place in the system as you sing or play.

Sports Trainer Design a new athletic game that exercises the circulatory system and respiratory system. With your teacher's permission, have volunteers play the game with you.

Medical Engineer Using materials of your choosing, build a model of the circulatory system and respiratory system. Show the actions of these systems on your model.

Emergency Medical Technician Learn about different First Aid techniques. Share what you learned with the class.

Playwright Write a skit that shows how the circulatory system and respiratory system change as a person at rest begins to exercise. Roles in the skit should include the parts of each system. If possible, have volunteers join you in performing the skit.

Commercial Artist Design an advertising poster that emphasizes health practices that are good for the circulatory and respiratory systems. If you can, display your poster in the school.

Glossary

air sac (er sak) A tiny sphere in the lung in which gas exchange takes place. (page F36)

artery (ärt′ər ē) A blood vessel that carries blood away from the heart. (page F16)

atrium (ā′trē əm) A chamber of the heart that receives blood from veins and pumps it into a ventricle. (page F18)

bronchial tube (brän′kē əl to͞ob) One of two tubes through which air enters the lungs from the trachea. (page F35)

capillary (kap′ə ler′ē) The smallest blood vessel, which connects a small artery and a vein. (page F16)

circulatory system (ser′kyo͞o lə tôr′e sis′təm) The system in the body that transports nutrients, oxygen, and other substances through the body; it includes the heart, blood, and blood vessels. (page F11)

diaphragm (dī′ə fram′) A muscle that forms the bottom of the chest cavity and that helps a person breathe. (page F32)

exhale (eks′hāl′) Breathe out. (page F32)

inhale (in′hāl′) Breathe in. (page F32)

lung (luŋ) The respiratory organ in which oxygen and carbon dioxide are exchanged. (page F35)

plasma (plaz′mə) The liquid part of blood. (page F12)

platelet (plāt′lit) A part of blood that helps form clots. (page F14)

red blood cell (red blud sel) A blood cell that carries oxygen from the lungs to the body cells. (page F13)

respiratory system (res′pər ə tôr′ē sis′təm) The system that exchanges oxygen and carbon dioxide. (page F30)

trachea (trā′kē ə) The tube in the throat through which air enters and leaves the chest area. (page F35)

vein (vān) A blood vessel that carries blood toward the heart. (page F17)

ventricle (ven′tri kəl) A chamber of the heart that pumps blood out of the heart to the body and lungs. (page F18)

white blood cell (hwīt blud sel) A blood cell that helps the body fight infection and disease. (page F15)

Unit F Index

Boldface numerals denote glossary terms. Italic numerals denote illustrations.

Credits

Photographs

2T David Madison; 3T David Madison; 4R David Madison; 12 C.C. Duncan/Medical Images Inc.; 13L Dennis Kunkel/CNRI/Phototake; 13R American Red Cross; 14R Manfred Kage/Peter Arnold, Inc.; 15T Manfred Kage/Peter Arnold, Inc.; 17 Lennart Nilsson, *Behold Man*, Little, Brown and Company; 20 Professors P.M. Motta & S. Correr/SPL/Photo Researchers; 26 David Madison; 27 David Madison; 38B David Madison; 40 David Madison; 46 Michel Hans/Agence Vandystadt /Allsport; 48 Lennart Nilsson/Boehringer Ingelheim International GmbH; 50–51 Shelby Thorner/David Madison; 52 Alec Duncan; 53C John Zoiner; 53TL Marcia W. Griffen/Earth Scenes; 53TR David Scharf/Peter Arnold, Inc.; 55 Workman Publishing Company, Inc.; 56BL Martin M. Rotker; 56R Stephen J. Krasemann/ DRK Photo; 56T Martin M. Rotker

Anne Dowie*: 47
Elliott Smith*: 8, 9, 25, 29, 41, 45, 59
GHP Studio*: 4L, 42–43, 49, 54B, 57, 58T
Ken Karp*: 2BR, 3B, 5, 7T, 11, 14L, 15B, 21, 30–34, 38T, 53BL, 58B
Lawrence Migdale*: 39
Tim Davis*: 1, 2BL, 6–7, 10, 35, 54T

Special thanks to the Boys and Girls Club of the Peninsula, San Mateo, California; Malcolm X Elementary School, Berkeley, California; Franklin Year-Round School, Oakland, California; Carl B. Munck Elementary School, Oakland, California; Hintil Ku Ka Child Care Center, Oakland, California.

*Photographed expressly for Addison-Wesley Publishing Company, Inc.

Illustrations

Nea Bisek 8, 25, 28, 41, 44, 59
Conery Calhoon 11, 16–17, 21, 31, 34, 36
Len Ebert 22
Jane McCreary 9, 19R, 29, 45
Gale Mueller 18, 19L, 24, 32, 33, 40
Randy Vergoustraete 60–61

Text

19 National Geographic Society, *The Incredible Machine* (Washington, DC: National Geographic Society). Copyright ©1986 by National Geographic Society.

22–23 Paul Pitts, *Racing the Sun* (New York: Avon Books, 1988). Copyright ©1988 by Paul Pitts.

55 American Heart Association, Middle School Heart Decisions, *Module II: Save-a-Sweet-Heart Teacher's Guide*, 1988, page 15.

55 American Lung Association, "Facts About Cigarette Smoking," 1990, page 1.

Index

Boldface numerals denote glossary terms. Italic numerals denote illustrations.

Credits

Photographs

Cover: Jim Pickerell/Tony Stone Images

Table of Contents: iiiL Ken Karp*; iiiR Frank Logue/Stock South; iiiL NASA; iiiR Nikolay Zurek*; ivL Ken Karp*; ivR Lawrence Manning/Westlight; vL D. C. Lowe/AllStock; vR GHP Studio*; viii Geoffrey Nilsen Photography*

*Photographed expressly for Addison-Wesley Publishing Company, Inc.

Illustration

Cover: Steve Musgrave